Salutations; a Festschrift for Burton Watson

Edited by Jesse Glass and Philip F. Williams

Tokyo: Ahadada/Ekleksographia, 2015

© 2015 Philip F. Williams and Jesse Glass

ISBN: 978-0-9964784-0-3

Published in Tokyo by Ahadada/Ekleksographia

Printed by Lightning Source
Layout management by Pure Energy Publishing, Seattle, WA

Table of Contents

Preface v
Jesse Glass

Introduction vii
Philip F. Williams

Part I: Prose

1 Zhang Dai in Nanjing: a Tribute to Burton Watson 1
    Duncan M. Campbell

2 Cultivators of the Stinky Quassia: a Cultural History of *Wenren* . . 21
    Victor H. Mair and Timothy Clifford

3 A Functionalist Scientific Worldview in the Early Chinese Science Fiction Story, "Tales of the New Mr. Bragadoccio" 46
    Hua Li

4 Hao Jing's Reflections on Cultural Change and Continuity 71
    Hoyt Cleveland Tillman

5 In Defense of Bodily Self-Sacrifice and Asceticism: The Making of a Virgin Saint in *Xingshiyan* 78
    Yenna Wu

6 Thinking of Burton Watson 104
    Robert E. Hegel

7 Pipings from Heaven 106
    Stephen Addiss

Part II: Poetry

8 Translation and Translucence in the Work of Burton Watson . . 108
    Lucas Klein

9 The Kindly Scholar Burton Watson 118
　Hiroaki Sato

10 Linked Verse 128
　Yoko Danno

11 Hagiwara Sakutarō's Arcane "Harmful Creatures" 130
　Robert Epp

12 Topicality and Arboreal Imagery in the *300 Tang Poems* 158
　Philip F. Williams

13 An Acrostic Eulogy for Burton Watson 170
　Jonathan Chaves

14 Salutation to Burton Watson 172
　Sam Hamill

15 From Primer to Second-level Reader: David Hawkes and Du Fu,
　an Appreciation 174
　William H. Nienhauser, Jr.

16 For Burton Watson 197
　Gary Snyder

17 The Moment Lasts Forever 198
　Philip Rowland

About the Contributors 199

Photography

Burton Watson by Andrea Augé 103, 196

Preface

Jesse Glass

When I made my exit from America I threw a party: poets, painters, cabaret singers, gallery owners, teachers, philosophers of the street, strangers and passersby looking for a bargain—everyone was welcome. Somehow I had managed to shake free from everything and everyone I thought I loved, reduced my worldly goods to a suitcase and a few boxes in friends' attics, and it was time to make my way to Japan the very next morning. But first we'd have a party: I'd play a record on my little black plastic machine, then give it away, and by the end of the night I gave the record player away, too; I made sure my suits, my hats, my ties, some paintings, a Haitian deity in repoussé steel, went walking out the door. My 1928 Underwood typewriter grew unsteady legs, too, after we'd typed dozens of drunken, communal, but surprisingly dry-eyed verses. I remember we'd all staggered down to the Milwaukee River an hour or two before sunrise, laughing at the lights reflected in the river, at the trees and at the few cold stars left in the sky. I was poorer and happier than I had been in a long time and I was not afraid. I kept referring in my mind to the one book I did not give away but would take with me on the plane, and keep with me through the coming years in countryside Japan, in south China, in Korea, and in Japan again: the book told me of trees that were useless, and best that way, and of a butcher who never needed to sharpen his knife, and of a giant bird and a vast fish and a skull existing in a perpetual dream of autumn, and of an unbearably ugly man who for some reason proved so attractive that everyone wanted to be near him and even princesses would fight to be his mistress, and of butterflies dreaming they were philosophers and philosophers dreaming they were butterflies. These stories nourished and consoled me then as they do even now. After many years, when I finally met the gentleman who gave me those precious stories, wrestling them expertly from the ancient Chinese into memorable English, I showed him the dog-eared, coffeestained, annotated, and deeply decrepit pages and he wrote on the fly-leaf of *Chuang Tzu: Basic Writings:* " October 22, 2005/ For Jesse Glass,/ In appreciation of a well-read copy, Burton."

    Due to the incredible generosity of Burton Watson with his gifts we all have been given a key to the intellectual riches of a part of the world that is just as crucial to the collective future of humanity as it is to its past. The stories, the poems, the teachings of great sages and the epic histories that Burton Watson has given us, both directly in his superb translations from the Chinese and the Japanese, and indirectly through his role as teacher and exemplar to dozens of other scholars, translators, poets, writers, and artists, continue to unpack their treasures. No, Burton, the appreciation, the pleasure, has been ours as well. Please accept this small gift from us, sensei.

Introduction

Philip F. Williams

Burton Watson (b. 1925) is the most prolific English-language translator of classical Chinese literature—defined broadly here to include not only *belles lettres*, but also various historical and philosophical texts that have often been read and appreciated as literature for many centuries in China and elsewhere in East Asia. During Watson's career of over half a century, he has also translated numerous great works of both classical and modern Japanese literature, along with writing various treatises on classical Chinese literature.[1] Watson's massive contribution to East Asian literary studies places him in the rarified company of other pioneering scholars and translators such as Arthur Waley (1889-1966), David Hawkes (1923-2009), and Donald Keene (b. 1922).

This festschrift of nearly twenty chapters by a similar number of contributors includes articles, essays, poems, and calligraphy in honor of Burton Watson. The first several chapters deal mainly with prose literature, while the second part of the book is about poetry. The editors' dedication of this volume to Burton Watson follows upon previous books that have been dedicated to him, such as Jonathan Chaves' *Heaven My Blanket, Earth My Pillow: Poems from Sung Dynasty China by Yang Wan-li* (White Pine Press, 2004) and John Timothy Wixted's *Handbook to Classical Japanese* (Cornell East Asia Series, 2006).

Endnote

[1]Three lists of selected translations and treatises by Burton Watson may be consulted below, with an emphasis on original editions instead of reprints. As far as the editors know, a truly comprehensive list of Watson's publications has yet to be compiled. Moreover, Watson has continued to publish new books and shorter works alike during the 2010s, and many of his older and sometimes out-of-print publications have been reprinted in new editions.

Selected Translations of Classical Chinese Works by Burton Watson

Ssu-ma Ch'ien: Grand Historian of China. New York: Columbia University Press, 1958.

Records of the Grand Historian of China. 2 vols. New York: Columbia University Press, 1961.

Hsün Tzu: Basic Writings. New York: Columbia University Press, 1963.

Mo Tzu: Basic Writings. New York: Columbia University Press, 1963.

Chuang Tzu: Basic Writings. New York: Columbia University Press, 1964.

Han Fei Tzu: Basic Writings. New York: Columbia University Press, 1964.

Su Tung-p'o: Selections from a Sung Poet. New York: Columbia University Press, 1965.

Complete Works of Chuang Tzu. New York: Columbia University Press, 1968.

Cold Mountain: 100 Poems by the T'ang Poet Han-shan. New York: Columbia University Press, 1970.

Chinese Rhyme-prose: Poems in the Fu Form from the Han and Six Dynasties Periods. New York: Columbia University Press, 1972.

The Old Man Who Does as He Pleases: Selections from the Poetry and Prose of Lu Yu. New York: Columbia University Press, 1973.

Courtier and Commoner in Ancient China: Selections from the History of the Former Han by Pan Ku. New York: Columbia University Press, 1974.

The Columbia Book of Chinese Poetry: From Early Times to the Thirteenth Century. New York: Columbia University Press, 1984.

The Tso Chuan: Selections from China's Oldest Narrative History. New York: Columbia University Press, 1989.
The Lotus Sutra. New York: Columbia University Press, 1993.
The Zen Teachings of Master Lin-chi: a Translation of the Lin-Chi lu. Boston: Shambhala Publications, 1993.
Selected Poems of Su Tung-p'o. Port Townsend, WA: Copper Canyon Press, 1994.
Sutra on the Exposition of Vimalakirti. New York: Columbia University Press, 1997.
Po Chü-i, Selected Poems. New York: Columbia University Press, 2000.
The Selected Poems of Du Fu. New York: Columbia University Press, 2002.
Late Poems of Lu You, the Old Man Who Does as He Pleases. Tokyo: Ahadada Books, 2007.
The Analects of Confucius. New York: Columbia University Press, 2009.

Selected Treatises on Classical Chinese Literature by Burton Watson

Early Chinese Literature. New York: Columbia University Press, 1962.
Chinese Lyricism: Shih Poetry from the Second to the Twelfth Century. New York: Columbia University Press, 1971.
"Tang Poetry: A Return to Basics." In *Finding Wisdom in East Asian Literary Classics.* Wm. Theodore de Bary, ed. New York: Columbia University Press, 2011. Pp. 149-158.

Selected Translations of Classical and Modern Japanese Literature by Burton Watson

Japanese Literature in Chinese. 2 vols. New York: Columbia University Press, 1975, 1976.
Ryōkan: Zen Monk-Poet of Japan. New York: Columbia University Press, 1977.
From the Country of Eight Islands: An Anthology of Japanese Poetry (by Hiroaki Sato and Burton Watson). Garden City, NY: Anchor

Press, 1981.

Grass Hill: Poems and Prose by the Japanese Monk Gensei. New York: Columbia University Press, 1983.

Kanshi: The Poetry of Ishikawa Jōzan and Other Edo-Period Poets. New York: North Point Press, 1990.

The Rainbow World: Japan in Essays and Translations. Seattle: Broken Moon Press, 1990.

Saigyō: Poems of a Mountain Home. New York: Columbia University Press, 1991.

Four Huts: Asian Writings on the Simple Life. Stephen Addiss, illustrator. Boston: Shambhala Publications, 1994.

The Wild Goose (by Mori Ōgai). Ann Arbor: University of Michigan Center for Japanese Studies, 1995.

The Letters of Nichiren. Philip Yampolsky, ed. New York: Columbia University Press, 1996.

Masaoka Shiki: Selected Poems. New York: Columbia University Press, 1998.

For All My Walking: Free-Verse Haiku of Taneda Santōka. New York: Columbia University Press, 2003.

The Tales of the Heike. Haruo Shirane, ed. New York: Columbia University Press, 2008.

Record of Miraculous Events in Japan: the Nihon ryōiki. New York: Columbia University Press, 2013.

1
Zhang Dai in Nanjing: A Tribute to Burton Watson

Duncan M. Campbell

I have never had the privilege of meeting Burton Watson in person. In an Australasian-based Sinological career of almost thirty years, however, few days would have gone by without my having had recourse to one or other of his books for either teaching or research purposes. In the case of the former especially, particularly his translations from classical Chinese—of the Han dynasty historian Sima Qian 司馬遷 (ca. 145 or 135-86 BCE), of the pre-Qin philosophers Zhuangzi 莊子, Han Feizi 韓非子, and Xunzi 荀子, of the Tang poet Bai Juyi 白居易 (772-846) or the Song poets Su Shi 蘇軾 (1037-1101) and Lu You 陸游 (1125-1209), for instance— enabled me to engage students with often difficult texts in fluent and easily accessible versions that were also precise and reliable. As a translator, Burton Watson is one of the few in the field who maintains equal facility when translating prose and poetry, religious classic and historical or philosophic text. Eliot Weinberger, discussing his twofold typology of translators of Chinese literature of the scholar (who is incapable of writing poetry) and of the poet (who knows no Chinese), justly claims that Watson is one of the few exceptions to the rule in the first category. By way of partial explanation, Weinberger continues by saying of him that he "…was also the first scholar whose work displayed an affinity with the modernist revolution in American poetry: absolute precision. Concision, and the use of everyday speech" (Weinberger and Paz, 25).[1]

Burton Watson has translated little if anything literary or historical that was produced in China after the Song dynasty (960-1279). As tribute to his lifetime's endeavors as a master craftsman in this most demanding of domains, however, I offer below (with short introduction) a number of items from the *Dream Memories of Taoan* [*Taoan mengyi* 陶庵夢憶] by the prolific late-Ming historian and essayist Zhang Dai 張岱 (1597-?1684).[2]

This selection of items from this late masterpiece of Chinese prose is focused on the southern Chinese city of Nanjing, in Zhang Dai's day the Secondary Capital [*Liudu* 留都] of a dynasty that was beginning to totter. Zhang Dai, from Shanyin 山陰 or present-day Shaoxing 紹興, spent some time living in this city during the winter months of 1638, the 11th year of the reign of the Chongzhen emperor of the Ming dynasty.[3] Zhang Dai was in the forty-second year of his life. He was to live at least as long again, but within less than a decade, the circumstances of his life were to change almost completely. It was doubtless not his first visit to the city and certainly we know that he was back there again in 1642; but it appears that it was this stay in Nanjing that left the strongest impressions on him—when he sat down almost a decade later to complete the book of vignettes from his past that has served to earn him his lasting reputation as one of the finest prose writers of the tradition, more than a dozen items were occasioned by his Nanjing days (and nights). By the time Zhang Dai sought to immortalize his memories, of course, his world of people and objects, of smells, tastes and sounds, had suffered what is often considered to have been the most cataclysmic dynastic transition of all Chinese history, and Zhang Dai himself had been reduced from the lap of luxury to self-imposed exile and arrant poverty.

Nanjing during the years before "The Earth crumbled and Heaven collapsed" [*diche tianbeng* 地坼天崩] must have been a restive and anxious place, however much, in Zhang Dai's account, the culture of refined splendor and indulgence of this late-Ming moment seemed largely unaffected, for the moment, by the looming crises.[4] Thomas Ebrey and Sara Yeung entitle their article introducing perhaps the finest product of the age, Hu Zhengyan's 胡正言 (1584/85-1673/74) *The Ten Bamboo Studio Collection of Calligraphy and Painting* [*Shizhu zhai shu hua pu* 十竹齋書畫譜], "The Wonder That Was Nanjing," and begin with Dickens's famous line: "It was the best of times, it was the worst of times" (Ebrey and Young 2012). Indeed, it was. The surrounding countryside was ravaged by drought and consequent famine and disease, as function of the last of what the historian Timothy Brook has described as the "nine sloughs of the Yuan and Ming dynasties."[5] Both before and after the brief interlude afforded him by his time in Nanjing, Zhang Dai was to be much involved in the attempts at the local level organized by his friend Qi Biaojia 祁彪佳 (1602-1645) to alleviate the famine and disease that stalked the countryside.

The bureaucratic factionalism that had been such a marked feature of the court during these years and which continued to inhibit any meaningful attempts to address the various dimensions of administrative and military failure, too, burst into the open in 1638 when 140 members of the Revival Society [Fushe 復社], gathered in Nanjing in preparation for the examinations of the next year, signed their names to a public denunciation of the playwright Ruan Dacheng 阮大鋮 (ca. 1587-1646), then living in retirement in Nanjing. Entitled "A Manifesto to Prevent Chaos in the Secondary Capital" ["Liudu fangluan gongjie" 留都防亂公揭] (often referred to in the secondary English-language scholarship as the "Proclamation of Nanjing"), the hatred for Ruan on the part of Revival Society members derived from Ruan's support in the mid-1620s for the eunuch faction led by Wei Zhongxian 魏忠賢 (1568-1627) in its vicious dispute with the Eastern Grove Academy faction 東林黨. The fall of Wei Zhongxian had forced Ruan Dacheng into retirement. Outraged by his revived prominence within Nanjing's cultural (particularly, dramatic) world, as glimpsed in Zhang Dai's account of the visit he paid upon him, as found below, the Revival Society's attack forced Ruan into further seclusion. Ruan was to be restored to office one further time, and briefly, after the suicide of the Chongzhen emperor and the fall of Beijing in 1644, as Vice-Minister of War at the court of the Southern Ming Prince of Fu in Nanjing. When the city surrendered to the Qing army in 1645 without a fight, Ruan too surrendered—many of his contemporaries chose suicide—only to die soon thereafter in obscure circumstances as he accompanied the Qing troops on their march into Fujian Province. Zhang Dai's judgment of this most reviled of late Ming figures ("…a man of extraordinary talent; regretfully, he is also a man riven by the remorselessness of his own ambition"), made only shortly after his death, seems a remarkably judicious one.⁶ The severe drought of these years had one particular consequence when in 1638 a well in the compound of the Upholding Heaven Temple 承天寺 in Suzhou dried up and, hidden within an iron casket, a text entitled *A History of the Heart* [*Xin shi* 心史] was found.⁷ Rabidly anti-Mongol in part, the work was attributed to the loyalist Song dynasty painter Zheng Sixiao 鄭思肖 (1241-1318), and was quickly copied, printed and circulated. Zhang Dai happened to be passing through Suzhou soon after the book's discovery; he notes the re-appearance of this book in his primer of knowledge necessary for any educated person, *Navigating By Night* [*Ye hang chuan* 夜航船] and writes a poem entitled "On Reading Zheng Suonan's *History of the Heart*" ["Du Zheng Suonan *Xin shi*" 讀鄭所南心史]. The title he later gave his magisterial history of the Ming dynasty makes explicit reference to Zheng's work. More generally, the book, as it circulated, provided Zhang and his contemporaries with a way of understanding their own plight as the continued existence of something by way of what they considered to constitute Chineseness, it was thought, was again being threatened by invasion by "barbarians" from the north.

For Zhang Dai more personally as well, 1638 proved a painful year. In the spring, his mother-in-law Liu Taijun 劉太君 (1579-1638) died, on exactly the same day in the fourth month that, nineteenth years earlier, his own mother had died, he tells us in the funeral address that he wrote on her behalf. A woman of indomitable disposition, she treated everyone with kindness and generosity, and her son-in-law had obviously been very fond of her. He wept for her, he said, as he had wept for his mother. Just as distressing was the death, in his fifty-fifth year and on the twentieth day of the eighth month, of Qin Yisheng 秦一生 (1584-1638), a family retainer and member of the family's acting troupe, as well as Zhang Dai's life-long companion. Early in the year, the two had paid a visit to the Temple of King Asoka 阿育王寺, not far from the coastal town of Ningbo 寧波, in the hope of viewing the vision that was said to manifest itself three of four times a year from the reliquary and which was granted visitors "in accordance with their karma" 隨人因緣現諸色相. Zhang Dai was granted a vision of Guanyin, but his companion "…failed to see anything, however often he looked at it; he grew panicky and his face reddened before he came out and departed in tears" 秦一生反覆視之訖無所見一生惶遽面發赤出涕而去. "And as it transpired,

Yisheng died in the eighth month of this same year" 一生果以是年八月死, Zhang Dai concludes his account of their visit, "Another instance of the extraordinary power of this relic" 奇驗若此. "Not a day would go by that Yisheng did not go roaming with me; his death leaves me suddenly completely bereft" 蓋一生無日不與岱游一生一死岱忽忽若有所失, Zhang Dai was to say in the Funeral Address he wrote for his companion.

Nanjing, it seemed, where by Zhang Dai's account as seen in the translations below the operatic performances continued unabated and late into the night, where the cultural world was the apotheosis of nonchalant, indulgent elegance and gorgeousness, offered Zhang Dai and his like-minded contemporaries a brief respite from the pressing cares of official and personal life. Finally, however, the dream faded, as had Zhang Dai's own. Nanjing was never again to recapture the splendor of this late-Ming moment; and forevermore, the gorgeous decadence and theatricality of that moment was to be associated, in the minds of those who sought to understand it, with inevitable dynastic collapse. A.C. Scott was later to characterize Nanjing as the "capital of dying regimes" (1982: 29).

Zhang Dai's *Dream Memories of Taoan* was in all likelihood completed sometime around 1647, although the first (and incomplete) printed version of the book was only to appear more than a hundred years later, in 1775. It is a book that is presented as a randomly arranged collection of memories snatched from the very cusp of oblivion as Zhang Dai is finally "about to awaken from the Great Dream" 余今大夢將寤 that has been his life. The Nanjing-related items translated below are found scattered throughout the eight fascicles into which Zhang Dai's book was divided, with little logic to their placement and certainly no chronological order. Significantly, however, the first two items of his work ("Bell Mountain" and "Pagoda for Requiting Benevolence") are both set in Nanjing, as below. All the items translated below are given in the order in which they appear in the earliest printed version of the text.

Bell Mountain

Thin clouds circulate around the summit of Bell Mountain [Zhongshan 鍾山], rising and falling slowly, their reds interfused with flashes of purple. People claim the phenomenon to be a manifestation of the "August Breath" of a king, this being a site where dragons molt and seek their shelter. Emperor Gao, the founder of the Ming, along with his ministers Liu Ji 劉基 (1311-1375), Xu Da 徐達 (1332-1385) and Tang He 湯和 (1326-1395), each individually selected a site for the emperor's mausoleum, hiding a chart marking the location each had selected in the sleeves of their gowns. When it was discovered that the site chosen by three of these men accorded, this site was decided upon.

    To the left of the entrance of the site chosen stood the tomb of Sun Quan 孫權 (182-252) of the Three Kingdoms period. When work was being done on the emperor's mausoleum, a request that it be moved was addressed to the emperor. "Sun Quan too was a true hero," the emperor replied, "leave him where he is. He can stand guard at the gate." When the tomb was excavated, the stupa of the Liang dynasty monk Baozhi 寶志 (418-514) was uncovered, within which it was discovered that his corpse had been preserved as if he was still alive, his fingernails having grown so long that they now encircled his body several times. When the troops tried to move him, they found that they could not lift him. Only once the emperor had himself come to pay obeisance to the monk, and had sworn to have him reinterred in a golden coffin within a silver casket, with a benefice of three hundred and sixty *mu* of arable land given over to provide for his continued veneration, could he be carried away and enshrined in a stupa within the Temple of the Numinous Valley [Linggusi 靈谷寺]. The monks here now number in the several thousand, with a daily consumption of grain that equals the total production of the estate. Once the emperor had been installed in his tomb, the area was closed off completely, and few knew where it was situated. All that is to be seen here are three gates, a single Sacrificial Hall, the Coffin Chamber itself, and an encircling and brush covered hill.

    During the seventh month of the *Renwu* year (1642), when Zhu Zhao 朱兆 was promoted to the post of Chamberlain for Ceremonials in order that he may officiate over the Ancestral Sacrifice of the fifteenth day of the first month, I was there to observe the ceremony. The Sacrificial Hall was a place of profound solemnity, with the Warm Pavilion annex only three *chi* away, all wreathed in Yellow Dragon wall hangings. Two armchairs had been placed in a row, adorned with yellow brocade and peacock feathers, the brocade embroidered with a facing dragon, all most splendidly done. The floor was laid in felt, and when walking upon it, one had to take one's shoes off and walk on tiptoe. If anyone uttered the slightest cough, a guard would immediately shout out: "Silence! Do not disturb the emperor." A seat next to the place of the emperor, slightly to the front, was that of Concubine Gong, the birthmother of the Yongle emperor (r. 1402-1424). When he was born, the Empress Xiaoci 孝慈皇后 pretended that he was her son, the affair having been shrouded in utmost secrecy. Further on down, forty-six seats had been arrayed to east and west, some seats taken, others not. The vessels for the sacrificial offerings were extremely simple and rustic: a vermillion wood platter, a wooden jug, and a wooden wine goblet, all coarsely carved. The platter held no more than three slices of meat, a pinch of rice-flour, several grains of millet, and a pot of pumpkin soup. On a side table in the Warm Pavilion were placed a single bronze brazier, two small chopstick containers, and two wine cups. On a larger side table next to this were placed the sacrificial ox and the sacrificial lamb. Perhaps it was different on other ceremonial occasions, but this was what I witnessed in this instance.

  On the day before the sacrifice, the Chamberlain for Ceremonials and his subordinate officials oversaw the opening of the middle gate of the pen where the sacrificial animals were housed, after which, accompanied by drum and pendant, the ox and lamb made their own ways out of their enclosure, before being covered with dragon blankets. When they reached the slaughter room, the ox's hooves were bound, each with its own rope. When the Chamberlain of Ceremonies and his subordinates arrived, the ox was presented to them, standing facing them head on. Before they had risen from their knees as they undertook the bows required of the ceremony, the ox's head had already ended up in the roasting pan. Once the head had been cooked, it was then taken to the Sacrificial Hall. At the fifth watch the next day, the Duke of Wei, Xu Hongji 徐弘基, arrived to oversee the ceremony, the Chamberlain of Ceremonials and his subordinate officials not forming part of the main group but rather standing in attendance in the Sacrificial Hall. By the time that the ceremony had been completed, the stench of the rotting ox and lamb had become quite overwhelming. On ordinary days, two sacrificial meals were presented during the course of each day, the Duke of Wei overseeing these ceremonies also, his attendance being required on a daily basis.

In the *Xuyin* (1638) year I was staying at Vulture Peak Temple when word spread that a black miasma had gathered around the Tomb of the Founding Emperor, before bursting its way upon the Ox and Dipper constellations, lingering there for a full hundred days. I rose one night in order to observe the phenomenon, catching sight of it. From the time of its appearance, roving bandits began to stalk the empire, and the alarm was raised at every quarter. In the *Renwu* year, Zhu Chunchen 朱純臣, the Duke of the Founding of the State, and Wang Yinghua 王應華 were tasked with the repair of the tomb, in the process of which they chopped down trees that had been growing there for three hundred years to use for firewood, and, in the removal of their trucks, digging down into the earth to a depth of several *zhang*. Those knowledgeable about such things maintained that in so doing, they had harmed the Veins of the Earth and had thus allowed the August Breath to escape. And now, indeed, we have experienced the calamity of the *Jiashen* year (1644), and even having Wang Yinghua decapitated and his corpse chopped up into little bits would not suffice to redeem this crime. For two hundred and eighty-two years the welfare of the Mausoleum of the Founding Emperor has been maintained and yet, this year, on the occasion of the Clear and Bright Festival of the Dead, not even a bowl of gruel was offered in sacrifice. To think about this makes one sob inconsolably.

Pagoda for Requiting Benevolence

Without question, the Pagoda for Requiting Benevolence [Baoenta 報恩塔] must be accounted one of China's greatest treasures, the finest product of the kilns of the Yongle emperor. Built during the early years of that emperor's reign, its construction would have been impossible were it not for the majestic spirit of the emperor's father, the founding emperor, for the immense wealth unleashed by the inauguration of his dynasty, and for the policies of the time that appointed to office all the most able of men, all of which derived from his courage, his wisdom, and his talents, such as were enough to swallow up the very pagoda itself.

The entire pagoda, from top to bottom, was garlanded with a million statues of the diamond body of Sakyamuni, each of which were made out of ten or so porcelain bricks, precisely cast so that when fitted together the clothing, the visages, even the beards and eyebrows of the figures, were perfect in their smallest detail; such was the magic of the manner of the joints and mortises. I hear that when the porcelain bricks were being fired for the pagoda, three of each design were made, one of which was used in the construction of the pagoda and the other two were buried, all of them having first been numbered. Nowadays, whenever a brick is damaged, the number of the damaged brick is reported to the Ministry of Works and its replacement is immediately unearthed, ensuring that the pagoda is always as new.

At night, the pagoda is always festooned with lanterns, these lanterns burning their way through a huge quantity of oil over the course of a year. When the sun stands high in the sky, and thick cloud or hazy mist wafts this way and that around the pagoda, a strange and wondrous light is emitted from its top, as if it were an incense brazier giving forth puffs of smoke, this phenomenon lasting a full half day before dispersing. And when, during the years of the reign of the Yongle emperor, envoys and their interpreters arrived here from the hundred or so barbarian lands across the seas, at sight of the pagoda they would invariably pay homage to it as they exclaimed about its wonderment, labelling it unparalleled throughout the four great continents.

Swallow Rock

Thrice have I passed by Swallow Rock [Yanziji 燕子磯], where the force of the waves is such that from here onwards the boatmen, with quick hands and straining shoulders, need to winch the boats upstream inch by inch, with hooks and iron hawsers. The sight, caught from the window of the cabin, of the angular and layered bones of the rock cliff looming up above one and seemingly holding back the flow of the water brings terror but little joy, for one had never imagined that the banks of the river here consisted of a realm such as this.

In the *Wuyin* year (1638), once I had arrived in the capital, I came here with Lü Jishi 呂吉士 by way of Guanyin's Gate 觀音門, and only then did I realize what a Buddha's Stage, an Immortal's Capital, I had previously ignored. We ascended Duke Guan's Hall that, straddling the lands of the kingdoms of Wu and Chu, was where Guan Yu had fought his battles. The numinous power of the place made our hair stand on end. We followed the contours of the hill to reach the top of Swallow Rock where we sat for a while in the kiosk on its summit watching the rippling water of the river down which the boats sped like arrows. Turning to the south, we walked to Guanyin Pavilion, which we ascended by way of a rope ladder. A monk's cloister stood beside the pavilion, with a sheer cliff of over a thousand *xun*, studded with giant rocks the color of iron. Several large maple trees overshadow all the other trees here, casting the whole area into a deep and chill shade. Appearing somewhat idiotic, a small tower stands facing the cliff, and here one could meditate facing the wall for a full ten years. Presently all the monk's cells and Buddha pavilions seem deliberately designed to back on to the cliff, perhaps by reason of the fact that they could not bear to face it.

When I returned home to Zhejiang at the end of this year, my friends Min Wenshui 閔汶水 and Moonlight Wang 王月生 came here with me to see me off, and we had a farewell drink together beneath the rock face.

The Tidal Bore at White Ocean[9]

On previous occasions when I had gone to Three Rivers [Sanjiang 三江] to view the tidal bore, it had transpired that there was in fact nothing much to be seen. By afternoon the word would spread that: "This year the tide is a submerged one," and so it proved, year after year.

In the eighth month of the *Wuyin* year (1638), when I attended the funeral of the Junior Preceptor Zhu Xieyuan 朱燮元, I visited White Ocean and was seated with Chen Hongshou 陳洪綬 and Qi Biaojia. When the shout went up that the sea wall was the spot from which to view the tidal bore, I hastened there, followed closely by both Chen Hongshou and Qi Biaojia. As we stood upon the embankment, we could see on the distant horizon the single line of the bore as it advanced towards us from Haining 海寧, heading straight for the embankment. As it drew nearer, we began to see the white crests, like a flock of tens of millions of goslings being herded towards us, their wings flapping as if about to take off in panicky flight. Nearer still and the bore began to billow foam and ice flakes flew in all directions, like a million snow lions descending upon the river, whipped forward by the thunder, ten thousand heads stretching up and none daring to fall behind. Nearer still it advanced towards us, as if driven by a typhoon, with a force that seemed about to crash against the banks and flood over them. The spectators scattered in panic, taking refuge below the embankment. When finally the bore reached the embankment where we stood, it smashed against it with all its power and plumes of water flew into the air and splashed up to a height of several *zhang*, drenching our faces. Then it rolled away to the right, smashed into Tortoise Hill [Guishan 龜山] and, with an extraordinary roar of anger, exploded into bits and pieces in the deep pond, like snowflakes dancing in the air. To see it dazzled one's eyes with fright and it was only after sitting down for some considerable time that I managed to regain my composure. The elders here maintain that the Zhe River [Zhejiang 浙江] tidal bore rises from the constriction of the river as it flows between Mounts Niche [Kanshan 龕山] and Red [Zheshan 赭山]. But White Ocean lies beyond these two mountains and here the tidal bore is even higher. I wonder why this is the case?

Houseboats of the Qinhuai

The houseboats of the Qinhuai River are designed to provide for overnighting, for socializing, and for the ultimate in gorgeous display, and although they are forbiddingly expensive to rent, not a night goes by that they are not fully occupied. Coming and going amidst the houseboats are the painted boats of musical troupes with flute and drum. And beyond the houseboats, the houses that line the river all have rooftop terraces, with crimson balustrades and intricately decorated windows, bamboo blinds and gauze canopies. On moonlit summer evenings after taking their baths, men and women sit here in the open, the jasmine scent of the women and girls, carried by the breeze and suffusing the water towers that line both sides of the river, proves intoxicating, as does the sight of the groups of women fanning themselves with silken fans or unhurriedly rebinding their hair prove seductive.

Each year, on the occasion of the Dragon Boat Festival on the fifth day of the fifth month, the women of the metropolis throng here in order to watch the lantern boats. The town's aficionados crowd into a myriad various little skiffs adorned with elaborate bullhorn lamps, strung from aft to stern and from one boat to another (up to a dozen boats in a line) like pearls on a string. The boats, twisting and turning this way and that, and rising and falling on the waves resemble flaming dragons and fiery sea serpents, spouting flames and fountains of water in all directions. And in the boats, amidst the drinking and the singing, the cymbals and drums, strings and pipes, played away with all the fury of a roiling pot of boiling water. The young girls of the town lent upon the balustrades laughing uproariously such that both the intermingled sound and sight of them both blinded the eye and deafened the ears. By midnight, however, the songs would tail off and the lanterns would start to gutter, whilst the assembled crowds, like stars strung across the sky, would begin to scatter. Zhong Xing 鍾惺 has composed a rhapsody entitled "The Lantern Boats of the Qinhuai River" ["Qinhuai he dengchuan fu" 秦淮河燈船賦] that gives exhaustive description of the scene.

Yao Yunzai's Paintings

Yao Yunzai's 姚允在 paintings are timeless; the artist himself, too, proved timeless. During the *Wuyin* year (1638) he was staying with the descendants of Duke of Wei, Xu Da (1332-1385), as an honored guest. For my part, I was living at Peach Leaf Ford [Taoye du 桃葉渡], spending my days with Min Wenshui 閔汶水 and Zeng Jing 曾鯨. I had not even a nodding acquaintance with Yao Yunzai, but nonetheless he came calling upon me one day, and the minute we caught sight of each other it was as if we had known each other all our lives. He immediately took up residence with me for the night, and, without letting me become aware of it, saw to having supplies provided for the kitchen. Whenever he was free of other commitments, he would drag me off with him to go drinking in the taverns that lined the Qinhuai River, and we would only head home once we had become completely soused. He was acquainted with all the most eminent figures of the capital, with the all the various officials and important monks, the literary figures and the famous courtesans, and he would insist on introducing me to all these people, without a single exception. After he has spent ten days with me, his servant suddenly appeared, and only then did I know that he had been accompanied all this time by his concubine. Yao Yunzai was a man of profound intelligence, but he wore it lightly. He found it hard to get along with people, preferring to plough a lone furrow, to the extent that others found him difficult to get to know. With me, however, for whatever reason, circumstances proved the opposite, and we could not see enough of each other.

On one occasion we went together to meet up with some friends at the Pagoda for Requiting Benevolence and someone brought out an album of over a hundred paintings, all by masters of the Song and Yuan dynasties. It was as if Yunzai's eyes were able to penetrate through the entire album at once, so intense was his concentration as he sat looking at the album, the color draining away from his face. Once we had returned to where we were staying, he produced a series of paintings for me, in imitation of the style of the Song painter Su Hanchen 蘇漢臣. One of these paintings depicted a child about to take a bath in a tub, with one foot already in the water, the other drawing back as if in alarm. A palace attendant squats at the side of the tub, one hand supporting the child, the other hand wiping away the snot from the child's nose. A palace lady sits to the side, a child who had just finished bathing sitting on her knees as she ties the bindings of its clothing. Another painting depicted a palace lady standing fully clothed in court attire, as if waiting, accompanied by two serving maids. One of the maids is holding up a tray on which are two cups that she is about to offer to guests. Another palace lady stands rearranging the tea whisk and so on, ensuring that everything is in its rightful place. When I later took another look at Su Hanchen's originals, I found that Yunzai's copies were exact in every detail.

Peng Tianxi's Acting

Peng Tianxi's 彭天錫 acting is a wonder throughout the empire, and each act of every play that he performs is done with deliberate vigor, with not a single word improvised. On one occasion, in order to have a particular play performed, he invited the playwright to take up residence at his house, expending several dozens of *taels* in this pursuit, and thus did the family fortunes of hundreds of thousands of *taels* flow through his hands. He spent three springs performing around the West Lake in Hangzhou, visiting Shaoxing also on five occasions and performing fifty or sixty times at my house there; and even then I did not experience everything that he was capable of. Tianxi tended to play either clown or painted-face roles, and in his inimitable impersonation, both evil ministers and imperial favorites become even more hateful; in his voice, they seemed even more crafty. He seemed able to assume completely the personality of the character he was playing such that I fear that Zhou himself, the evil last emperor of the Shang dynasty, could not have appeared more evil. With knotted brow and blazing eyes, his stare was, quite literally, as if daggers drawn, his laugh always concealed a barb, and his spectral air and murderous intent emanated a fearful fog of insinuation. In truth, at his disposal Tianxi had a veritable bellyful of history, a bellyful of landscape, a bellyful of sly tricks, and a bellyful of grievances that had no other venue for their venting apart from when he was on stage.

On one occasion, when watching a marvelous opera, I was overcome with a sense of remorse that I could not wrap the performance up in finest brocade so that it could be passed on and thus become immortal. This feeling I liken to what we experience when we happen to catch a glimpse of a bright moon hanging high within the sky, or as we savor the taste of a freshly-brewed cup of fine tea, both things that can provide us the gratification of but a moment, their passing to then occasion a lifetime's regret at their passing. Whenever Huan Yi 桓伊 (d. ca. 392) happened to see a lovely stretch of scenery, he would exclaim: "Ah, what can I say?! What can I say?" In truth, whenever one encounters some matchless splendor, words prove woefully inadequate.

Moonlight Wang

The courtesans of Song Quarter [Quzhong 曲中] in Nanjing thought it beneath their dignity to associate with the tarts of Crimson Market [Zhushi 朱市]. But Moonlight Wang, born to a tart of Crimson Market and who spent thirty years of her life in Song Quarter, was quite beyond compare. Her complexion was as white as a Fujianese orchid recently bloomed, she moved with elegant and refined grace, and her long and slender fingers were like the stalks of a red water caltrop jutting out of the surface of the water. She was dignified and sparing of both word and laughter, to the extent that even the most ingenious teasing on the part of her fellow courtesans or other good-for-nothings could never bring the slightest smile to her lips.

Her calligraphy in the Regular Script was excellent, and she could paint orchids, bamboo, and narcissus. She could also understand Wu dialect songs, but was reluctant to sing them herself. Even members of the imperial family and the rich and powerful old men of Nanjing could not command her attendance. Whenever a rich merchant or important man managed to secure her services to preside over a half-day's banquet, her invitation (along with a consideration) would need to have been sent to her the day before, and the consideration would have totaled at least five *taels*, if not as much as ten; and even in such circumstances, she was fastidious about the invitations she would accept. Anyone wanting a somewhat longer-term relationship with her would need to send her the betrothal gifts at least several months in advance, and even then they would be left waiting for a reply for a year or so.

She loved drinking tea and was a close friend of Old Man Min; whatever the weather or however important the banquet at which she was expected, she would always insist on going to Old Man's Min house to share a pot or two of tea with him before setting off. Whenever someone she had met pleased her, she would drag him off to meet Old Man Min. On one occasion, Old Man Min's neighbor, a rich merchant, was hosting a party for a dozen or so girls from Song Quarter, and everyone was sitting in a circle drinking to excess in the midst of laughter and tomfoolery. Moonlight dawdled on the balcony, leaning on the balustrade with a winsome but somewhat embarrassed look on her face; chagrined, the girls fled in shame to an inner room in order to avoid her withering look.

Moonlight was as aloof and dispassionate as a solitary flowering apricot under the chill light of the moon, blossoming nobly despite the frost and ice. She did not enjoy associating with vulgar types; whenever such a man happened to sit down beside her, she would rise to her feet as if he did not exist. On one occasion her lips began to quiver, whereupon the good-for-nothings there at the time leapt up with excitement and went off to report to their master: "Moonlight's about to speak!" Fooled into thinking that it was an auspicious sign, everyone came running to take a look. Her face reddened and her lips soon ceased quivering. After the master had entreated her countless times, she finally uttered a reluctant word or two: "I'm off home."

Ruan Dacheng's Operas

Ruan Dacheng's players pay much attention to dramaturgy, to the logic of the plots of their plays, and to the continuity between the acts—not at all like the laxness of other troupes in these respects. And the plays they perform are all composed by their master, each sentence beautifully turned and the playwright's conceits perfectly realized, again, not at all like the shapelessness of the plays performed by other troupes. Whenever they perform, each and every play is remarkable, each and every character performed is remarkable, each and every performance is remarkable, each and every line sung is remarkable, and each and every word declaimed is remarkable. With each of the three plays I saw performed at his house, *Ten Cases of Mistaken Identity* [*Shi cuo ren* 十錯認], *Pearl Beads* [*Moni zhu* 摩尼珠] and *Swallow Messenger* [*Yanzi jian* 燕子箋], each sequence or moment of transition, each impromptu gag and comic interlude, each facial expression or glare of the eyes, was fully explained by the master before the performance began. And because the players understood fully both the meaning and the connotations of the lines they were performing, understood the role they were playing, each and every word they uttered was done so with conviction, such that excellence of their performance stayed long in one's mind. As to the Dragon Lanterns and Purple Lass of *Ten Cases of Mistaken Identity*, the mounted performance of *Pearl Beads* or the monkey opera of the same play, the flying swallows, dancing elephants, the Persian presenting the treasure, or the decoration of the notepaper of *Swallow Messenger*, all these were exquisitely represented, making the performance even more memorable.

Ruan Dacheng is a man of extraordinary talent; regretfully, he is also a man riven by the remorselessness of his own ambition. For this reason, his plays are seven-tenths invective against the ways the age, and only three-tenths ridicule, containing much slander at the expense of the Eastern Grove Academy faction, and seeking to defend the reputation of the faction of the eunuch Wei Zhongxian, such that they provoke the upright gentleman to disgust and are, for this reason, nowhere as famous as they should be. Assessed simply as plays, however, each one of them is innovative and as sharp as an arrowhead; not one of them retreats into cliché.

Endnotes

[1] On Watson's strengths as a translator, see Klein 2014.

[2] For short biographies of Zhang Dai in English, see Hummel 53-54 and Nienhauser 220-221. In Chinese, see Xia Xianchun 1989 and Hu Yimin 2002a and 2002b. For a full-length English-language treatment of the life of this extraordinary man, see Spence 2007. Philip Kafalas offers numerous translations of items from this work (2007). Biographies of many of the figures mentioned in the translations above may be found in Goodrich and Fang 1970. This, too, is a book I consult on an almost daily basis. L. Carrington Goodrich was Burton Watson's teacher; Chaoying Fang was instrumental in the establishment of the Menzies Library at the Australian National University, a library that I had much occasion to use during my years of teaching in Canberra. Such are the hidden skeins of a Sinological career. These present translations were initially prepared for a special issue of the *China Heritage Quarterly* focused on Nanjing; I am grateful for the care with which Geremie Barmé read and commented upon my drafts, and also for the encouragement given me by Zhu Yayun, the guest editor for that issue.

[3] One can reconstruct the chronological details of Zhang Dai's life only in broadest outline from his writings. Working from the texts translated below and information given elsewhere in his corpus, we can guess that Zhang Dai arrived in Nanjing sometime early in the ninth month of 1638, after having attended the funeral spoken of in "The Tidal Bore at White Ocean," translated below. The end of the year sees him back in Shaoxing, his friends Min Wenshui and Moonlight Wang having bid him farewell at Swallow Rock. His stay in Nanjing appears not to have been continuous; we know that he went off hunting at Ox Mountain sometime during the winter, and he also makes note of a visit he made to Hangzhou early in the ninth month.

[4] This expression is that of Wai-yee Li 1993. She begins her discussion of this moment with an item from Zhang Dai's *Dream Memories of Taoan* describing a visit that he paid to Jinshan Temple in the middle of the night one day after the Mid-Autumn festival of 1629, and during which he had his opera troupe perform in the main hall—to the consternation of the monks thus aroused from their slumbers.

She concludes this section of her argument: "To recapitulate: Zhang Dai's entry on the nocturnal performance at the Jinshan Temple sums up several aspects of late-Ming sensibility. First, it shows how the fascination with dreams and illusions is also the celebration of the human capacity to produce them, a token of implied freedom and autonomy for the dreaming, imagining, or remembering self. Second, the transitions in the passage show a heightened consciousness of the narrow, shifting margin between being within and without the illusion, between being dreamer and dreamed, and the ironic implications that arise therefrom. Finally, in linking the dialectics of enchantment and disenchantment with a nostalgic and elegiac mood, Zhang Dai represents the late-Ming obsession with problems of self-expression and truth-telling. Fascination with dreams and illusions is then linked to the problem of self-representation" (49-50; Romanization altered).

[5] "The final wave of famine of the Ming dynasty started in 1632, escalated to vast proportions in 1639, and remained severe for two more years. Neither the Yuan nor the Ming had previously suffered a disaster on this scale," for which, see Brook 2010: 71. One (and possibly fatal) token of the crises that faced the Chongzhen emperor (r. 1628-1644), apart from widespread peasant rebellion and the incursions of an expanding Manchu polity that had already declared its imperial ambitions, was the collapse of the state's finances; by 1644, "80 percent of counties had stopped forwarding any taxes at all. The central treasury was empty" (Brook 252).

[6] On the factionalism that so marred the final years of the Ming dynasty, see, in Chinese, Xie Guozhen 2004. On the Revival Society, see Atwell 1975. On Ruan Dacheng, see Hardie 2007. On the Southern Ming generally, see Struve 1984.

[7] Doubts about the authenticity of this text, and story of its recovery, continue to be voiced.

[8] The allusion is to that passage from the "Discussion on Making All Things Equal" chapter of the *Zhuangzi* 莊子 wherein Zhangwuzi 長梧子 addresses Ququezi 瞿鵲子: "He who dreams of drinking wine may weep when morning comes; he who dreams of weeping may in the morning go off to hunt. While he is dreaming he does not know it is a dream, and in his dream he may even try to interpret a dream. Only after he wakes does he know it was a dream. And someday there will be a great awakening when we know that this is all a great

dream," for which see Zhuangzi 1968: 47.

⁹White Ocean Township [Baiyangzhen 白洋鎮] is about 30 *li* north-west of Shaoxing 紹興. The famed Qiantang tidal bore occurs towards the beginning and the middle of each month, with those of the spring and the autumn equinoxes usually proving to be especially spectacular and sometimes rising to a height of between eighteen to twenty-four feet.

Works Cited

Atwell, William S. "From Education to Politics: The Fu She." In *The Unfolding of Neo-Confucianism*. Wm. Theodore de Bary, ed. New York: Columbia University Press, 1975. Pp. 333-367.

Brook, Timothy. *The Troubled Empire: China in the Yuan and Ming Dynasties*. Cambridge: Harvard University Press, 2010.

Ebrey, Thomas and Sara Yeung. "The Wonder That Was Nanjing." *Kaikodo Journal* XXVIII (Spring 2012): 13-20.

Goodrich, L. Carrington and Chaoying Fang, eds. *Dictionary of Ming Biography, 1368-1644*. New York: Columbia University Press, 1970.

Hardie, Alison. "Conflicting Discourse and the Discourse of Conflict: Eremitism and the Pastoral in the Poetry of Ruan Dacheng (c. 1587-1646)." In *Reading China: Fiction, History and the Dynamics of Discourse. Essays in Honour of Professor Glen Dudbridge*. Daria Berg, ed. Leiden: Brill, 2007. Pp. 111-146.

Hu Yimin 胡益民. *Zhang Dai pingzhuan* 張岱評傳 [A Critical Biography of Zhang Dai]. Nanjing: Nanjing University Press, 2002a.

---. *Zhang Dai yanjiu* 張岱研究 [Research on Zhang Dai]. Hefei: Anhui jiaoyu chubanshe, 2002b.

Hummel, Arthur W., ed. *Eminent Chinese of the Ch'ing Period, 1644-1912*. Washington: U.S. Government Printing Office, 1943.

Kafalas, Philip A. *In Limpid Dream: Nostalgia and Zhang Dai's Reminiscences of the Ming*. Norwalk, CT: EastBridge, 2007.

Klein, Lucas. "Not Altogether an Illusion: Translation and Translucence in the Work of Burton Watson." *World Literature Today* 88.3 (August 2014): 1-9.

Li, Wai-yee. *Enchantment and Disenchantment: Love and Illusion in Chinese*

Literature. Princeton: Princeton University Press, 1993.

Nienhauser, William H., Jr., ed. *The Indiana Companion to Traditional Chinese Literature.* 2nd edition. Bloomington: Indiana University Press, 1986.

Scott, A.C. *Actors are Madmen: Notebook of a Theatregoer in China.* Madison: University of Wisconsin Press, 1982.

Spence, Jonathan D. *Return to Dragon Mountain: Memories of a Late Ming Man.* New York: Viking, 2007.

Struve, Lynn. *The Southern Ming, 1644-1662.* New Haven: Yale University Press, 1984.

Weinberger, Eliot and Octavio Paz. *Nineteen Ways of Looking at Wang Wei.* Mount Kisco, NY: Moyer Bell, 1987.

Xia Xianchun 夏咸淳. *Mingmo qicai—Zhang Dai lun* 明末奇才—張岱論 [A Late Ming Genius—On Zhang Dai]. Shanghai: Shehui kexueyuan, 1989.

Xie Guozhen 謝國楨. *Ming Qing zhi ji dangshe yundong kao* 明清之際黨社運動考 [An Investigation of the Factional Movements of the Ming and Qing Dynasties]. Shanghai: Shanghai shudian, 2004.

Zhuangzi 莊子. *The Complete Works of Chuang Tzu.* Burton Watson, trans. New York: Columbia University Press, 1968.

2
Cultivators of the Stinky Quassia: A Cultural History of *Wenren*

Victor H. Mair and Timothy Clifford

In 1934 the writer, translator, and bon vivant Lin Yutang 林語堂 (1895–1976) defended his essay magazine *Renjian shi* 人間世 [This Human World] from the criticism of leftist writers:

> Thus Yutang says: "*This Human World*'s promotion of the familiar essay cannot revive the nation, nor can it destroy the nation. My only thought was merely to put out a nice magazine; for the most part, it was merely to promote a certain type of prose style."
> 故語堂曰：人間世提倡小品，不能興國，亦不能亡國，只想辦一好好的雜誌而已，最多亦只是提倡一種散文筆調而已。(Lin 102)

How should we understand Lin's insistence on the triviality of his literary project? As an ironic posture? Political frustration? Cowardice? Unwillingness or inability to criticize or transcend a dominant discourse of moralistic literature?

We will return to this question below. First, we should note that Lin Yutang was writing in the midst of a *xiaopin* 小品 [familiar essay] renaissance, during which his books and articles, along with those of Zhou Zuoren 周作人 (1885–1967), Yu Pingbo 俞平伯 (1900–1990), Zhu Ziqing 朱自清 (1898–1948), and others, both fed and rode a wave of interest in the late-Ming *xiaopin* genre and the apolitical world of flower arranging, tea sampling, and curio collecting that the genre seemed to encapsulate. By declaring his self-avowedly trivial concerns in print, Lin was deliberately evoking the morally and politically fraught image of the traditional *wenren* 文人 [literary man].

This essay is not about Lin Yutang, but rather the pre-twentieth-century concept of *wenren* with which he was playing.[1] Specifically, this essay attempts a longue-durée cultural history of *wenren* centered on the problem of "trivial" writing. It asks: How should we understand the powerful ideal—or, more often, anti-ideal—of *wenren*? How has it developed and how has its significance changed over time? Who have been the key figures in shaping its development? What sort of relationship has it had with other cultural ideals, such as that of *ru* 儒 [classicist]? What has it meant to call someone a *wenren* or to claim to be a *wenren*? Why has the idea of *wenren* continued to both allure and offend readers after the collapse of the imperial *ancien* régime and the civil service examination system? Most importantly, how should we understand the idea of "trivial" writing in Chinese literary history?

In early usage, the term *wenren* was bound up with the mysterious term *wen* 文. The earliest occurrences of *wenren* are in the *Shujing* 書經 [Documents Classic] and the *Shijing* 詩經 [Poetry Classic]. The *Shujing* passage reads as follows:

> "Uncle Yi-he, you render still more glorious your illustrious ancestor. You were the first to imitate the example of Wen and Wu, collecting the scattered powers, and continuing the all but broken line of your sovereign. Your filial piety goes back to your accomplished ancestor [*wenren*], and is equal to his. You have done much to repair my losses, and defend me in my difficulties, and of you, being such, I am full of admiration."
> 父義和！汝克紹乃顯祖，汝肇刑文、武，用會紹乃辟，追孝于前文人。汝多修，扞我于艱，若汝，予嘉。(*Shang shu zhengyi*)

The *Shijing* poem "Jianghan" (江漢) reads as follows:

> "I give you a large libation-cup of jade,
> And a jar of herb-flavored spirits from the black millet.
> I have made announcement to the accomplished one [*wenren*],
> And confer on you hills, lands, and fields.

In Qizhou shall you receive investiture,
According as your ancestor received his."
Hu bowed with his head to the ground, and said,
"May the Son of Heaven live forever!"
釐爾圭瓚、秬鬯一卣。
告于文人、錫山土田。
于周受命、自召祖命。
虎拜稽首、天子萬年。(*Mao shi zhengyi*)

Later commentators would gloss both of these usages as *wende zhi ren* 文德之人, but—as is so often the case in Chinese lexicography—rather than clarifying the issue, this gloss merely redirects our attention to another unknown variable, namely *wende* 文德 (Morohashi 5:583). Lothar von Falkenhausen's explanation of wen is helpful here. Von Falkenhausen notes that in the *Shijing* and *Shujing*, *wen* means "patterned" only in a few instances in which it is also used as an epithet in early bronze inscriptions. Based on this evidence, he supports the earlier view of Arthur Waley that *wen* is usually "a stock epithet for ancestors" in early texts, and thus follows Legge in translating *wenren* as "accomplished ancestor" (von Falkenhausen 1). Von Falkenhausen carefully distinguishes this meaning of *wen* from the more familiar nexus of "pattern/ritual display/written script/civil learning/cultural accomplishment." He admits that *wen* as a ritual epithet is still semantically very close to *wen* as "ornament/ritual," but cautions that "the word *wen* as used in the ritual contexts explored in this paper may well be quite distinct in origin from *wen*, 'ornament'" (von Falkenhausen 61).

In contrast to von Falkenhausen, and in a slightly later historical context, Martin Kern defines *wen* as a fluid referent to historically contingent modes of privileged cultural forms (Kern 45). Kern's article is also important for our purposes because it posits a crucial shift in the meaning of *wen* and the "status of the literary text" (Kern 61). Kern argues that during the late Western and Eastern Han, "*wenzhang*—the appropriate appearance—was found less in sensual emblems and increasingly in correct writings that were based on canonical learning: *wenxue*, in the Han sense of the word" (Kern 76). In other words, the meaning of *wen* still centered on ritual appropriateness and refinedness, but now this appropriateness/refinedness was thought of as manifesting itself primarily through literary patterning. The concept of culture/civilization and of writing/literature would henceforth be fused in the idea of "this culture/writing" [*siwen* 斯文], of which the classicists [*ru* 儒] assumed stewardship, although, as we will see, the connotation of the term *wenren* also changed with the literary and scholarly mores of later historical periods.

Before moving on to these periods, it may be helpful to say a word about *ru* 儒. The origins of the word *ru* are obscure. The *Shuowen jiezi* 說文解字 defines it as "soft/yielding" [*rou* 柔], as a "term of address for a classical scholar" [術士之偁], and classifies it as a semanto-phonetic compound [從人需聲].[2] This graphic analysis, however, obscures possible phonological connections with words such as *nuo/ru* 懦/臑 [weak, timid], *ru* 孺 [child], *ru* 濡 [to moisten], *ru* 乳 [breast], *ru* 溽 [moist, rich-tasting], *ru* 醹 [rich, intoxicating], *nong* 濃/醲 [strong, viscous] whose meanings revolve around a sensory impression of the softness or tenderness of liquid (milk, water, and wine) and flesh (a mother's breasts, mother and child).[3] From the Warring States period through the Han, the term *ru* came to refer to the textual custodians of the governmental ideals and ritual traditions that Confucius compiled and transmitted in the form of the Six Classics [*liu yi* 六藝].[4] Although we see criticism of the so-called "vulgar *Ru*" (*su ru* 俗儒) in both Mozi and Xunzi, it is significant that the *ru* ideal was never as ambiguous as that of *wenren* in late imperial China. Indeed, as we continue to trace the cultural history of *wenren*, we might ask whether any well-educated Chinese seriously considered themselves *wenren*—or whether it was mainly used as an ironic foil for the Ruist ideal.

The centuries following the fall of the Han were marked by political fragmentation, war, and large-scale human dislocations and migrations. At the same time, the popularity of literary salons among the southern gentry and courts, as well as the development of the nine rank civil service selection system [*jiupin zhongzheng zhi* 九品中正制] and an attendant intellectual interest in personality types and the aesthetics of personality led to a new interest in belletristic writing and literary skill. We must be careful not to reduce the whole of medieval literary writing to Liu Xie's 劉勰 distinction between *wen* 文 ("patterned," i.e. rhymed, belletristic writing) and *bi* 筆 (unrhymed, utilitarian writing), but when the *Wenxin diaolong* 文心彫龍 [The Literary Mind Carves Dragons], Xiao Tong's preface to the

Wenxuan 文選 [Selections of Refined Literature], Lu Ji's *Wen fu* 文賦 [Rhapsody on Literature], the *Shishuo xinyu* 世說新語 [New Account of Tales of the World], and other medieval texts are read together, we see a clear interest in literary skill and genre, as well as in the cosmological, mental, and biological mechanisms of literary creation.

The term *wenren* occurs in several texts from this period. The most famous usage, which Morohashi Tetsuji identifies as the locus classicus for the idiom "literary men disparage one another" [*wenren xiang qing* 文人相輕] (Morohashi 5:583), is the first line of Cao Pi's *Lun wen* 論文:

> Literary men [*wenren*] disparage one another—it's always been that way. The relation between Fu Yi [d. 90] and Ban Gu was nothing less than the relation of a younger brother to an elder brother. Yet Ban Gu belittled him, writing in a letter to his elder brother Ban Zhao: "Wuzhong [Fu Yi] became Imperial Librarian through his facility in composition: whenever he used his writing brush, he couldn't stop himself." (Owen 58–59)

As Stephen Owen observes, Cao Pi's attitude towards these "literary men" is conflicted: on the one hand, he mocks their insecurity and contentiousness; on the other, when faced with the inevitability of death, he recognizes the "fine writings" [*wenzhang* 文章] of these "literary men," as "the supreme achievement in the business of state and a splendor that does not decay."

It should be noted that the "literary men" described by Cao Pi do not engage in "pure" or "independent" literature, but rather produce ritual/political writings with an awareness of artistic skill and a desire for posthumous reputation. Cao Pi both disparages and admires these literary men. Other medieval authors discuss *wenren* in a similarly ambivalent way. In the Wenzhang 文章 [Refined Writing] chapter of Yan Zhitui's 顏之推 (531–591) *Yanshi jiaxun* 顏氏家訓, after describing how each genre of "fine writing" originates in one of the Five Classics, Yan Zhitui writes about *wenren*:

> As for cultivating one's native animus and leisurely remonstrating, savoring their flavor is also a pleasurable affair. If one has surplus strength after performing one's duties, then it is permissible to engage in it.[5] However, from ancient times

many literary men [*wenren*] have descended into frivolity.
至於陶冶性靈，從容諷諫，入其滋味，亦樂事也。行有餘力，則可習之。然而自古文人，多陷輕薄。(*Yanshi jiaxun jijie* 顏氏家訓集解)

Yan Zhitui then launches into a lengthy list of the personal and literary flaws of famous past "literary men," at one point criticizing Ban Gu for having "stolen his father's history" [班固盜竊父史]. The *Sanguo zhi* 三國志 records a letter from Emperor Wen to Wu Zhi:

> When I observe the literary men of ancient and modern times, I find that they generally do not trouble themselves over trifles, yet few are able to establish themselves posthumously through reputation and moral conduct."
> 觀古今文人，類不護細行，鮮能以名節自立。(*Sanguo zhi* 三國志)

After appraising several contemporary literary men, Emperor Wen concludes "It is just that these various masters do not measure up to the ancients; they are but the outstanding talents of one era" 諸子但為未及古人，自一時之儁也. Here we see another important aspect of the medieval sense of *wen*: it is temporally bound, merely the literary remnants of the "outstanding talents of one era," and not the timeless moral truths recorded by the ancients. Wai-yee Li writes of the contradictory nature of *wen* in *Wenxin diaolong*: "On the one hand, it is the outward manifestation of a moral-cosmological system based on order, unity, and continuity. On the other hand, it tends toward excess, intensity, and imbalance, especially as realized in literature" (Li 2001: 202). This same "dialectic of excess and restraint" characterizes other medieval discussions of *wen* as well as the paradigm of the "literary man." The "literary man" harmonizes heaven and earth and participates in the great affairs of the state, but is also driven by the desire to surmount his contemporaries and secure his posthumous reputation through literary talent.

What role did *ru* play during this unsettled era in which adepts of "fine writing" [*wenzhang*] staked their legacies on their literary talents? Did the moral ambiguity of the idea of *wenren* proceed from the *ru* ideal? In the *Xingpin* 行品 [Classes of Comportment] chapter of the *Baopuzi* 抱朴子, passages describing the comportment of *wenren* 文人 and *ruren* 儒人 are almost adjacent, separated only by *wuren* 武人. The entry for *wenren* reads as follows:

> Those who wield luxuriant rhetoric in order to establish their words, and whose diction is magnificent and apt are literary men.
> 摘銳藻以立言，辭炳蔚而清允者，文人也。⁶

The entry for *ruren* reads as follows:

> Those who sift the profundities of the *Three Tombs* and *Eight Ropes*, and who restore past words in order to fully comprehend principle are scholarly men.
> 甄墳、索之淵奧，該前言以窮理者，儒人也。⁷

Here we see a clear contrast between the *wenren* and *ruren*: *wenren* look toward posterity and try to secure their reputation through literary skill; *ruren* look toward the past, sifting through classics and "restoring" past words in order to "fully comprehend principle." We might also note that in the case of Ge Hong, this Ruist ideal is basically a form of self-study and self-cultivation—there is no mention of governance. Furthermore, these character types are not contradictory, and might even be complementary. Anne Cheng has translated a passage from Ge Hong's self-introduction to the *Baopuzi*:

> I have perfectly mastered the Five Classics and written a work of philosophy, just so that later ages would know that I was a scholar of literary accomplishment [*wenru*] (Cheng 118).
> 念精治五經，著一部子書，令後世知其為文儒而已。

In the same vein, Xiao Yi's 蕭繹 *Jinlouzi* 金樓子 identifies both *ru* and *wen* not as conflicting ideals, but rather as progressive stages in self-study/self-cultivation:

> Wang Zhongren said: One who explicates a single classic is a classical scholar [*rusheng*]; one who broadly comprehends the ancient and modern is a polymath [*tongren*]; one who submits memorials to the throne is a literary man [*wenren*]; one who is able to refine his thoughts, compose fine writing, and link together sections and chapters is an awesome classicist

[*hongru*]; Liu Xiang and Yang Xiong are exemplars of awesome classicists. I suspect that the classical scholar turns into the polymath, that the polymath is the literary man, and that the literary man turns into the awesome classicist.

王仲任言：夫說一經者為儒生，博古今者為通人，上書奏事者為文人，能精思著文連篇章為鴻儒，若劉向揚雄之列是也。蓋儒生轉通人，通人為文人，文人轉鴻儒也。[8]

It seems that the medieval period saw an enlargement of the concept of *wen* into one that not only included the field of *belles lettres*, but also valued it as the "supreme achievement in the business of state and a splendor that does not decay." *Wenren* were thus those who cultivated literary skill, either in public or private life, primarily in order to secure posthumous reputation. The business of *ru*, which here we might define as "classical studies," i.e. the study of pre-Han texts (not limited to the *Analects* and *Mencius*), was also contained within this broad, polysemic concept of *wen*. Classical studies might be pursued with an awareness of and desire to cultivate literary skill, as with Ge Hong, but there was not yet an intellectual need to define literary skill in relation to an essentialized *Dao*, nor was the cultivation of literary skill much associated with careerism, as it would be after the introduction of civil service literary examinations in the Tang. As we read in Cao Pi and Yan Zhitui, *wenren* could sometimes be frivolous and vain, but these personal flaws associated with the cultivation of literary skill did not yet represent a threat to the orthodox transmission of the moral truths of the classics.

Both David McMullen and Peter Bol argue that this model of classical learning as a subfield of *wen* persisted through the Tang, which Bol calls a "literary society" (Bol 27; McMullen). While this general esteem among classically literate society (which, we must not forget, represented a tiny percentage of the total population, and in which membership was stringently controlled by educational practices as well as by the nature of the Chinese script) demonstrates continuity with the medieval period, three important changes took place during the Tang, all of which would alter the cultural status of *wen* and of "literary men" [*wenren*]. The first was the introduction of a civil service examination system based in large part on *belles lettres*; the second was the An Lushan rebellion; the third was the concept of "ancient-style prose" [*guwen* 古文] as developed by Han Yu.

As David McMullen and Benjamin Elman describe, two types of civil service examinations developed in the early Tang. The first, known as *mingjing* 明經, required expository essays on the classics. The second, known as the *jinshi* 進士, tested the examinee's ability to compose poems and rhapsodies [*fu* 賦]. While Elman cautions against attributing too great a role to literary examinations in selecting officials during the Tang, noting "the great majority of literati officials during Tang times...were not products of the examination system," it is evident that the practice had an enormous cultural impact (Elman 8). Charles Hartman traces a "shift in emphasis among officials of the central government from martial [*wu*] to literary [*wen*] values" and describes Han Yu's literary and political thought as a reaction against the "hereditary practice of literary 'worm-carving' solely for the purpose of passing the examinations and obtaining office" that characterized Tang literary society and literary examinations (Hartman 122).

Although it avoided total collapse, the Tang state emerged from the An Lushan rebellion with its authority fragmented and decentered. Like the literati of the early Qing, late Tang literati searched for cultural reasons for the recent disaster. The literary examinations were one convenient target. McMullen writes, "In the post-rebellion period, critics of the literary emphasis that the *jinshi* had acquired advocated the use of Han and post-Han histories for the curricula" (McMullen 128). In medieval times, literary dilettantism—the practice of *wenren*—was viewed at worst as a personal flaw; similarly, early Tang cultivators of literary skill might be faulted for careerism. However, the moral ambiguity of *wen* and "fine writing" [*wenzhang*] became considerably more troubling after the An Lushan rebellion. Scholar-officials did not blame literary dilettantism for the near-collapse of the Tang empire—as they frequently did following the fall of the Ming—but many did assign it deeper moral and political significance.

Han Yu was one such scholar-official. Hartman argues that *guwen* as formulated by Han Yu represented "an attempt to manifest in words that quality of the Sage's mind described as *cheng* 誠 'sincere, integral'" and in which "'antiquity' can be understood as a spiritual state roughly synonymous with *cheng*." Han Yu's *guwen* was therefore not simply a prose style (indeed, as Hartman notes, Han Yu's *guwen* style encompassed poetry and prose), but a kind of "Confucian enlightenment" in which dualities such as antiquity vs. modernity, literature vs. learning, public vs. private, and poetry vs. prose all dissolve (Hartman 14). The philosopher Li Ao 李翱 was another such literatus. His "Letter to my Younger Cousin, Correcting his Writing" 寄從弟正辭書 reads as follows:

> You must not believe those who maintain that literature is merely a skill. What they call a "skill" is only writing which our modern age enjoys and which has become popular in recent times. Any work that can attain to the Ancients has perforce a style of humanity and justice [*renyi* 仁義], and it is hardly proper to call this a "skill."
> 汝勿信人號文章為一藝。夫所謂一藝者, 乃時世所好之文, 或有盛名於近代者是也。其能到古人者, 則仁義之辭也, 惡得以一藝而名之哉? (Hartman 214)

This narrow focus on Han Yu and Li Ao is not meant to give the impression that the earlier concept of belles lettres as "the great business of state and a splendor that does not decay" had been overturned; rather, it is merely highlighting a new understanding of wen that would be taken up and reworked by Song literati. Furthermore, one might argue that the concept of *guwen* as formulated by Han Yu and Li Ao represented a potential threat to classicism as it had been practiced since the Han in that "antiquity" could now be understood as an internal state that one might attain through literary-moral cultivation, rather than a body of knowledge and practices to be reconstituted and maintained through textual scholarship. As we move on to the idea of *wenren* and *wenrenhua* 文人畫 in the Song, we might wonder whether Song *guwen* could accommodate an idea of *wenren* or whether literati such as Su Shi 蘇軾 articulated the wenren paradigm in opposition to *guwen*.

As in the Tang, literary examinations in the Northern and Southern Song were central to literati life,[9] and as with Tang literati, Song literati defined *wen* in relation to or in opposition to the examination regime. Ronald Egan notes that Song *guwen* also "began as a protest against the required use of the Current Style in the examinations" (Egan 1984: 13). At the same time, the *guwen* promoted by Ouyang Xiu 歐陽修, Su Shi, and others in the Northern Song was only one iteration of *wen*, a concept which by the

Song had grown so inclusive that, as Peter Bol notes, both belletristic writers and classical scholars could lay claim to "*siwen*, This Culture of Ours" (Bol 16–17). Moreover, like the scholar-officials of the late Tang, Southern Song literati too looked for signs of literary decadence that they felt surely must have brought about the loss of the North. What notions of *wenren* emerged in this period, during which the meaning of *wen* was indeterminate and fiercely contested?

Su Shi is frequently identified as the prototype of the disengaged, aestheticized *wenren* of the late empire. Although Su Shi's numerous theoretical writings on painting and calligraphy would provide ample reading material for *wenren* of the Yuan and later dynasties, Egan convincingly demonstrates that Su Shi's conception of *wenren* differs from later conceptions of *wenren*, and emphasizes Su Shi's "repeated statements about refined literature being a *mo* ('extremity'), and related aesthetic pursuits being even less significant" (Egan 1994: 374). At the same time, one might argue that Su Shi's insistence on the irrelevance and unimportance of fine writing, calligraphy, and painting even while demonstrating an obvious interest in and appreciation for such practices is not necessarily a devaluation or dismissal of aesthetic pursuits; rather, it might also be a way to preserve a space for less morally encumbered literary and artistic practice. In this way, Su Shi does anticipate one of the central aspects of the late imperial *wenren* paradigm: an insistence on the triviality of one's aesthetic obsessions.

Indeed, as Egan also notes, this is precisely what Zhu Xi disliked about Su Shi (1994: 360). Although Learning of the Way [*Daoxue* 道學] did not really take form until the centuries following Zhu Xi's death, Zhu Xi's criticisms of Su Shi can tell us much about the subsequent antipathy among Learning of the Way adherents toward "literary men." First, the germination of Learning of the Way during the Southern Song reconfigured the relationship between "literary man" and "classical scholar" (Bol 3). Hilde De Weerdt describes the gradual synthesis of *guwen* and Learning of the Way thought in the Southern Song through comparing two Song prose anthologies: Lü Zuqian's 呂祖謙 (1137–1181) earlier *Guwen guanjian* 古文關鍵 [Key to Ancient-style Prose], more of a guide to argumentative rhetoric and examination prose, and Zhen Dexiu's 真德秀 (1178–1235) later *Wenzhang zhengzong* 文章正宗 [Orthodox Ancestor of Refined Writing], in which we see a clear emphasis on individual moral cultivation.[10] The engineers of this synthesis relegated writing itself to a secondary or instrumental role: writing was an extremity [*mo* 末], not a foundation [*ben* 本]; a branch [*zhi* 枝], not a root [*gen* 根]; a means of conveying the Way and not the Way itself. In other words, writing itself is trivial; it is significant only insofar as it illuminates or acts as a vehicle for the cosmic moral Way. Egan translates one of Zhu Xi's critiques of Su Shi:

> Someone asked, "How does East Slope [Su Shi] compare with Master Han [Yu]?"
> Zhu Xi replied, "In rectitude he does not measure up to Han."
> "What about Master Ou [yang Xiu]?"
> "He is shallow."
> After some time, Zhu Xi added, "Such persons as Su Shi sought to establish themselves as men of letters [*wenren*]. When they studied, all they investigated was the causes of the rise and fall of dynasties in ancient and modern times. They wrote, but never exerted any effort at cultivating their own person. They spent their days doing nothing more than reciting poetry, drinking wine, and telling jokes" (Egan 1994: 360).

Zhu Xi's negative image of "men of letters" as exemplified by Su Shi is quite clear: *wenren* devote themselves to trivial literary and historical pursuits and other pleasurable activities rather than personal moral cultivation through intensive study of the Four Books.

Yoshikawa Kōjirō argues that Yuan dynasty *wenren* such as Yang Weizhen 楊維楨 (1296–1370) represented a new type of figure in Chinese history, an "attitude toward life in which literature and the arts were made supreme" (Yoshikawa and Wixted 84). Yoshikawa employs what he views as the Song attitude toward literary writing, in which figures such as Su Shi were "considered to be better as literary figures or poets by virtue of having talent and responsibility in political and philosophical affairs," as a foil for the unabashed aestheticism of the Yuan *wenren* ideal (Yoshikawa and Wixted 84).

Our analysis up to this point gives us a unique opportunity to appraise Yoshikawa's argument. We have seen how, prior to the Southern Song, *wenren* referred to those skilled in belletristic composition. Although during this period, as we have seen, *wenren* and *ruren* were differentiated and *wenren* were sometimes chastised for their vanity and frivolousness, literary cultivation was not considered necessarily antithetical to moral cultivation, and it was certainly not considered antithetical to classical erudition. During this period the ideal was to be a *wenru* 文儒, a cultured classicist. The *wenru* ideal changed little with the introduction of literary examinations in the Tang and Northern Song, despite Han Yu's reimagining of literary writing in terms of moral cultivation. The real change came in the Southern Song and early Yuan, when Learning of the Way thought percolated and developed in southern lineages and private academies; it was also during this period that literary writing was conceptually differentiated from, subjugated to, and reconciled with the Way of Confucius and Mencius by Learning of the Way progenitors such as Zhou Dunyi 周敦頤 (1017–1073), Cheng Yi 程頤 (1033–1107), and Zhu Xi. The collection of ideas and pedagogical practices which would later be codified as "*Daoxue*" in the early Ming more rigidly defined moral cultivation in terms of stilling the "human mind" [*renxin* 人心] and attaining the "mind of the Way" [*Daoxin* 道心] through intensive study of the Four Books; this new model of moral cultivation regarded literary skill (as exemplified by the *wenren*) and classical erudition (as exemplified by the *ruren*) as both trivial and, in excess, morally deleterious.

Therefore, it would seem that it was not the image of the Yuan aesthete-eccentric renouncing political affairs and composing poetry behind closed doors that was new—Yuan eccentric *wenren* were clearly playing the part of medieval eccentrics like the Age of Division's Seven Sages of the Bamboo Grove—but rather the moral ambiguity of *wen* in Learning of the Way thought that shaped the appropriation of this image. The reluctant literatus Song Lian 宋濂 (1310–1381)—invariably classified as a "Ming writer" even though he did most of his writing before the establishment of the Ming—is a case in point. Song Lian regretted his early obsession with "ancient-style phraseology" [*guwenci* 古文辭], and his biography in the *Ming shi* 明史 [History of the Ming] records that he "considered himself a classicist" [濂自命儒者]. The Hongwu Emperor would describe Song Lian's talents in a less flattering manner:

> Although you, Lian, are broadly learned in ancient and modern affairs, it is a pity that you lack ability in practical matters, and with every issue waver without resolve. If I were to appoint you

official proofreader, you would be more than up to the task; but if I were to employ you in carrying out concrete business, you would be sorely lacking. Nevertheless, nowadays there are very few classical scholars who conceive of writing as you do, and I recall that you have long served me. To specially appoint you Hanlin academician is also something worthy of celebrating! 爾濂雖博通古今，惜乎臨事無爲，每事牽制弗決。若使爾檢閱則有餘，用之於施行則甚有不足。然方今儒者以文如斯者甚少，朕念卿相從久矣，特授卿翰林學士承旨，亦宜懋哉！ [11]

In the emperor's view, what distinguishes Song Lian from contemporary *ru* is not his literary and scholarly talents, but his understanding of literary writing. What is more difficult is how to define Song Lian's unique understanding of *wen*. By recanting his earlier literary beliefs, Song Lian was clearly trying to distance himself from a kind of *wenren* anti-ideal; and in essays like *Huachuan shushe ji* 華川書社記 and *Xu Jiaoshou wenji xu* 徐教授文集序 he defends *wen* against the charge of triviality and attempts to imbue it with cosmic significance, but does so by describing it as the vehicle or external expression of—i.e., as secondary to—the Way. Likewise, because of his lack of ability in practical matters, he was consigned to an official position of great prestige but ultimately—in the context of the early Ming—secondary importance.

As we move into the Ming, we should note that the main difficulty with saying anything further about Yuan *wenren* identity is how to separate *wenren* identity in the Yuan from its large-scale commodification and popularization in Ming-Qing commercial print. Rather than trying to peel back these layers of representation, the remainder of this essay will deal with representation itself, arguing that the key event shaping our modern understanding of *wenren* was the development of late-Ming print culture and the commercial propagation of *wenren* identity.

As Katherine Carlitz writes of late Ming printed dramatic texts, print gave literati a sense of self and community but not a "permanent hold on intellectual property" (Carlitz 297). That is to say, by reducing the *wenren* ideal to an image, a set of tropes and visual motifs, "print made the images of literati selfhood available, in principle, to all" (Carlitz 297). The ease with which *wenren* identity could be appropriated in the late Ming is particularly evident in the practices of printers like the Wanli-era (1572–1620) Yu Xiangdou 余象斗. Yu Xiangdou was born into a Fujian family that had been involved in printing since the Yuan. He is notable first, for being one of the most successful Jianyang publishers, and second, for including a detailed self-portrait in his printed books in which the markers of literati [*wenren*] identity are on full display.

The printer Yu Xiangdou as a *wenren*

Yu Xiangdou's self-portrait is suffused with the trappings of the cultured literatus. The inscribed lintel above his head reads Santai guan 三台館, the name of his publishing house, and couplet on the posts beside him reads, "A round, red sun on the verge of shining out its rays, and in an instant, ten thousand *li* of clear sky" 一輪紅日展依際，萬里青雲指顧間. He sits before a painted screen on which a fisherman lifts his head to gaze at the moon. An inkstone, two brushes, an empty notebook, and a small stack of books are arrayed on the desk before him. He sits comfortably at his desk with his elbows leaning on his notebook and gives directions to his servants. The servant to his right appears to be offering a steaming cup of tea. Another tends the stove. In front of his desk is a flowering plant placed on a stand with elegantly curved legs. Another servant boy sweeps in front of what appears to be a small, fenced duck pond. A closed gate inscribed with the name "Gate of Cultivation" (*yanghuamen* 養化門, which could also be a playful pun on *yanghuamen* 養花門, "gate of cultivating flowers") identifies the courtyard as a private, domestic space. Ornamental rocks, trees, and what appears to be mist also serve to frame the scene.

The caption at the top of the portrait reads "Portrait of the Santai Mountain Man, Yu Yangzhi [Xiangdou]" 三台山人余仰止影圖. The term "mountain man" [*shanren* 山人] needs further explication, as it is essential to late Ming commercial appropriations and redefinitions of traditional images of reclusion, and in particular the Yuan *wenren* ideal. In a discussion of the late Ming celebrity-*wenren* Chen Jiru 陳繼儒 (1558–1639) as a "mountain man," Jamie Greenbaum notes that, in the mid-sixteenth century, the word served as "an umbrella term for different styles of reclusion," and was used in the names of both actual retirees and office-holders. Greenbaum translates Yuan Hongdao's criticism of the word: "Since the Jiajing period, the practice of retiring to live in the mountains and woods in order to get a good name for oneself has become a type of game" and concludes that, "to add to the apparently unrestrained usage by individuals, publishers soon seized on the term and. . .simply used *shanren* rather than the personal name of an author on the cover of a book" (Greenbaum 172). Yu Xiangdou was one such *shanren*. Chen Jiru was another. Like Yu Xiangdou, Chen Jiru is representative of the late Ming commercialization of the *wenren* image. After failing the provincial examination twice, Chen Jiru renounced official life by either tearing up his cap or burning his robe and cap and presenting the following declaration to the local prefect:

> To participate in worldly affairs makes for a life full of clamor; to dissociate oneself from them makes for a peaceful life. To support one's parents through working in the government, or to do so through personal attendance, amount to the same thing. My father is approaching seventy and I would like to sweeten his later years. I, myself, am not yet thirty, but already dislike the vulgar world. To spend one's life in a calculating way reproducing examination papers is like the image of a flower reflected in a mirror—it is insubstantial. I intend to take the rest of my life into my own hands and spend it happily, communing with nature (Greenbaum 18).

Chen subsequently built himself a rather lavish retreat in Suzhou, began experimenting with alchemy, and took on the role of medieval recluse as exemplified by figures such as Ge Hong. Chen began compiling books on alchemy and other subjects in the 1590s, either on his own or more probably with a team of underemployed licentiates, and over the next few decades attained fame across the empire.

As Greenbaum notes, the primary difficulty in studying Chen the man as opposed to Chen the personality is that his name became in effect a brand, and was inscribed on many prefaces, colophons, and book covers to which he had no personal connection. Greenbaum also argues that his apparent lack of contact with Li Zhi 李贄 (1527–1602) and the Yuan brothers (although he was friends with the famed official and literary archaist Wang Shizhen 王世貞 and the painter Dong Qichang 董其昌), suggests that "Chen was not a serious literary thinker, and that this conception of Chen must be separated from his fame as a writer" (Greenbaum 18). We would argue that, to the contrary, the way Chen embodied all that is *wenren* for his middlebrow, urban readership is inseparable from his "literary thought," and furthermore that the immense influence of his literary thought on late-Ming literary culture was due precisely to its deliberate lack of seriousness—to its trivial preoccupations and political irrelevance.

The commercialized image of *wenren* as connoisseur of

tea, wine, drama, novels, *objets d'art*, and anything else trivial did not end with the fall of the Ming; it persisted into the Qing most notably in Li Yu's *Xianqing ouji* 閒情偶寄 [Random Expressions of Idle Feeling].¹² At the same time, many Qing scholars disapproved of this commercially propagated obsession with sensual pleasure, collectible objects, and minor literary genres. This strain of thought is evident in the comments of the *Siku quanshu* editors on late-Ming *xiaopin* collections. Most of these were excluded from the *Siku quanshu*, although the editors thought them significant enough to merit entries in the *cunmu* 存目 section. The abstract for Cao Rong's 曹溶 *Juanpu shizhi ji* 倦圃蒔植記 reads as follows:

> Rong's knowledge base is rich, so in his citations there is much worthy of attention. It is just that his choice of words often verges on the effete, and still cannot throw off the habits of late-Ming *xiaopin*.
> 溶學本贍博，故引據多有可觀。惟下語頗涉纖仄，尚未脫明季小品積習。¹³

It seems that the *Siku* editors associated late-Ming *xiaopin* with the Ming editorial habit of chopping up and recycling old texts,¹⁴ effete prose style, attention to trivial matters [*suosui* 瑣碎], and professional recluses. The entry for Chen Zhi's 陳直 *Shouqin yanglao xinshu* 壽親養老新書 reads as follows:

> Often the diction and intent are effete, gathering up trivial matters. Ming Dynasty "pure speech" *xiaopin* in fact originates in this.¹⁵
> 往往詞意纖仄，採掇瑣碎。明季清言小品，實亦濫觴於此。¹⁶

The *Siku* editors frequently liken the literary practices of Chen Jiru and his ilk to the "pure conversation" of "abstruse learning" [*xuanxue* 玄學] and medieval literary salons that they believed brought ruin upon the Jin dynasty [*qingtan wangguo* 清談亡國]. The entry for Shen Daqia's 沈大洽 *Shuzhai feiyu* 蔬齋剕語 reads as follows:

> It seems to be of the same class as Zhao Huanguang and Chen Jiru. The first two chapters are informal *xiaopin*. They are neither Confucian nor Buddhist, and forcedly affect a style of

"pure speech." They do not escape the banalities of late Ming "mountain men."
蓋亦趙宦光陳繼儒之類。前二卷皆隨筆小品。不儒不釋。強作清言。不出明季山人之窠臼。[17]

The Ming loyalist Gu Yanwu 顧炎武 (1613–1682) also condemned the "pure conversation" of late-Ming literary men and classical scholars, but in comments like the following he seems to have had eight-legged examination essays [*baguwen* 八股文] in mind rather than *xiaopin*:

> Everyone knows that the five barbarians' plunging China into chaos originated from the protracted disaster of "pure conversation." But who knows that today's pure conversation is even more disastrous than that of the past? Ancient pure conversation conversed on Laozi and Zhuangzi. Modern pure conversation converses on Confucius and Mencius—it leaves out the obvious aspects without obtaining the subtleties, and places the branches first without probing the roots.
> 五胡亂華，本於清談之流禍，人人知之。孰知今日之清談，有甚於前代者。昔之清談談老莊，今之清談談孔孟，未得其精而已遺其粗，未究其本而先其末。(Gu 402)

As Lung-chang Young demonstrates, like Han Yu and Ouyang Xiu, Gu Yanwu and Huang Zongxi 黃宗羲 held the civil examination system responsible for the moral and intellectual degradation of both fine writing and classical scholarship (Young 1987). Indeed, Gu Yanwu's criticisms of the Ming examination system echo Zhu Xi's argument that, with Su Shi, fine writing and historical scholarship become equally trivial and insubstantial because both are divorced from the fundamental task of moral cultivation.

Likewise, as in the Southern Song, the Qing literati reaction against morally vapid literary frivolity was triggered by social upheaval and a changing intellectual and literary landscape. Benjamin Elman has described the rise of evidential learning [*kaozhengxue* 考證學] in terms of the development of Jiangnan-region "academic communities" bound together by "associations and institutions for the propagation of knowledge," "family lineages that had excelled in classical studies," and the resulting "consensus of ideas about how to find and verify knowledge" (Elman 2001: xxvi). In turn, Theodore Huters has described the nineteenth-century emergence of the Tongcheng 桐城 and Wenxuan 文選 schools of prose as a reaction to the "new classicism" of empirical learning, as well as a "struggle over writing between those striving to preserve the medium as the central portion of a unified field of knowledge [the Tongcheng School] and those seeking to elevate letters by splitting them off from ordinary knowledge [the Wenxuan School]" (Huters 1987: 95). In a separate monograph, Huters identifies the continuities between this debate and the concept of *wenxue* 文學 [literature] as it developed in the late 19th and early 20th centuries (Huters 2005).

It is not our intent to reduce the cultural history of *wenren* to a linear progression from belletristic writer to careerist examinee to politically oppressed aesthete recluse to commodified mountain man to morally degenerate literary dilletante. Qing *wenren*—even if they, like most premodern writers, would have balked at being called *wenren*—hoped for literary immortality just as medieval writers did. And even while Gu Yanwu railed against the examination system, Wu Jingzi 吳敬梓 (1701–1754)[18] ridiculed the hypocritical literati class associated with it, and Zhang Xuecheng 章學誠 (1738–1801) criticized an overly prescriptive prose pedagogy that sprang up in response to it,[19] Qing literati generally acquiesced in a kind of love-hate relationship with the examinations and accepted the examination system as fundamental to their collective identity— much as Song, Yuan, and Ming literati did. Nor are we positing a trans-historical, essentialized "literati spirit." Rather, we have tried to give a sense of how, when, and why new ways of thinking about *wenren* emerged, how they were conceived of in relation to classical scholarship and individual moral cultivation, and how they interacted with and reshaped the always heterogeneous, polysemic, and contested field of *wen*.

As for the fate of the *wenren* ideal or anti-ideal after the end of the imperial system, we might once more return to the issue of trivial writing. As it was formulated during and after the Yuan, the *wenren* ideal seems less about the imperial system and civil examinations specifically, and more about insisting on the utter triviality of the very thing with which one is obsessed. This insistence, in turn, provokes moral scrutiny. This dialectic did not end with the imperial system; in fact, it was central to debates over the meaning and purpose of *wenxue* 文學 through the first half of the twentieth century, particularly during the renaissance of lyrical prose in the 1920s and 1930s. Although one might object to considering twentieth-century writers like Lin Yutang and Zhou Zuoren *wenren* on the grounds that were merely playing at being *wenren*, we hope that the above analysis has demonstrated that the set of traits we now associate with the "*wenren* ideal" were in fact propagated by late imperial commercial publishers precisely for the purpose of playing the part.

In his *Zhongguo xin wenxue de yuanliu* 中國新文學的源流 [The Origin of China's New Literature], Zhou Zuoren claims that "literature is useless" 文學無用. Like Lin Yutang, Zhou was writing against the belief that literature could save China, which he viewed as heir to Qing dynasty literary moralism. The idea of preserving something by insisting on its "uselessness" was not new in China. One finds precisely these sentiments in the *Zhuangzi*:

> Now you, sir, have a big tree and are bothered by its uselessness. Why don't you plant it in Nevernever Land with its wide, open spaces? There you can roam in nonaction by its side and sleep carefreely beneath it. Your Stinky Quassia's life will not be cut short by axes, nor will anything else harm it. Being useless, how could it ever come to grief?
> 今子有大樹，患其無用，何不樹之於無何有之鄉，廣莫之野，彷徨乎無為其側，逍遙乎寢臥其下？不夭斤斧，物無害者，無所可用，安所困苦哉！(Mair 1998: 9)

This essay has argued that the trivialization of literary writing in late imperial China opened up a discursive space for amoral literary play and unapologetic displays of skill—the business of *wenren*. Literary self-marginalization mirrored political disengagement, and both late imperial "*wenren*" and modern "writers" jealously guarded the uselessness of their Stinky Quassia.

Endnotes

[1] For a thorough discussion of the *xiaopin* essay in 1930s China, see Laughlin 2008.

[2] "Ru 儒," *Shuowen jiezi* 說文解字, http://www.shuowen.org/view/4937.

[3] For definitions, etymologies, and phonetic reconstructions, see Schuessler 2007: 445.

[4] See Lai and Xin 157–79, Nylan 5-20, and Cheng 101–18.

[5] This passage is an allusion to the *Analects* passage, "The Master said, 'A youth, when at home, should be filial, and, abroad, respectful to his elders. He should be earnest and truthful. He should overflow in love to all, and cultivate the friendship of the good. When he has time and opportunity, after the performance of these things, he should employ them in polite studies.'" 子曰: 弟子入則孝，出則弟，謹而信，汎愛眾，而親仁。行有餘力，則以學文。I read the *zhi* 之 in Liu Xie's 行有餘力，則可習之 as referring to *wen* 文 (James Legge, trans.).

[6] Our translation. "Baopuzi," *Chinese Text Project*, http://ctext.org/baopuzi.

[7] Our translation, *ibid*.

[8] Our translation. "Jinlouzi," *Chinese Text Project*, accessed May 29, 2014, http://ctext.org/jinlouzi.

[9] See De Weerdt 2007.

[10] See De Weerdt 1999 and De Weerdt 2007.

[11] For a discussion of these events, see Guo 1993.3: 17.

[12] For critical discussions of the *Xianqing ouji*, see Hanan 1988 and Sieber 2000. For connoisseurship culture and literary culture in the late Ming, see Li 1995.

[13] *Siku quanshu zongmu tiyao*, zibu 子部, 116:26, *Pulu lei cunmu* 譜錄類存目. *Scripta Sinica* version, accessed May 30, 2014, hanji.sinica.edu.tw/.

[14] On this habit, see He.

[15] The editors write that the "pure speech" of Ming *xiaopin* "originate in this" because it was a Song dynasty work.

[16] *Siku quanshu zongmu tiyao*, zibu, 103:13, *Yijia lei* 醫家類, *Scripta Sinica* version, accessed May 30, 2014.

[17] *Siku quanshu zongmu tiyao*, zibu, 125:35, *Zajia lei cunmu* 雜家類存目, *Scripta Sinica* version, accessed May 30, 2014.

[18] Author of the satirical novel *Rulin waishi* 儒林外史 [Unofficial History of the Literati]. For a critical study, see Shang 2003.

[19] On Zhang Xuecheng, see Ridley 1973 and Nivison 1966.

Works Cited

Bol, Peter. *"This Culture of Ours": Intellectual Transitions in T'ang and Sung China*. Stanford: Stanford University Press, 1992.

Carlitz, Katherine. "Printing as Performance: Literati Playwright-Publishers of the Late Ming." In *Printing and Book Culture in Late Imperial China*. Cynthia Joanne Brokaw and Kai-wing Chow, eds. Berkeley: University of California Press, 2005.

Cheng, Anne. "What Did It Mean to Be a Ru in Han Times?" *Asia Major*, Third Series 14.2 (2001): 101-118.

De Weerdt, Hilde. "Canon Formation and Examination Culture: The Construction of 'Guwen' and 'Daoxue' Canons." *Journal of Song-Yuan Studies* 29 (1999): 91-134.

---. *Competition over Content: Negotiating Standards for the Civil Service Examinations in Imperial China (1127–1279)*. Cambridge: Harvard University Asia Center, 2007.

Egan, Ronald. *The Literary Works of Ou-yang Hsiu (1007–72)*. Cambridge: Cambridge University Press, 1984.

---. *Word, Image, and Deed in the Life of Su Shi*. Cambridge: Council on East Asian Studies, Harvard University, 1994.

Elman, Benjamin. *A Cultural History of Civil Examinations in Late Imperial China*. Berkeley: University of California Press, 2000.

---. *From Philosophy to Philology: Intellectual and Social Aspects of Change in Late Imperial China*. Los Angeles: UCLA Asian Pacific Monograph Series, 2001.

Greenbaum, Jamie. *Chen Jiru (1558–1639): The Background to Development and Subsequent Uses of Literary Personae*. Leiden: Brill, 2007.

Gu Yanwu 顧炎武. "Fuzi zhi yanxing yu tiandao" 夫子之言性與天道 [The Pedants Discussing Human Nature and the Heavenly Way]. In *Ri zhi lu* 日知錄. Chen Yuan 陳垣, ed. Hefei: Anhui daxue chubanshe, 2007.

Guo Yuheng 郭豫衡. *Zhongguo sanwen shi* 中国散文史 [A History of Chinese Prose Literature]. 3 vols. Shanghai: Shanghai guji chubanshe, 1993.

Hanan, Patrick. *The Invention of Li Yu*. Cambridge, Mass: Harvard University Press, 1988.

Hartman, Charles. *Han Yü and the T'ang Search for Unity*. Princeton: Princeton University Press, 1986.

He, Yuming. *Home and the World: Editing the "Glorious Ming" in Woodblock-Printed Books of the Sixteenth and Seventeenth Centuries.* Cambridge: Harvard University Asia Center, 2013.

Huters, Theodore. *Bringing the World Home: Appropriating the West in Late Qing and Early Republican China.* Honolulu: University of Hawai'i Press, 2005.

---. 1987. "From Writing to Literature: The Development of Late Qing Theories of Prose," *Harvard Journal of Asiatic Studies* 47.1 (1987): 51-96.

Kern, Martin. 2001. "Ritual, Text, and the Formation of the Canon: Historical Transitions of 'Wen' in Early China." *T'oung Pao* Second Series, 87.1/3 (2001): 43-91.

Lai, Chen, and Xin, Yan. "'Ru': Xunzi's Thoughts on Ru and Its Significance." *Frontiers of Philosophy in China* 4.2 (June 2009): 157–179.

Laughlin, Charles. *The Literature of Leisure and Chinese Modernity.* Honolulu: University of Hawaii Press, 2008.

Legge, James. "Charge to the Marquis Wen." Chinese Text Project, http://ctext.org/shang-shu/charge-to-the-marquis-wen.

---. "Jiang Han." *Chinese Text Project*, http://ctext.org/book-of-poetry/jiang-han.

Li, Wai-yee. "Between 'Literary Mind' and 'Carving Dragons': Order and Excess in *Wenxin diaolong.*" In *A Chinese Literary Mind: Culture, Creativity, and Rhetoric in Wenxin diaolong.* Cai Zong-qi, ed. Stanford: Stanford University Press, 2001. Pp. 193-225, 275-282.

---. "The Collector, the Connoisseur, and Late-Ming Sensibility." *T'oung Pao* Second Series 81.4/5 (1995): 269–302.

Lin Yutang. "Xiaopinwen zhi yixu" 小品文之遺緒 [The Cause of the Informal Essay Left to us by Our Forefathers]. In *Xiaopinwen yishu tan* 小品文藝術談 [On the Art of the Informal Essay]. Li Ning 李寧, ed. Beijing: Zhongguo guangbo dianshi chubanshe, 1990. Pp. 101-107.

Mair, Victor H. *Wandering on the Way: Early Taoist Tales and Parables of Chuang Tzu.* Honolulu: University of Hawai'i Press, 1998.

Mao shi zhengyi 毛詩正義 [An Orthdox Interpretation of the Mao Commentary on the *Classic of Poetry*]. In *Shi san jing zhu shu (biao dian ben)* 十三經注疏 (標點本) 3:1458. Beijing: Beijing daxue chubanshe, 1999.

McMullen, David. *State and Scholars in T'ang China*. Cambridge: Cambridge University Press, 1988.

Morohashi Tetsuji, ed. *Dai Kan-Wa jiten*. Tokyo: Taishukan Shoten, 1990-2001.

Nivison, David S. *The Life and Thought of Chang Hsüeh-ch'eng*. Stanford: Stanford University Press, 1966.

Nylan, Michael. "Kongzi and Mozi, the Classicists (Ru 儒) and the Mohists (Mo 墨) in Classical-Era Thinking." *Oriens Extremus* 48 (2009): 1-20.

Owen, Stephen Owen, ed. *Readings in Chinese Literary Thought*. Cambridge: Council on East Asian Studies, Harvard University, 1992.

Ridley, Charles P. *Educational Theory and Practice in Late Imperial China: The Teaching of Writing as a Specific Case*. Stanford: Stanford University, 1973.

Sanguo zhi 三國志 [A Record of the Three Kingdoms]. *Wei shu* 魏書, *juan* 21, *liezhuan* 21, *Scripta Sinica* 漢籍電子文件資料庫.

Schuessler, Axel. *ABC Etymological Dictionary of Old Chinese*. Honolulu: University of Hawai'i Press, 2007.

Shang shu zhengyi 尚書正義 [An Orthodox Interpretation of the *Classic of Documents*]. In *Shisan jing zhu shu (biaodian ben)* 十三經注疏 (標點本) 2:654. Beijing: Beijing daxue chubanshe, 1999.

Shang, Wei. *Rulin Waishi and Cultural Transformation in Late Imperial China*. Cambridge: Harvard University Asia Center, 2003.

Sieber, Patricia. "Seeing the World Through 'Xianqing Ouji' (1671): Visuality, Performance, and Narratives of Modernity." *Modern Chinese Literature and Culture* 12.2 (2000): 1-43.

Von Falkenhausen, Lothar. "The Concept of Wen in the Ancient Chinese Ancestral Cult." *Chinese Literature: Essays, Articles, and Reviews* 18 (1996): 1-22.

Yan Zhitui. *Yanshi jiaxun jijie* 顏氏家訓集解 [Collected Commentaries on the Yan Family Precepts]. *Juan* 4, "Wenzhang" 文章 Section 9, *Scripta Sinica* 漢籍電子文件資料庫.

Yoshikawa, Kōjirō and John Timothy Wixted. *Five Hundred Years of Chinese Poetry, 1150-1650: The Chin, Yuan, and Ming Dynasties*. Princeton, NJ: Princeton University Press, 1989.

Young, Lung-chang. "Ku Yen-Wu's Views on the Ming Examination System." *Ming Studies* 23 (1987): 48-63.

3

A Functionalist Scientific Worldview in the Early Chinese Science Fiction Story "Tales of the New Mr. Braggadocio"

Hua Li

Introduction

Science-popularization science fiction has been a major literary genre in China since science fiction became a transplanted Chinese literary genre in the late Qing years of the early 20th century. During this emergence of Chinese science fiction, Xu Nianci 徐念慈 (1875–1908) and Lu Xun 魯迅 (1881-1936) called for the penning of science fiction as a tool for popularizing science and technology among lay readers. This function is reflected in early Chinese science fiction works such as *Tales of the Moon Colony* [*Yueqiu zhimin di xiaoshuo* 月球殖民地小說, 1904] and "Tales of the New Mr. Braggadocio" [*Xin faluo xiansheng tan* 新法螺先生譚, 1905].

In the 1930s and 1940s, Gu Junzheng 顧均正 (1902-1980) further developed the genre by incorporating scientific ideas into the aesthetic framework of a given science fiction narrative with tortuous plots. He attempted to improve his readers' understanding of science and technology through the vehicle of his short-story collection *Under the North Pole* [*Zai beiji xia* 在北極下, 1940]. Later in the century during the 1950s and 1980s, science-popularization science fiction rose to the status of one of the top literary genres in China. These works contained detailed and rigorous descriptions of scientific concepts and principles. This emphasis on exploring technology and science through fiction laid the groundwork for a more imaginative or "hard" Chinese science fiction that has flourished since the 1990s.

This chapter examines the pioneering Chinese science-fiction story "Tales of the New Mr. Braggadocio," which was written by Xu Nianci under his pen name Donghai Juewo 東海覺我 in 1905.[1] This story reflects the growing influence of modern science and the spread of a functionalist scientific worldview among many late Qing intellectuals. I will explain this by examining the literary scene and the standing of modern science at the time the story was written, by exploring the story's scientific neologisms and related terminology, and by surveying the story's readership.

"Tales of the New Mr. Braggadocio" was the second earliest Chinese science fiction work. The literary critic and science fiction writer Ye Yonglie 葉永烈 discovered this long-neglected story during the early 1980s when browsing through an old collection entitled *New Braggadocio* [*Xin faluo* 新法螺], which had been published by the Fiction Grove Society [*Xiaoshuo lin she* 小說林社] in Shanghai during June 1905. Both the front and back covers of the collection were festooned with the neologism *kexue xiaoshuo* 科學小說 [scientific fiction] to indicate the genre of the fiction therein. The collection includes three stories: Xu Nianci's "Tales of the New Mr. Braggadocio" plus Tian Xiaosheng's 天笑生 (pseudonym of Bao Tianxiao 包天笑, 1876-1973) two Chinese translations from the Japanese, "Tales of Mr. Braggadocio" and "Supplementary Tales of Mr. Braggadocio." The term *faluo* 法螺 is taken directly from the Japanese word *hora*, and means "boasting" or "a big lie" (it is also a Buddhist term referring to the shell of a triton that monks sometimes use in ceremonies). In the Japanese translation of an 18th-century German collection of short stories, Iwaya Sazanami 嚴谷小波 (1869-1933) drew upon the term *faluo* as a clever nickname for the protagonist Baron Münchhausen in Rudolf Erich Raspe's (1736-1794) *The Surprising Adventures of Baron Münchhausen* (1781) in order to emphasize the implausibility of the protagonist's fanciful adventures. Xu Nianci adapted his "Tales of the New Mr. Braggadocio" from Bao Tianxiao's two translated stories.

Xu Nianci's piece was written one year later than *Tales of the Moon Colony*. *Tales of the Moon Colony* has generally been identified as the first piece of Chinese science fiction. It was written in 1904 by an anonymous author with the pen name Huangjiang Diaosou 荒江釣叟. *Tales of the Moon Colony* is an incomplete work that was serialized off and on in 35 installments within the magazine *Illustrated Fiction* [*Xiuxiang xiaoshuo* 繡像小說] in 1904. The novel is an imitation of *Five Weeks on a Balloon* by Jules Verne (1828–1905), and is a key source for many literary watchwords that figure prominently in Lu Xun's fiction, such as China as the "sick man of Asia" that confines its denizens inside a cultural "iron house" and incites many of them to "cannibalism" (Isaacson 50). Because of the unfinished nature of *Tales of the Moon Colony*, "Tales of the New Mr. Braggadocio" can be considered the earliest complete science fiction narrative in China.[2]

Since about 2005, Chinese science fiction has attracted the attention of an increasing number of Chinese and Western critics. Wu Yan, Mingwei Song, and other literary critics have noticed some recurring science fiction motifs in contemporary Chinese science fiction, and have traced many of their origins back to early 20th-century science fiction by Liang Qichao 梁啟超 (1873-1929), Lu Xun, Xu Nianci, and Lao She 老舍 (1899-1966). Xu Nianci's "Tales of the New Mr. Braggadocio" has been read by various academic critics to explain why Chinese science fiction emerged around the turn of the 20th century. In two of the most recent studies of "Tales of the New Mr. Braggadocio," both authors situate their discussion of the story within the discourse of orientalism, colonialism, imperialism, and Marxism. For example, Nathaniel Isaacson relates "the emergence of sci-fi to the European colonial project" and offers the following conclusion: "Science fiction as a literary category emerged in China as a product of what Tani Barlow has identified as 'colonial modernity'" (33-54). In a similar ideological vein, Shaoling Ma argues that the brain-based electricity which Xu Nianci describes in "Tales of the New Mr. Braggadocio" is a "daring commentary on political economy through science fiction"—and that the story "demonstrates the relevance of Marxist critique as a way of understanding early twentieth-century Chinese science fiction" (69). Both critics are preoccupied with the allegedly overwhelming foreign impact on the production of early Chinese science fiction. Their approach contends that the emergence of Chinese science fiction narratives such as "Tales of the New Mr. Braggadocio" was caused by Western colonialist incursions in China, and reveals anxieties among many Chinese intellectuals and writers about the encounter between China and various foreign powers during the late Qing period. However, the reading of the story that I offer below does not try to clothe Xu Nianci in the garb of a Marxist or anti-colonialist ideologue, but instead focuses on his heartfelt preoccupation with championing modern science as an efficient and proven tool of national development.

A Revolution in Fiction and the Function of Science Fiction

The introduction and reception of Western science fiction in China at the turn of the 20th century catalyzed the formation of science fiction as a transplanted Chinese literary genre. Meanwhile, early Chinese science fiction was also a product of the "revolution in fiction" [xiaoshuojie geming 小說界革命] advocated by Liang Qichao in the late Qing period. The introduction of foreign novels to China through translation was crucial to the rise of new Chinese fiction. Beginning in 1899, Liang Qichao called for "a revolution in poetry," "a revolution in prose," and "a revolution in fiction"—and endeavored to make them a reality by restructuring Chinese literature on the basis of various models derived from foreign literature.[3]

Among the three literary "revolutions," the one in fiction gained the most traction, contributing to the emergence of the new genres of political fiction, detective fiction, science fiction, and romance fiction in early 20th-century China. Liang Qichao first discussed the "revolution in fiction" in his treatise "On the Relationship between Fiction and the Government of the People" in 1902 (1:50-54). He called for writing a non-traditional type of socially engaged fiction that could be aimed at transforming Chinese society in a way that traditional fiction never did. Liang concluded his treatise with reformist zeal: "Therefore, if we want to reform collective governance in the present day, we must start with a revolution in fiction. If we want to rejuvenate the people, we must start with new fiction" (1:54).

Liang's call for a new type of engagé fiction is thus based on its potential ability to advance social reform and contribute to the well-being of the populace. His emphasis on the function of fiction to transform society derived from his favoring of socially engaged foreign fiction over traditional vernacular Chinese fiction. After the failure of the Hundred Days' Reform of 1898 within the Qing court, he fled the Empress Dowager's ensuing crackdown on reformists and found political asylum in Japan. There he rapidly came to view the new Japanese literary genre of the political novel as a tool for carrying out political and social struggle in China.

Liang Qichao and his contemporaries started to carefully select an assemblage of foreign novels for translation into Chinese. A given literary work's potential for enlightening the reading public and reforming society became their main criterion for selecting foreign novels to translate. Specifically, theme, plot, subject matter, and narrative style were the four elements they considered, while theme held priority over the other three. The foreign narratives Liang and his fellow reformers selected reflect the themes of democracy, liberty, national self-determination, human rights, modern science, and other progressive ideologies and modes of thought. Naturally, the genres of political fiction, socially engaged fiction, and science fiction were their first choices. This also explains why new fiction written during the late Qing period often contained lengthy political commentary. In addition, foreign fiction with intricate and convoluted plot structure, lively subject matter, and unusual narrative styles also attracted late Qing Chinese translators—including many works of detective fiction and romantic fiction (Chen 11). However, compared with political fiction, socially engaged fiction, and science fiction, detective fiction and romance fiction were viewed more commonly as popular entertainment rather than as works of mass edification. As one form of "new fiction," from the very beginning Chinese science fiction was typically saddled with the task of reforming society and viewed as a tool for political and social reform. This is one of the critical differences between early Chinese science fiction and its even earlier Western counterpart.

"Tales of the New Mr. Braggadocio" emerged from precisely this socio-cultural backdrop and literary scene. In addition, the introduction of modern science to China through Euro-American missionary work in the 19th century also helped lay the foundation for the emergence of Chinese science fiction. "British and American missionaries viewed science as emblematic of their superior knowledge systems. Their introduction of modern science and medicine to China was not only a missionary tactic; it was a way of showcasing the wealth and power of Western nations" (Elman 112). These missionaries funded new translations, newspapers, and schools in China as early as the 1830s. For example, the joint missionary-merchant Publication Society for the Diffusion of Useful Knowledge in China was founded in 1834, and "initiated an ambitious plan to present in Chinese works on history, geography, natural history, medicine, mechanics, natural theology, and other subjects" (Elman 103). For example, Inkstone Press (the former London Missionary Society Press) was founded in Shanghai in 1842. It was the first publisher to introduce modern science in China beyond the five treaty ports established that same year by Sino-British Treaty of Nanjing (Elman 117). These publications helped Qing intellectuals and officials develop a better grasp of the new maritime world they faced after the First Opium War (1839-1842). By the time Chinese science fiction began to appear at the turn of the 20th century, many Chinese writers and intellectuals had already absorbed a basic grounding in modern science, and were able to infuse their literary works with this knowledge. Xu Nianci was one of these writers.

Xu Nianci, born in Zhaowen (present-day Changshu), Jiangsu in 1875, studied English, Japanese, and mathematics along with the traditional Chinese curriculum during his formative years, and passed the county-level imperial civil service examination at the age of 21.[4] In 1897, he established a Chinese-Western school with his friends in Changshu, and taught history, geography, and mathematics for six years. Xu began to translate foreign literary works in 1903, during the autumn of which he founded the Fiction Grove Society in Shanghai with the novelist Zeng Pu 曾樸 (1872–1935) and other friends. The Fiction Grove Society published Xu's "Tale of the New Mr. Braggadocio" in book form in 1905.[5]

Xu Nianci was an ardent promoter of science fiction. He worked on the translation and writing of science fiction from 1903 until he died of an illness in 1908. Before writing "Tales of the New Mr. Braggadocio," Xu Nianci translated some works of science fiction such as *New Stage* [*Xin wutai* 新舞臺] by the Japanese writer Shunrō Oshikawa 押川春浪 (1876–1914) in 1904, and "His Wisdom: The Defender" [*Hei xingxing* 黑行星] by Simon Newcomb (1835–1909) in 1905 (Yu 14). As co-founder of the literary journal *Fiction Grove*, he used this magazine as a megaphone for promoting science fiction. In the first issue of *Fiction Grove*, he published an essay entitled "The Origin of *Fiction Grove*," in which he writes: "Journeys outward to the moon and inward to the center of the earth change with each passing day. These voyages originate from scientific ideals, go beyond the confines of nature, and bring about progress" (Yu 13-14). He regarded science fiction as a tonic for advancing the consciousness of humankind, and disapproved of many Chinese writers' preference for detective novels, which he scorned as an idle diversion. Xu Nianci believed that for the sake of the future of Chinese society, its literary translators should specialize in translations of military novels, adventure novels, and science fiction. In this same issue, he began to serialize the science fiction novella "Electric Crown" [*Dian guan* 電冠], which was translated by the woman writer Chen Hongbi 陳鴻璧 (1884–1966).[6] This journal increasingly focused on publishing science fiction written by Chinese writers, including lengthy works of science fiction in book form.

Modern Science and Its Social Function

Xu's educational background and literary experience are reflected in his story "Tales of the New Mr. Braggadocio." The protagonist is presented as an intellectual who appreciates all kinds of Western knowledge, and has interests in polytechnic and general information, rather than solely in literary research. The story showcases the scientific worldview, modern science, neologisms, various classifications of knowledge, and the formation of scientific institutions. More importantly, science and technology are presented as inseparable from their social function and their role in national development.

In the story, the first-person narrator recounts his adventures on Earth and in space. He is blown afar by a gust of wind to the Himalayas, and gains the ability to separate his physical body from his soul. His soul lightens up and is divided into four pieces due to an accidental fall.[7] One quarter of his soul is joined to his physical body and drops to the center of the earth by means of the force of gravity. At the center of the earth, he meets a Chinese ancestor who is disappointed with his offspring—i.e., the protagonist's contemporaries. The remaining three-quarters of his soul flies away beyond Earth's atmosphere and almost crashes into the moon, hence causing a volcanic eruption on the moon. After this collision with the moon, his soul continues to fly even further from Earth, eventually alighting upon Mercury, where he witnesses the technology of human rejuvenation. After leaving Mercury, he travels to Venus, on which he finds his own travel diary that he lost five years earlier while on a trek to the North Pole. Next, the protagonist recalls his earlier voyage by hot-air balloon to the North Pole and his encounter with polar bears there. After visiting Venus, his soul orbits around the sun before eventually returning to Earth, specifically the Mediterranean Sea, where it rejoins with his physical body and the remaining quarter of his soul. Lost and afloat in the Mediterranean Sea, the protagonist is rescued by a Chinese ship and returns to Shanghai. In Shanghai, the protagonist uses so-called brain electricity [*nao dianbo* 腦電波] that he had obtained during his adventures to train ordinary people to develop their own brain electricity. However, his promotion of brain electricity somehow aggravates the problem of worldwide unemployment, so he finally feels compelled to shut down his brain electricity training sessions.

Like many of his contemporaries, Xu Nianci attempted to tie his stories to science, considering this sort of fiction to be a means of promoting scientific knowledge. This stance has become a common one within what came to be known as *kepu xing kehuan* [science-popularization science fiction 科普型小說] in the PRC, especially during the 1950s and 1980s. Xu Nianci was wholly justified in identifying the genre of his story as *kexue xiaoshuo* ("scientific fiction," to distinguish it from the standard contemporary rendering of "science fiction" as *kehuan xiaoshuo* 科幻小說) because the story includes several themes that were widespread in this new type of fiction. These include voyages into space and other unexplored realms, specifically the moon, Mercury, Venus, and the center of the earth, encounters with aliens (on Mercury and Venus); and a wide range of frames of time. These typical science fiction motifs are more than just narrative devices. They reflect the various aspects of modern science that many Chinese intellectuals knew about or found interesting, and reveal these intellectuals' perceptions about the social function of modern science and technology.

The space that is explored by the protagonist in the story is typical of settings that imaginary explorations in early Western science fiction use: Earth itself, outer space, and the interior of Earth (Seed 8). In "Tales of the New Mr. Braggadocio," one of the plot lines is the journey into space, whose unlimited expanse gives license to an outward push of the author's imagination. As in early Western science fiction, the use of anti-gravity devices is self-evidently a pretext for rapidly covering the enormous distances of space. Xu Nianci uses a gust of wind to initiate his narrative of various faraway excursions. Later in the story, the protagonist's travel diary is conveyed to Venus on a hot-air balloon.

Xu Nianci gives only perfunctory attention to the voyage itself, such as his protagonist's transit from the Himalayas to the hollow center of Earth or to the supposedly inhabited planets of Mercury and Venus. The space voyage functions as a device for defamiliarizing ourselves from ordinary terrestrial ways, thereby enabling extraterrestrial perspectives to be constructed on Earth. The voyage into space also creates an aesthetic of estrangement, which is indispensible for science fiction. It offers a convenient transit to other worlds, and more importantly offers sites for metaphysical and cultural speculation.

Aside from using the voyage into space as a narrative device, Xu also uses it to introduce modern astronomy to Chinese readers. In 1849, the American medical missionary Benjamin Hobson (1816-1873) wrote the *Summary of Astronomy* in addition to his various works on Western medicine. He presented to his Chinese students the Copernican solar system in terms of Newtonian gravitation, though he pointed to God as the author of the works of creation (Elman 111). Western astronomy attracted the interest of many Chinese literati who associated it with traditional Chinese mathematical astronomy. The New Mr. Braggadocio's travel in the solar system reveals Xu's knowledge about Newtonian mechanics based on gravitational pull.

The New Mr. Braggadocio has experienced various unusual phenomena on faraway planets such as alien humanoids and brain-changing technology on Mercury, and the potential mining of precious metals and gems from mollusks on Venus. The aliens in science fiction are by definition always imagined through reference to familiar human groups and other animal species. In "The New Mr. Braggadocio," the aliens are in forms of humanoids on Mercury and treasure-bearing mollusks on Venus. They tend to be described in terms that are linked with that period's ethnic or "racial" hierarchies, which I will discuss in more detail later in this chapter.

The rejuvenation technology on Mercury is suggestive of Chinese intellectuals' knowledge of modern Western medicine at that time. As early as the 1850s, Benjamin Hobson translated Western medical works into classical Chinese, and produced a series of works to educate his medical students in China. For example, his *Treatise on Physiology* presented the basics of modern anatomy, introducing his Chinese readership to the untraditional medical idea of the centrality of the brain and the nervous system (Elman 105). Xu's description of the workings of the brain in his story underlines the fact that knowledge of modern Western medicine in late-Qing China was not limited to Chinese medical students and scientists, for it extended to ordinary men of letters like Xu Nianci. This episode also echoes Liang Qichao's call for rejuvenating the Chinese people and transforming the mentality of the populace. In the story, Xu transformed Liang's conceptual abstraction into a concrete occurrence. The inhabitants on Mercury could refill the brain of an old or dead creature with a young brain and thereby transform it into a newly revitalized creature. After observing the operation, the protagonist plans to start a similar business in Shanghai dedicated to reforming and rejuvenating the brains of the Chinese populace.

Along with outer space, another destination of the New Mr. Braggadocio is the center of the earth. As observed by David Seed, "Hollow-earth narratives developed in the late 19th century as a separate subgenre partly out of the theories of John Cleves Symmes, Jr., who believed that the Earth had openings at the North and South Poles" (8). In the wake of Symmes' conjectures about these non-existent openings, a flurry of narratives about traveling to the center of the earth occurred in early Western science fiction writing. In Xu's story, the protagonist dives to the center of the earth, and eventually travels back to Earth's surface, winding up in the Mediterranean Sea. The center-of-the-earth narrative tends to gloss over many of the physical difficulties of imagining how this deep interior region might appear, merely assuming that it would retain most of the ordinary characteristics of life and landforms present at Earth's surface. This voyage to the center of the earth also echoes Jules Verne's *A Journey to the Center of the Earth*, which was translated into Chinese under the title *Dixin youji* 地心遊記 by Lu Xun in 1906. In "The New Mr. Braggadocio," the center of the earth that the protagonist visits is directly underneath Henan province (roughly the center of China proper); this embodies the fantasy of traveling back into humankind's evolutionary past. Within the center of the earth, the passage of time is on a different scale: one day in the center of the earth is equivalent to six hundred years on Earth's surface.

While underground, the New Mr. Braggadocio meets an old man surnamed Huang 黃 who symbolizes the ancestor of the Chinese ethnicity. Old Huang can observe his descendants on Earth's surface through a special lens. Here, Xu draws upon the voice of this old man to inject authorial political commentary on Chinese society: 65% of the population is addicted to opium; many non-addicts are sick, superstitious, or hanker after money to the exclusion of everything else, while only 8% of the population retains a kindly and virtuous nature and remains uncorrupted. The various percentages of the population are represented by different colors of gases in test tubes, as if in a chemistry lab. Though Xu does not present the chemical terminology of the gases in Chinese, this analogy implies that chemicals are at the root of all matter, a modern Western idea that strongly contrasts with the traditional Chinese concept of the five phases of all matter [*yinyang wuxing* 陰陽五行].

The Chinese ancestor Old Huang asks the protagonist to express his sadness and disappointment to his Chinese descendants and help awaken them from complacency in the face of the aforementioned dire circumstances. The old man's disappointment with his descendants betrays the author's evolution-inspired ideas about the rise and decline of societies. In the wake of Yan Fu's 嚴復 (1854-1921) watershed translation of Herbert Spencer's *The Study of Sociology* into Chinese in 1902, Spencer's idiosyncratic twist on Darwinian evolutionary thought had become a common prism through which Chinese intellectuals and writers sought to understand their own history, society, and prospects for future development. In his book *Developmental Fairy Tales*, Andrew Jones argues that the "vernacularization" of evolution-inspired developmental thought has shaped the narrative mode of modern Chinese literature. Western science fiction in the form of "evolutionary adventure tales" such as Edward Bellamy's *Looking Backward: 2000–1887* inspired Chinese "narratives of national development" (Jones 28-47).

In "The New Mr. Braggadocio," Xu recasts such developmental thinking in the form of speculative fiction. The ancestor's disappointment derives from his apparently newfound belief in Spencerian social evolution and progress. This episode is similar to the one on Venus. On Venus, when the New Mr. Braggadocio touches the bodies of these mollusks, which are the most advanced and high-ranking inhabitants of the planet, he can feel the warmth of these surprisingly warm-blooded creatures. He laments that people on Earth have instead reverted back to the state of cold-blooded creatures. These two episodes demonstrate that Spencer's misguided "application of evolutionary theory to questions of social, cultural, and geopolitical import resulted in an intense and productive anxiety about their [Chinese] historical agency as intellectuals entrusted with the task of building a modern nation" (Jones 10).

After one quarter of the protagonist's soul returns to Earth from outer space and reconnects with the other three quarters of his soul along with his physical body, the New Mr. Braggadocio falls into the Mediterranean Sea. There he encounters some ships from China's navy. This episode is a reflection of the relative weakness of China's navy during the late Qing. In 1841, Wei Yuan 魏源 (1794-1856) wrote *A Treatise on the Maritime Countries* [*Haiguo tu zhi* 海國圖志]. He advocated the strengthening of Qing military defenses "that included construction of a navy yard and arsenal near Guangzhou where Westerners could teach the Chinese how to build ships and manufacture arms" (Elman 104). During the 1860s, arsenals and shipyards were established in some Chinese ports for creating better munitions and ships for defending the coast, such as the Jiangnan Arsenal in Shanghai and the Fuzhou Navy Yard. However, because of inferior training, poor coordination, mediocre leadership, and general mismanagement, the numerically superior Qing Navy with its many up-to-date warships suffered a crushing defeat at the hands of the Japanese Navy in the Sino-Japanese war of 1894-95. In the story, the advanced modern fleet established by patriotic Chinese volunteers not only reflects the social reality of China's ineffectual navy, but also echoes many late Qing intellectuals' call for a revitalized Chinese military.

The protagonist's travels to outer space and the center of the earth, along with his encounter with Chinese naval vessels on the other side of the world, showcase the author's knowledge of modern astronomy, Western medicine, physics, chemistry, and shipbuilding. Xu also reveals his knowledge of light and electricity through the protagonist's ability to literally illuminate himself and generate "brain electricity." After the protagonist accidentally falls down, he somehow gains the ability to light himself up like a firefly and generate brain electricity. The author introduces his readers to modern scientific concepts of light and heat by contrasting the new type of light that the New Mr. Braggadocio generates in his body with sunlight. Meanwhile, he also inserts political commentary about some of China's thorny social problems. When the New Mr. Braggadocio obtains the ability to illuminate himself, he shines light on both the West and the East, and hence has a chance to observe and compare the two regions. In contrast with the bright and apparently civilized Western world, he finds that his home country of China seems stuck in darkness, and his fellow Chinese are either fast asleep or else mindlessly indulging themselves in physical pleasure. He laments that his fellow Chinese cannot wake up from their somnolent state, and thus are unable to catch up with the Western world and construct a truly civilized order in China. This image of China and its people resonates with China's image as a sleeping giant at that time. The author's regret reveals his vision of China's future as a truly civilized society.

Aside from discussing modern science and technology, the story also ushered in a lot of new terms. The largest impact that translated work had upon late Qing new fiction in China was probably its importation of new terminology. In the early period of translating foreign literature, some translators directly transcribed the pronunciation of a given foreign word into Chinese and used an annotation to explain its meaning. For example, the word "captain" was often transliterated as *jiabidan* 甲必丹 instead of translated literally as *shangwei* 上尉. In contrast, other terminology was imported through a literal translation of the meaning, such as with *tianxin* 甜心 for "sweetheart." In addition, many new political terms were borrowed from Japanese renditions and used in translated works, novels, and newspaper articles, such as *zongtong* 總統 [president], *zujie* 租界 [foreign concession], *xianfa* 憲法 [constitution], *guohui* 國會 [congress], *lianbang* 聯邦 [federal], and *yiyuan* 議員 [member of parliament].

Shanghae Serial was the first publication in China to use contemporary terms for science in the 1850s. In the introduction of the first issue of *Shanghae Serial*, the editor Alexander Wylie (1815-1887) "stressed the value of science for understanding the world, and introduced the Chinese to terminology for its most important fields: chemistry, geography, animals and plants, astronomy, calculus, electricity, mechanics, fluid mechanics, and optics and sound"

(Elman, 116). During the 1870s and 1880s, the need for a consensus on terminology was critical to the success of Chinese science textbooks and primers. Western missionaries and Chinese translators worked together to compile specialized vocabularies in 85 fields. As a result, over 9000 terms were incorporated in Justus Doolittle's 1872 dictionary of the Chinese language. Many of these terms originated from ancient Chinese texts in traditional medicine, indigenous mathematics, and traditional astronomy—and often made for a poor fit with Western scientific terminology. So by the end of the 19th century, many Chinese literati had instead turned to Japanese terminology for their new Chinese vocabulary of modern science. "By 1903, state and private schools were increasingly borrowing from Japanese translations to enunciate the modern classifications of the social sciences, natural sciences, and applied sciences" (Elman 212-13).

In "Tales of the New Mr. Braggadocio," the new terms adopted were mainly related to the natural and social sciences, such as *zongjiao* 宗教 [religion], *mixin* 迷信 [superstition], *kexue* 科學 [science], *kuangwu jie* 礦物界 [mineral kingdom], *zhiwu jie* 植物界 [plant kingdom], *linghun* 靈魂 [soul], *xian wei jing* 顯微鏡 [microscope], *huxi xitong* 呼吸系統 [respiratory system], *shenjing xitong* 神經系統 [nervous system], *weixing* 衛星 [satellite], *baifenzhi* 百分之 [percentage], *qiangchang dongwu* 腔腸動物 [coelenterata], and *ruanti dongwu* 軟體動物 [mollusks]. As for the place names, an example is *Aibolaisi feng* 艾伯萊斯峰 as the transliteration of Mount Everest. The importation of new terminology helped smooth the way for the introduction of various classics of Western civilization and modern science to China, and it also reveals new classifications of knowledge. Meanwhile, the inclusion of these new terms also made the language of narration more expressive and diverse.

Scientific Worldview, Readership, and Language

The Chinese literary critic Wu Yan argues that early Chinese science fiction during the late Qing was a cultural experiment responding to the need for social change and reform. Intellectuals and writers such as Liang Qichao, Lu Xun, Zhou Zuoren 周作人, and Mao Dun 矛盾 were all advocates of this cultural experiment. In their eyes, the features of science revealed in science fiction represent accurate principles [*jingque de xueli* 精確的學理] in modern Western culture. It represents a mode of thought [*sixiang fangshi* 思想方式] that furthers the endeavor of understanding and transforming nature (97-100). It is a kind of knowledge derived from empirical and experimental thought, and reflects a "scientific worldview based on axiomatic principles" [*gongli shijie guan* 公理世界觀] to replace the traditional Chinese "worldview based on heavenly principles" [*tianli shijie guan* 天理世界觀] (Wang 140). The Chinese critic Wang Hui has argued that this imported worldview "paved the way for the division and specialization of knowledge and institutions in modern society" (140). Viewing the New Mr. Braggadocio's adventures from the perspective of the relationship between modern science, its social function, and its role in national development, Xu's story illustrates Wang's point that "the issue of science itself is a social issue" (140). Similar to the scientific journals published around the same time, such as Yaquan Magazine [*Yaquan zazhi* 亞泉雜誌, 1907], World of Science [*Kexue shijie* 科學世界, 1903] and A Glimpse of Science [*Kexue yiban* 科學一斑, 1907], "Tales of the New Mr. Braggadocio" displays a functionalist scientific worldview.

The purpose of writing about travels to outer space and the center of Earth, illustrations of modern science and technology, and the adoption of new terms is to convey a functionalist scientific perspective to the Chinese populace and thereby help move the country forward. So who were the anticipated readers of the story? Xu Nianci modestly indicates at the beginning of the story that his writing amounts to "casual and playful simulation" [*xizhuan* 戲撰] of the translated work "Tales of Mr. Braggadocio," and is designed merely to "entertain villagers" (1). Bao Tianxiao makes similar self-deprecating comments in the preface to his translated works. However, the prefaces to both Bao's and Xu's works of fiction reveal a dilemma. Each claims that the translation and writing of tales are for the purpose of entertaining women and fellow villagers—the targeted readership of new fiction. However, these tales were written in the classical or literary idiom, which would not be intelligible to such a poorly educated readership at that time. In actuality, practically all of the readers of these narrative works were literati like Bao Tianxiao and Xu Nianci themselves.

"Tales of the New Mr. Braggadocio" was written in the classical literary language partly because it was imitating the diction of Bao Tianxiao's translation, and partly because many other late Qing novels and practically all prose essays were also still written in the classical idiom at that time. During the late Qing, five types of diction coexisted in fiction writing: vernacular, literary-idiom, dialect, rhythmical prose [*pianwen* 駢文], and the translation style. Among them, vernacular novels and literary-language stories were the most popular varieties. Vernacular and literary idioms sometimes interpenetrated, and often co-existed within the same story (Chen 192). Some new works of fiction were even written entirely in the classical literary language instead of the vernacular idiom.

If we examine the imperatives of the "revolution in fiction," it would help us understand why the classical literary language still played a major role in late Qing "new fiction." One of the imperatives of the "revolution in fiction" was based on the recognition that "Among those who can read, there might be some people who do not read classics, but there are very few who do not read fiction" (Kang 1:29). Since new fiction was often considered instrumental to social reform and thus became the vehicle of new ideas, it should be easy for the reader to understand when new ideas and schools of thought were conveyed through fiction. Therefore, Liang Qichao clearly indicated the necessity of using the vernacular language for fiction in his essay "On the Relationship between Fiction and Ruling the Populace": "In terms of language, literary language is less effective than vernacular language, and serious discussion is less effective than allegory" (1:52). Other scholars such as Guan Daru also expressed a similar idea: "Fiction has the advantage of popularity and gets through to ordinary people, and vernacular language is the only means of gaining popularity and getting through to ordinary people" (Guan 1:399). Theoretically, vernacular language should have been the preferred choice of new-fiction novelists. Many writers at the time indeed favored vernacular language because of its growing popularity. In late Qing newspapers, journals and magazines, many articles were translated from the literary language to the vernacular language.

However, Liang Qichao clearly perceived the limits of vernacular Chinese. He did not advocate completely abandoning literary language, but only chose vernacular language for the specific purpose of spreading new ideas to the general reader. In private, Liang Qichao and many other writers still used the literary language to write essays embodying complicated ideas and lyrical expressiveness. There are two major reasons why such late Qing writers sensed the inadequacy of using the vernacular language[8] to convey complex ideas. On the one hand, the vernacular language had not yet been refined as a literary idiom to the extent that it would become later in the 20th century. On the other hand, it had something to do with the educational and cultural background of these writers. The literary or classical idiom had been the primary mode of diction that they had used for writing since their days of youth. Their infrequent encounter with vernacular texts led many late Qing writers and scholars to express frustration with reading and writing the vernacular language. With respect to reading, for those late Qing literati, "Reading a book written entirely in the vernacular language was far less easy than reading something written in the literary idiom" (Yao 1:151). In the publishing market at that time, novels written in literary idiom consequently tended to sell better than those written in the vernacular language. In addition, considering the literary merits of literature, many writers preferred to use literary language because of its elegance, concision, and allusiveness. Therefore, it is not surprising that many writers and translators used the classical literary idiom when writing fiction or translating foreign literature during the late Qing.[9]

The utilization of literary language in new fiction and translated works also reveals something about the actual late Qing readership. For these readers, it typically felt more natural to read a text written in the classical literary language than one written entirely in the vernacular. Therefore, when late Qing writers of fiction chose a type of prose, they were on the horns of a dilemma. In theory, drawing upon the vernacular was in accordance with the literary trends of the time. On the other hand, the shallowness of the vernacular language at that time limited the expression of more complicated modern ideas as well as aesthetic expressiveness in fiction. Though compared with the vernacular language the literary idiom was more confined, stiff, and divorced from the rhythms of spoken Chinese, its subtlety, complexity, and elegance were qualities largely lacking in vernacular language. So it is not surprising that late Qing writers and translators who had significant aesthetic concerns would often choose the literary idiom for their texts. Bao Tianxiao recalls the literary scene in the late Qing: "The trend of this period was that vernacular stories were not very well received by readers. The stories written in the classical literary language were considered higher in value" (169). When Bao translated "Tales of Mr. Braggadocio" and "Supplementary Tales of Mr. Braggadocio," he naturally chose the classical literary idiom for both of his renditions. So when Xu Nianci adapted parts of Bao Tianxiao's translated narratives in his own story "Tales of the New Mr. Braggadocio," he also chose the literary idiom.

Aside from these dilemmas of readership and language, the story is also problematic in the way it presents various scientific principles. Much of what the story presents as scientific knowledge and technology is merely speculative and lacking in scientific grounding, and often violates the very laws of science that Xu Nianci had intended to exalt. Many of the author's speculations are mere fantasies rather than bona fide fiction, at least if measured by the mainstream contemporary approach to science fiction, namely imagination based on scientific laws, or "cognitive estrangement."

In his book *Metamorphoses of Science Fiction*, Darko Suvin argues for an understanding of science fiction as the "literature of cognitive estrangement" (4). He defines science fiction as "a literary genre whose necessary and sufficient conditions are the presence and interaction of estrangement and cognition, and whose main formal device is an imaginative framework alternative to the author's empirical environment" (8). In this definition, "Concepts of science are for cognition, and fiction for estrangement" (13). The framework of "cognitive estrangement" distinguishes the genre of science fiction from both realist literature and meta-empirical genres such as the fairy tale, mythology, and fantasy narratives. Estrangement distinguishes science fiction from literature of a realist, naturalist, or empirical bent. Estrangement also signifies a break with the empirical world, but is at the same time beyond the confines of reality with the help of "novum" (a strange newness), which forms the aesthetic framework of the narrative. Cognition distinguishes science fiction from myths, fairy tales, folk tales, and fantasy narratives. If we examine Xu's "New Braggadocio" in terms of Suvin's "cognitive estrangement," it is not a bona fide work of science fiction. The story's portrayal of voyages to both outer space and the center of the earth creates an atmosphere of strange newness, but various "technologies" and "sciences" conjured forth by the author are indifferent to cognitive possibilities in the empirical world. For example, a gust of wind blows the protagonist all the way to the Himalayas and later even to outer space; and a hot-air balloon transports his travel diary as far as Venus; naturally, these scenarios confound the empirical law of gravity. When writing the story, Xu generally draws upon literary imagination as an end unto itself and seldom bothers to consider the scientific plausibility of the scenarios he has concocted. The story thus often fails to provide evidence for the propositions it puts forward. It merely expresses the author's longing to prod China's status quo into a change for the better. This creates a discrepancy between the content of actually existing Chinese science fiction and Chinese intellectuals' relatively sober scientific viewpoints. From this perspective, "Tales of the New Mr. Braggadocio" is far from a full-fledged example of science fiction, for it reads more like science fantasy.

Conclusion

"Tales of the New Mr. Braggadocio" is an ideal text for examining the rise of early Chinese science fiction. Though Xu Nianci modestly indicates at the beginning of the story that his writing is a "casual and playful simulation" of the recently translated work "Tales of Mr. Braggadocio," the composition of the story of the New Mr. Braggadocio embodies a number of new late Qing literary developments. These developments include the influence of translated Western literary works, the introduction and broadening of modern scientific knowledge in China, and Chinese writers' response to the call for a "revolution in fiction," and their increasingly functionalist scientific worldview.

Though Xu labeled his story *kexue xiaoshuo*, it is not a bona fide work of science fiction. To be sure, the story's portrayal of voyages to both outer space and the center of the earth creates an atmosphere of strange newness that is characteristic of the genre. However, various "technologies" and "sciences" conjured forth by the author are often indifferent to the demands of basic scientific plausibility. Instead, he avidly displays the functions of modern science and technology as mere tools for modernizing China and freeing the country from treaty-port spheres of foreign domination. Xu's adoption of classical language, inclusion of new terminology, and use of Western-influenced punctuation, syntax and neologisms correspond with general trends of late Qing new fiction—and involve compromise and negotiation among vernacular Chinese, classical Chinese, and the foreign-influenced translation style. Influenced by political fiction of that era, the narrative incorporates lengthy political commentary, Spencerian notions about societies and nations in a struggle for "survival of the fittest," and authorial visions of a new political system and society. Although set in outer space and the center of the earth, the New Mr. Braggadocio's experiences are understood to be about the moment contemporary to its author's time, including various anxieties and hopes that were characteristic of this point in history. The view of science reflected in this story does not only praise and showcase modern science and technology. It focuses more on displaying the functions of modern science and technology so as to achieve the goals of transforming Chinese society, fortifying the nation and contributing to its rise in the world, and freeing the country from foreign incursion and treaty-port infringement of Chinese sovereignty. This functionalist scientific worldview would often re-appear in later Chinese science fiction narratives throughout the 20th century.

Endnotes

[1] There are various translations of the story entitled "Xin faluo xiansheng tan." Nathaniel Isaacson translated it as "New Tales of Mr. Braggadocio." See Nathaniel Isaacson, "New Tales of Mr. Braggadocio," *Renditions* 77–78 (Autumn 2012): 15–38. Shaoling Ma translated the title as "A Tale of New Mr. Braggadocio." See Shaoling Ma, "'A Tale of New Mr. Braggadocio': Narrative Subjectivity and Brain Electricity in Late Qing Science Fiction," *Science Fiction Studies* 40.1 (March 2013): 55-72. I translated the title as "Tales of the New Mr. Braggadocio" to reflect the fact that the protagonist in Xu's story is a completely different character from the Japanese version's Mr. Braggadocio and the original German version's Baron von Münchhausen.

[2] Ye Yonglie, "1904 Zhongguo kehuan xiaoshuo shanguang de qidian" [1904: The Glittering Beginning of Chinese Science Fiction], *Shijie kehuan bolan* [Review of World Science Fiction] 1 (2005): 4–6.

³Chen Pingyuan offers a detailed discussion of Liang Qichao's "revolution in fiction" and the birth of new fiction during the late Qing in the first chapter of his book. Chen Pingyuan, "Xin xiaoshuo de dansheng" [The Birth of China's New Fiction], in *Zhongguo xiandai xiaoshuo de qidian:Qingmo Minchu xiaoshuo yanjiu* [The Starting Point of Modern Chinese Fiction: Research on Chinese Fiction of the Late Qing and Early Republic] (Beijing: Beijing University Press, 2005), pp. 1–23. Unless otherwise indicated, all English translations in this article are mine.

⁴Xu Nianci's real name was Xu Zhengyi 徐蒸乂; Xu Nianci was originally his alternate name, though it has become the standard way of referring to him. He wrote and published literary works under the pseudonyms Juewo and Donghai Juewo.

⁵The book was entitled *Xin faluo* [New Braggadocio], in which Xu's "Tales of Mr. New Braggadocio" and Bao Tianxiao's two Chinese translations of both "Tales of Mr. Braggadocio" and "Sequel to Tales of Mr. Braggadocio" were included. See Donghai Juewo and Tian Xiaosheng, *Xin faluo* [New Braggadocio] (Shanghai: Fiction Grove Society, 1905).

⁶Twenty-five chapters of *Electric Crown* were serialized from issue no. 1 (1907) to no. 8 (1908) in *Fiction Grove*.

⁷Shaoling Ma explains the split of the New Mr. Braggadocio's body as the duality of mind and body. The narrator "I" becomes the third-person narrator who is attached to neither spirit nor physical body. She argues that "the splitting of New Braggadocio posits another half over and above the Cartesian duality of mind and body." Ma also presents an in-depth analysis of brain electricity in the Marxist framework of fixed and circulating capital. Ma, " 'A Tale of New Mr. Braggadocio': Narrative Subjectivity and Brain Electricity in Late Qing Science Fiction."

⁸For example, a late Qing writer named Yu Cheng expresses his frustrations with the vernacular in an essay: "When the literati of our generation lift our pen to write, it is difficult to write with shallowness instead of profundity, and with vulgarity instead of elegance... It is a hundred times more challenging to write in the vernacular than in the literary idiom" (Yu 1:509).

⁹For example, when Liang Qichao translated Jules Verne's *Two Years' Vacation* (1888) into Chinese as *Shiwu xiao haojie* [Fifteen Heroes] in 1902, he originally planned to draw upon the vernacular and

follow the narrative style of the Ming-Qing novels *Water Margin* and *A Dream of Red Mansions*. However, he found it was very difficult to render it in the vernacular idiom. Instead, using literary language seemed to produce "twice as much to show for half the effort" [*laoban gongbei*] required for a vernacular version (Liang 1:64). Similarly, when Lu Xun translated Jules Verne's *From the Earth to the Moon* (1865) as *Yuejie lüxing* in 1903, he originally planned to translate it into vernacular Chinese, but he found that "using vernacular languages is repetitious and redundant [*Chunyong suyu, fuxian rongfan*]," so he decided to "draw upon the literary language" (Zhou 1:68).

Works Cited

Bao Tianxiao 包天笑. "Yi xiaoshuo de kaishi" 譯小說的開始 [When Beginning to Translate Fiction]. In *Zhongguo xiandai xiaoshuo de qidian: qingmo minchu xiaoshuo yanjiu* 中國現代小說的起點: 清末民初小說研究 [The Starting Point of Modern Chinese Fiction: Research on Chinese Fiction of the Late Qing and Early Republic]. Beijing: Beijing University Press, 2005. P. 169.

--- (Tian Xiaosheng 天笑生, pseud.). "Faluo xiansheng tan" 法螺先生譚 [Tales of Mr. Braggadocio]. In *Qingmo minchu xiaoshuo shuxi: kexue juan* 清末民初小說書系: 科學卷 [Fiction of the Late Qing and Early Republic: Science Fiction]. Beijing: Zhongguo wenlian chuban gongsi, 1997. Pp. 21-37.

Chen Pingyuan 陳平原. *Zhongguo xiandai xiaoshuo de qidian: qingmo minchu xiaoshuo yanjiu* 中國現代小說的起點: 清末民初小說研究 [The Starting Point of Modern Chinese Fiction: Research on Chinese Fiction of the Late Qing and Early Republic]. Beijing: Beijing University Press, 2005.

---and Xia Xiaohong 夏曉虹, eds. *Ershi shiji zhongguo xiaoshuo lilun ziliao* 二十世紀中國小說理論資料, 1897-1916 [Original Theoretical Materials of 20th-century Chinese Fiction, 1897-1916]. Vol. 1. Beijing: Beijing University Press, 1997.

Elman, Benjamin A. *A Cultural History of Modern Science in China*. Cambridge: Harvard University Press, 2006.

---. *On Their Own Terms: Science in China, 1550-1900*. Cambridge: Harvard University Press, 2005.

Guan Daru 管達如. "Shuo xiaoshuo" 說小說 [On Fiction]. In *Ershi*

shiji zhongguo xiaoshuo lilun ziliao, Chen Pingyuan and Xia Xiaohong, eds. Vol. 1. Beijing: Beijing University Press, 1997. Pp. 397-412.

Isaacson, Nathaniel. "New Tales of Mr. Braggadocio." *Renditions* 77 & 78 (Autumn 2012): 15–38.

---. "Science Fiction for the Nation: Tales of the Moon Colony and the Birth of Modern Chinese Fiction." *Science Fiction Studies* 40.1 (March 2013): 33–54.

Iwaya Sazanami 嚴谷小波. *Horakurabe* 法螺くらべ. Tokyo: Hakubunkan, 1904.

Jones, Andrew F. *Developmental Fairy Tales: Evolutionary Thinking and Modern Chinese Culture*. Cambridge: Harvard University Press, 2011.

Kang Youwei 康有為. "Riben shumu zhi shiyu" 日本書目志識語 [Foreword to a Catalogue of Japanese Book Titles]. In *Ershi shiji zhongguo xiaoshuo lilun ziliao* [Original Theoretical Materials of 20th Century Chinese Fiction, 1897-1916]. Chen Pingyuan and Xia Xiaohong, eds. Vol. 1. Beijing: Beijing University Press, 1997. P. 29.

Liang Qichao 梁啟超. "Lun xiaoshuo yu qunzhi zhi guanxi" 論小說與群治之關係 [On the Relationship Between Fiction and Ruling the Populace]. In *Ershi shiji zhongguo xiaoshuo lilun ziliao* [Original Theoretical Materials of 20th Century Chinese Fiction, 1897-1916]. Chen Pingyuan and Xia Xiaohong, eds. Vol. 1. Beijing: Beijing University Press, 1997. Pp. 50-54.

---. "*Shiwu xiao haojie* yihou yu" 十五小豪傑譯后語 [Postscript to the Translation of Two Years' Vacation]. In *Ershi shiji zhongguo xiaoshuo lilun ziliao* [Original Theoretical Materials of 20th Century Chinese Fiction, 1897-1916]. Chen Pingyuan and Xia Xiaohong, eds. Vol. 1. Beijing: Beijing University Press, 1997. P. 64.

Lu Xun 魯迅. "Yuejie lüxing bianyan" 月界旅行辨言 [Preface to *From the Earth to the Moon*]. In *Ershi shiji zhongguo xiaoshuo lilun ziliao*. Chen Pingyuan and Xia Xiaohong, eds. Vol. 1. Beijing: Beijing University Press, 1997. Pp. 67-68.

---. *Zhongguo xiaoshuo shilüe* 中國小說史略 [A Short History of Chinese Fiction]. Beijing: Renmin wenxue chubanshe, 1973.

Ma, Shaoling. "'A Tale of New Mr. Braggadocio': Narrative Subjectivity and Brain Electricity in Late Qing Science

Fiction." *Science Fiction Studies* 40.1 (March 2013): 55–72.
Raspe, Rudolph Erich. *The Adventures of Münchhausen*. London: Max Parrish, 1950.
Seed, David. *Science Fiction: A Very Short Introduction*. Oxford: Oxford University Press, 2011.
Suvin, Darko. *Metamorphoses of Science Fiction*. New Haven: Yale University Press, 1979.
Verne, Jules. *Didi lüxing* [Journey to the Center of the Earth]. Lu Xun, trans. Nanjing: Qixin shuju, 1906.
Wang Hui. *The End of the Revolution: China and the Limits of Modernity*. London: Verso, 2009.
---. *China from Empire to Nation-State*. Michael Gibbs Hill, trans. Cambridge: Harvard University Press, 2014.
Wu Jianren 吳趼人, "Zhongguo zhentan an mouyan" 中國偵探案牟言 [Preface to Chinese Detective Cases]. In *Ershi shiji zhongguo xiaoshuo lilun ziliao*. Chen Pingyuan and Xia Xiaohong, eds. Vol. 1. Beijing: Beijing University Press, 1997. Pp. 211-213.
Wu Yan 吳岩 and Fang Xiaoqing 方曉慶. "Zhongguo zaoqi kehuan xiaoshuo de kexue guan" 中國早期科幻小說的科學觀 [The Scientific View in Early Chinese Science Fiction]. *Ziran bianzhengfa yanjiu* 自然辯證法研究 [Research on the Dialectics of Nature] 24. 4 (April 2008): 97–100.
Xu Nianci 徐念慈. "Xin faluo xiansheng tan" 新法螺先生譚 [Tales of the New Mr. Braggadocio]. In *Qingmo Minchu xiaoshuo shuxi: kexue juan* 清末民初小說書系：科學卷 [Fiction of the Late Qing and Early Republic: Science Fiction]. Yu Runqi 于潤琦, ed. Beijing: Zhongguo wenlian chuban gongsi, 1997. Pp.1-20.
Yao Pengtu 姚鵬圖. "Lun baihua xiaoshuo" 論白話小說 [On Vernacular Fiction]. In *Ershi shiji zhongguo xiaoshuo lilun ziliao*. Chen Pingyuan and Xia Xiaohong, eds. Vol. 1. Beijing: Beijing University Press, 1997. Pp. 150-152.
Ye Yonglie 葉永烈. "1904 Zhongguo kehuan xiaoshuo shanguang de qidian" 1904 中國科幻小說閃光的起點 [1904: the Glittering Beginning of Chinese Science Fiction]. *Shijie kehuan bolan* 世界科幻博覽 [Review of World Science Fiction] 1 (2005): 4–6.
Yu Cheng 宇澄. "*Xiaoshuohai* fakan ci" 小說海發刊詞 [Foreword to *Sea of Fiction*]. In *Ershi shiji zhongguo xiaoshuo lilun ziliao*. Chen Pingyuan and Xia Xiaohong, eds. Vol. 1. Beijing: Beijing University Press, 1997. Pp. 509-510.

Yu Runqi 于潤琦. "Woguo qingmo minchu de duanpian xiaoshuo" 我國清末民初的短篇小說 [Chinese Short Stories at the End of Qing and Beginning of the Republic]. In *Qingmo minchu xiaoshuo shuxi: kexue juan*. Yu Runqi, ed. Beijing: Zhongguo wenlian chuban gongsi, 1997. Pp. 1-17.

Zheng Jun 鄭軍. "Kehuan zonglan" 科幻縱覽 [A Review of Science Fiction]. http://culture.163.com/editor/qihuan/050104/050104_107007.html (accessed 10 May 2012).

4

郝經對文化轉變與連續的反省
Hao Jing's Reflections on Cultural Change and Continuity

Hoyt Cleveland Tillman (田 浩)

Abstract

To commemorate Burton Watson's contributions to our understanding of Chinese intellectual history, I offer this short essay from one of my recent projects even though it focuses on a period that is different from those upon which he primarily focuses. Also to honor his major contributions to the translation of Chinese texts into English, I think it appropriate to provide an example of translation traffic going in the opposite direction. The bridges he and others built for intellectual interaction across the Pacific have contributed to having major scholars in East Asia, such as Lau Nap-yin 柳立言, offer to translate selected Western scholarship into Chinese. Professor Lau earned his Ph.D. at Princeton University with Professor James T.C. Liu 劉子健 and then began a splendid career as a Song dynasty historian in the Institute of History and Philology at Academia Sinica. In addition to my gratitude to Lau Nap-yin, I also appreciate my longtime unit, Peking University's Center for Study of Ancient Chinese History (Zhongguo Gudaishi Yanjiu Zhongxin) and Director Rong Xinjiang 榮新江, for having granted me permission to revise and republish this essay that appeared in the retirement festschrift honoring another friend Li Xiaocong 李孝聰; that volume, edited by Cheng Yinong 成一農, appeared in the Center's series published by Beijing's Zhonghua shuju in 2012. This short essay thus also celebrates the international collaborations and friendships across the Pacific for which Professor Watson and others of his generation paved paths.

Hao Jing (1223-1275) dedicated much of his energy not only to actively serving the Mongols after their conquest of North China in order to protect as many people and preserve as much culture as possible in such turbulent times, but also to reflect on history and culture. First, he regarded the Song dynasty as the zenith of a new stage of classical scholarship that was a logical or methodological culmination of the commentary tradition; however, he did not follow Zhu Xi in giving priority to the *Four Books* over the *Five Classics*. Second, Hao Jing hailed the establishment of an enduring intellectual lineage (*Daoxue*) during the Song as something that Tang Confucians never accomplished. Even though *Daoxue*, according to Hao Jing, "attained its grand completion in Zhu Xi," the Mongols' establishment of the Supreme Ultimate Academy in Yenjing (Beijing) meant that this lineage of *Dao* learning was conveyed to North China's center of political culture and thus ultimately filled the Realm of All-Under-Heaven. Hence, the revival of the transmission of the *Dao* and the spread of *Dao* learning throughout China was an important step toward retrieving cultural unity—a cultural unity potentially far beyond what the Tang or the Song had achieved. Third, Hao Jing's apparent enthusiasm about the progress evident in these Song cultural developments did not (despite the claims of some scholars in China today) extend to his evaluation of the Song dynasty as a whole. Ultimately, he regarded history and a government's actual accomplishments in implementing the *Dao* as crucial criteria for evaluating degree of progress and legitimacy. A much fuller discussion of these and other issues regarding Hao Jing's place in Chinese history and culture is available in Tillman's 2012 book.

Text

在蒙古征服的混亂歲月中，郝經 (1223-1275) 從實際經驗出發，反省和評價唐宋政治和文化的轉變。蒙古兵馬入侵，郝家從老家山西逃入金境，不久生下郝經。年青時，郝經從金境遷移至蒙古平定的順天府（後稱保定）。成長後，他成為忽必烈（元世祖，1260-1294在位）在蒙古內部崛起時的重要謀臣。1260年，忽必烈即帝位並鞏固政權，派他為國信使，至南宋要求宋人履行之前訂立的和約。宋臣恐怕郝經替四面楚歌的宋帝帶來不利的消息,危害他們的地位,於是將他囚禁,使他不能到達首都臨安。在元兵入侵的壓力下,宋廷才釋放郝經 (Song, 12:157.3698-3709)。1275年,郝經終於回到燕京向忽必烈述職,幾個月後便去世,南宋也在1276年降元。他一生大部分在宋、金和元朝渡過,他戮力仕元,在亂世中不但盡力保存生命和文化,也對歷史和文化作出反省。順此方向引發,我利用元人的反省來探討唐宋的轉變,部分是因為黃寬重的近著 (2006 & 2009) 有效地利用元人的深刻觀察來探討宋末的社會和文化轉變;此外,不久前柳立言的論文 (2005 & 2006)也指出近代學人探索唐宋變革時所容易犯的錯誤。也許我利用郝經的反省作為出發點,可有所創獲。

郝經對唐宋文化轉變和連續的反省值得注意,有些對今天的研究者仍具意義。例如在經學研究裡,他認為唐代既是漢代訓詁之學的完成,也是議論之學的開始,後者在宋代達到高峰。在〈經史〉一文裡,郝經認為:「訓詁之學,始於漢而備於唐。議論之學,始於唐而備於宋。」 兩者的研究方法均有過分之處:訓詁者或至於穿鑿,議論者或至於高遠。郝經認為,救弊之方在於「學經者不溺於訓詁,不流於穿鑿,不惑於議論,不尼於高遠,而知聖人之常道,則善學者也。」這個理想幾乎難以實現,因為釋經之學已經歷三變:訓詁於漢,疏釋於唐,議論於宋,三變而經之法已盡,後世無以復加,惟致力保持和利用這三種研究方法。另方面,郝經悲觀地指出,近世學者務於進取,治經時碎裂章句,學術水平大降。在〈經史〉一文裡,郝經先將唐代視為漢學至宋學的過渡,復認為唐代擁有自己的疏釋傳統 (Hao 1988: 19.9a-10b, p. 648; 1999a: 19.11b-13b; 1999b: 138.256-57)。無論何者,宋代是經學研究一個新階段的高峰,是傳統釋經之學的邏輯或方法的極致。雖然他敦促學者避免傳統經學研究的過當,他批評近世進一步支離破碎和放棄經典的完整性。

郝經對經典的討論讓他跟宋代經學的研究產生一種複雜的關係。他取名為「經」,的確潛心於經典,很早就把五經記誦,並熟悉主要的注釋。不但如此,跟宋代學者一樣,他尤其著意於《易》和《春秋》,有不少著述。在〈春秋〉一文裡,他說:

> 《易》載聖人之心,《春秋》載聖人之迹。心、迹,一也,何遠之有?…蓋《易》窮理之書,而《春秋》盡性之書也。《易》由正以推變,《春秋》由變以返正者也。(Hao 1988: 18.7b-8a, p. 639; 1999a: 18.9b-10a; 1999b: 127.242)

不像朱熹(1130-1200),他沒有把四書置於五經之上。在〈五經論〉的序言裡,他把《禮》放在其他四經之後 (Hao 1988: 18.1a, p. 636; 1999a: 18.1ab; 1999b: 127.236) ,而朱熹把其中〈大學〉和〈中庸〉兩篇

的地位抬高 (Tillman 159-71; Yin & Tillman)。

其次,郝經讚揚宋儒能夠建立一個持之久遠的學統,成就超越唐儒。在1255年,他為燕京太極書院撰寫〈周子祠堂碑〉,認為「道之統一,其傳有二焉:尊而王,其統在位,則以位傳;化而聖,其統在心,則以心傳。位傳者,人人得之,故常有在不忘;心傳者,非其人則不可得,是以或絕或續,不得而常也。」從孔子到孟子,道只靠心傳,不能靠位傳,而且孟子之後,其道不傳。即使是王通(584-617) 和韓愈 (768-824) 等一代大儒,「以道自任」,不能傳其學於後世,聖人之統也不能永久恢復。周敦頤則 (1017-1073) 大不同,其學「範圍天地,窮神知化,盡性至命。…發前聖之蘊奧,先儒之所未言,為道學宗。…一傳而得程顥 (1032-1086)、程頤 (1033-1107)、張載 (1011-1077)…卒之集大成于朱熹。」二百年來,朱子之學遍及四方,太極書院在燕京建立,標示道統已傳至北方的政治文化中心,終而充沛於天地,乃漢以來所未有 (Hao 1988: 34.8b-10b, pp. 782-83; 1999a: 34.11a-13a; 1999b: 133.405-406)。簡言之,道之再傳及道學之推廣至全國各地,是文化統一的重要里程,雖然在蒙古控制之下,此文化統一可超越唐代。

郝經的上述兩個觀點亦隱約出現在近代學術論著裡。徐洪興在2006年出版《道學思潮》,認為唐宋文化轉變的重點,在宋代經學(以義理之學為中心)的興盛、儒學(尤其是道學)在政府和社會上取得優勢、古文運動的興起,和道學對佛道兩教的抗拒 (Xu 84-177)。近代學人時常將漢唐章句之學和宋代義理之學截然二分,但John Makeham細心研究朱熹的《論語集注》,提出相反的看法,認為朱熹繼續利用漢及漢以後哲學論述的方法和概念,只是未為人發覺。為闡明這論點,他分析朱熹對人性的看法,指出它是出自情與理之間的特殊關係。理基於性,從性可直達於理。假如朱熹對人性的理論是源自黃侃 (488-545) 和王弼 (226-249) 的著作,就表示從漢唐到宋代,有一個連續的思想和傳注傳統 (Makeham 171)。

第三,郝經雖然對宋代的文化發展流露讚歎之情,但並不表示他對宋代作為一個整體也有相同的評價。有些現代學人的確從郝經的著作裡找到証據,認為他對南宋十分欽佩。例如秦鴻昌認為,郝經代表「漢統思想」,亦即郝經尤其推崇漢人建立的文化價值和王朝。他又認為,郝經的謀和,是為了永保宋朝。他從郝經所奏〈使宋譯文〉的措詞推論,郝經使宋,目的就是謀和。郝經竭盡全力,化解南北矛盾,並堅持他的夢想,要在南方與北方各立一朝。他的實際意圖,是讓南宋長久維持下去 (Qin 200)。白綱也認為,雖然郝經的身分是蒙古國信使,但他不認為元朝是正統王朝,南宋才是。在〈上宋主陳請歸國萬言書〉裡,郝經甚至說:「嘗以為漢氏之治似乎夏,李唐之治似乎商,而貴朝享國之久則似乎周,可以為後三代」(Bai 89)。

然而，在郝經論著的較大脈絡裡，其實顯示元朝較宋朝更具正統。例如在前述的〈上宋主陳請歸國萬言書〉裡，不能過於強調他對宋廷的讚美，而應看到他僅是根據國祚的長短來比較宋代和周代，而宋代的三百餘年實在遠遠比不上周代的八百載。在〈復與宋國丞相論本朝兵亂書〉裡，郝經甚至稱讚忽必烈「甚得夷夏之心，有漢唐英主之風，…其為天下主無疑也」(Hao 1988: 38.7b-8a, p. 830; 1999a: 38.9a; 1999b: 122.121)。拙作在其他地方一再指出，郝經一般以「天下」與「國家」指稱北方的蒙古 (Tillman 148-149)。更明顯的，是在〈时务〉一文裡郝經宣稱：「堯舜而下，三代而已矣。三代而下，二漢而已矣。後世不可及也。」(Hao 1988: 19.13a, p. 650; 1999a: 19.16b; 1999b: 128.259)。

因此，從郝經的文集裡，我們可以提出三個基調來檢視唐宋變奏：一是經學研究，認為宋以後已無新方法。二是道學的傳播和道統的確立，認為宋超越前代。三是王朝正統，認為郝經以元朝而不是以南宋為正統。就像柳立言先生在會議時的評論提到，乍看之下，第一和第二個基調與第三個基調有點矛盾，一方面承認宋代以經學和道學超越前代，即文化上的優越，另方面又認為元才是正統；那麼，是不是元代的經學和道學都超越南宋？假如元朝和南宋都擁有道學，為何是元代的優勝而不是南宋？從〈時務〉一文看來，郝經用了一個標準，在最後幾句：

以是知天之所與，不在于地而在于人，不在于人而在于道，不在于道而在于必行力為之而已矣。嗚呼，後世有三代二漢之地，有三代二漢之民，而不能為元魏苻秦之治者，悲夫 (Hao 1988: 19.13b, p. 650; 1999a: 19.17b; 1999b: 128.259-60)。

似乎是說，元代能將堯舜之道付諸實行（必行力為之），故優於南宋的知道堯舜之道而不能行。此外，在〈刪注刑統賦序〉裡，郝經亦認為金朝泰和律「粲粲一代之典，與唐、漢比隆，詎元魏、高齊之得厠其列也。…國家今地過于金，而民物繁庶，龍飛鳳舞，殆四十年。…必欲致治，創法立制，其先務也」(Hao 1988: 30.12ab, p. 741; 1999a: 30.15b-16a; 1999b: 124.186-87)。似乎也是以務實的「創法立制」為標準。另外在〈經史〉一文裡，他以「史」為重要的標準 (Hao 1988: 19.9a-10b, p. 640; 1999a: 19.11b-13b; 1999b: 138.256-57)。分析〈周子祠堂碑〉、〈太極書院記〉、〈送漢上趙先生序〉等文以後，拙作在其他地方指出，郝經認為元代已繼承道統 (Tillman 136-158)。但是對經典研究方面，好像還沒這樣清楚。

簡言之，郝經雖然盛讚宋代文化的進步，特別是道學和宋學的發展，但對宋代整體似乎流於悲觀。無怪乎他存世的主要歷史論著《續後漢書》把重點放在接續漢代的歷史，連唐代都不大著意。總的來說，郝經只在文化領域明顯看到唐宋的進步與轉變，尤其是道學的發展及其重建法古的傳統，而且元代已經開始超過宋代。

中央研究院歷史語言研究所柳立言譯

Works Cited

Bai Gang 白纲. "Lun Hao Jing de zhengzhi qingxiang" 論郝經的政治傾向 [On Hao Jing's Political Orientation] *Zhongguo Renmin Daxue shubao ciliao zhongxin baokan ciliao xuanhui* 中國人民大學書報資料中心報刊資料選匯, 2 (1986): 83-96; reprinted from *Zhongguoshi yanjiu*中國史研究, 4 (1985):101-115.

Hao Jing郝经. *Hao Wenzhonggong Lingchuan wenji* 郝文忠公陵川文集 [Hao Jing's Lingchuan Miscellany]. Ming Zhengde 2nd year [1507] edition in Peking University Rare Books Collection, n.p. Photographic reproduction of this edition was also published by Bejing tushuguan guji chuban bianjizu. In *Beijing tushuguan guji zhenben congkan*北京圖書館古籍珍本叢刊. Beijing: Shumu wenxuan chubanshe, 1988.

---. *Lingchuan ji* 陵川集 [The Lingchuan Collection]. Wenyuange Siku quanshu dianziban. Hong Kong: Dizhi wenhua, 1999a.

---. *Lingchuan wenji* 陵川文集 [Lingchuan Miscellany]. In *Quan Yuan wen* 全元文, vol. 4. Nanjing: Jiangsu guji chubanshe, 1999b.

Huang K'uan-ch'ung 黃寬重. *Songdai de jiazu yu shehui* 宋代的家族與社會[Clans and Society of the Song Dynasty]. Taipei: Dongda tushu gongsi, 2006.

---. "Zhengzhi, diyu yu jiazu --- Song Yuan shiqi Siming shizu de shuaiti" 政治、地域與家族——宋元時期四明士族的衰替 [Politics, Region, and Clan: the Decline of Siming's Gentry during the Song-Yuan Period]. *Xin shixue* 新史學 20.2 (2009):1-41.

Lau Nap-yin柳立言. "He wei 'Tang-Song biange'?" 何謂"唐宋變革"? [What Was the "Tang-Song Reform"?] *Zhonghua wenshi luncong* 中華文史論叢 81 (2006): 125-171.

---. "Songdai de shehui liudong yu falü wenhua: zhongchan zhi jia de falü"? 宋代的社會流動與法律文化：中產之家的法律? [Social

Mobility and Legal Culture During the Song Era]. *Tang yanjiu* 唐研究 11 (2005): 117-158.

Makeham, John. *Transmitters and Creators: Chinese Commentators and Commentaries on the Analects*. Cambridge: Harvard University Asia Center, 2003.

Qin Hongchang 秦鸿昌. *Hao Jing zhuan* 郝经传 [A Biography of Hao Jing]. Taiyuan: Shanxi guji chubanshe, 2001.

Song Lian宋濂. *Yuanshi* 元史 [History of the Yuan]. Beijing: Zhonghua shuju, 1976.

Tillman, Hoyt Cleveland. "Part Two: The Collision and Amalgamation of Song, Jin, and Yuan Cultural Thinking." In Christian Soffel and Hoyt Cleveland Tillman, *Cultural Authority and Political Culture in China: Exploring Issues with the* Zhongyong *and the* Daotong *during the Song, Jin and Yuan Dynasties*. Stuttgart, Germany: Franz Steiner Verlag, 2012. Pp. 111-188.

Xu Hongxing 徐洪興. "Daoxue sichao" 道學思潮 [Currents in Confucian Thought]. In Yin Jizuo 尹繼佐and Zhou Shan 周山, eds., *Zhongguo xueshu xixiangshi*中國學朮思潮史. Shanghai: Shanghai shehui kexue chubanshe, 2006.

Yin, Hui and Hoyt Tillman. "The Confucian Canon's Pivotal and Problematic Middle Era: Reflecting on the Northern Song Masters and Zhu Xi." *Dao: A Journal of Comparative Philosophy* 14.1 (March 2015): 95-105.

5

In Defense of Bodily Self-Sacrifice and Asceticism: The Making of a Virgin Saint in *Xingshiyan* 型世言

Yenna Wu

Introduction

Xingshiyan 型世言 [Exemplary Stories for the World] is a late Ming collection of forty stories possibly written by Lu Renlong 陸人龍 and published around 1631-1632 (Chan 4-12). Little is known about Lu Renlong, though his older brother Lu Yunlong 陸雲龍 was a well-recognized writer and publisher in Hangzhou during the late Ming.¹ After somehow being lost in oblivion for many years, this collection was miraculously resurrected in 1987 when the Chinese-French scholar Chan Hing-Ho [Chen Qinghao 陳慶浩] discovered a copy of this work while doing research in the archives of the Kyujanggak Royal Library of Seoul National University in South Korea.² Many of the forty stories, however, had existed previously under different titles or in revised versions in the extant copies of three later story-collections: *Huanying* 幻影, *Sanke pai'an jingqi* 三刻拍案驚奇, and (Bieben) *Erke pai'an jingqi* (別本)二刻拍案驚奇 (Chan 12-36; Quan 37-73).

This chapter focuses on the fourth story in this collection, entitled "Cunxin yuange shenming, piangan dunsu zumu" 寸心遠格神明，片肝頓蘇祖母 ["An Inch of Heart Reaches the Deities from Afar; a Sliver of Liver Revives Grandma Instantly"] (hereafter "Cunxin yuange shenming"). The story highlights the theme of filial piety and the act of *gegu liaoqin* 割股療親 or *gegu jiuqin* 割股救

親, which literally means to cut the flesh from one's thigh in order to make it into a medicine that would help one's parent or grandparent recover from a serious illness. The term *gegu* includes cutting off flesh from one's arm or other parts of the body to cure one's parent or grandparent. In this story, a filial girl named Chen Miaozhen 陳妙珍 saves her grandmother from practically incurable illnesses by performing the act of *gegu*–cutting off a slice of flesh from her upper arm—on one occasion, and the act of *gegan* 割肝—cutting off a slice of flesh from her own liver—on another. Miaozhen also refuses to marry, even after her grandmother dies.

Moral instruction and entertainment are two of the multiple functions served by *Xingshiyan*, which to some extent continues to follow in the footsteps of its immediate predecessors such as Feng Menglong's (1574-1646) three famous story-collections.[3] Scholars have observed that *Xingshiyan*'s central concept is to "punish the wicked and praise the good" [*cheng'e yangshan* 懲惡揚善] (Quan 172-173). Although some criticize its stories for advocating "feudal" ethics and values, others find the stories to be of socio-historical and artistic interest.[4]

For those who condemn *Xingshiyan* as a "mirror" reflecting "feudal" moral teachings, a story like "Cunxin yuange shenming" that eulogizes such filial behaviors as a girl's *gegu* and *gegan* as well as her vow of chastity exposes precisely the "cruelty" of the "feudal" morality. Denouncing the belief in curing illnesses by *gegu* as absurd and unscientific, Wei Wenzhe goes so far as to contend that because of the compulsory requirement of being filial, Miaozhen first suffers from physical injury and almost loses her life, and later decides not to marry, thereby "destroying her own youth, life, and happiness" (190-191). Rather than contending with the "Marxist" approach that flatly denounces traditional ethics as "feudal" moral teachings, however, I propose to examine how the author represents Miaozhen's *gegu* and asceticism, and to explore some of the cultural contexts surrounding these issues.

So far modern scholars have qualified the act of *gegu* [*ko-ku*] differently, depending on their perspectives. The literary scholar Jonathan Chaves (1986) refers to *gegu* as "acts of self-mutilation in the hope of curing a parent's illness, acts which sometimes end in death" (405), or as "acts of filial self-mutilation" (413). However, the historian T'ien Ju-K'ang (1988) criticizes the practice as "the most notorious self-mortifying filial rite" and as "medical cannibalism" (152). Key Ray Chong (1990) refers to this practice as "filial piety-related cannibalism" (165). Discussing more from a medical perspective and being less critical than T'ien Ju-K'ang, two M.D.'s, Thomas S. N. Chen and Peter S. Y. Chen (1998), introduce the practice of *gegu* as "an unusual form of medical cannibalism, arising in China" (25). In their view, "The social significance of *ko-ku* [*gegu*] far overshadowed the nominal purpose of a medical cure" (25). An expert on Chinese religion, Chün-fang Yü (1997; 2001) at first thought of referring to *gegu* as "filial cannibalism" or "cannibalistic filiality," but later considered the use of the word "cannibalism" inappropriate (1997: 154; 2001: 340-341). She argues that in discussing the practice of cannibalism, the emphasis is on the "consumer" who eats "the flesh of his or her victim," whereas in the case of *gegu*, the chronicler's focus is on the "victim," and the parent was unaware of "eating human flesh, for it was always prepared with other ingredients and served in disguise as a soup or gruel" (2001: 341).

I follow Chaves and Yü in not referring to *gegu* as a cannibalistic practice. In particular, finding Yü's argument persuasive and her perspective pertinent to my examination of this story, I would emphasize the subject that offers her flesh to the parent or grandparent, and explore the act of *gegu* in the contexts of Confucian discourse on filial piety and of Buddhist discourse on bodily sacrifice. Regarding the practice of *gegu* as an ethical irony or dilemma, I would look into how Lu Renlong presents the act and resolves the irony. Finally, I would also briefly discuss how Lu justifies Miaozhen's asceticism, and how the story is connected to some extent with the syncretizing of the Three Teachings [*sanjiao heyi* 三教合一] and the lay Buddhist movement [*jushi fojiao* 居士佛教] in the late Ming.

The Story and its Precursors

The heroine Chen Miaozhen 陳妙珍 hails from a humble family in a mountainous region. Her father dies from illness when she is two years old, while her mother remarries after three years' mourning. Miaozhen lives alone with her grandmother, who plays the role of a mother in caring for and instructing her. Their only meager income is from leasing the family land to some tenant farmers.

When Miaozhen is thirteen years old, her aging grandmother falls ill. None of the medicines that Miaozhen manages to procure can cure her. Miaozhen then slices a piece of flesh off from her upper left arm, mixes it with rice to make gruel, and offers the gruel to her grandmother. Having eaten the gruel, the grandmother recovers. However, after a few days, the grandmother finds out about Miaozhen's flesh-slicing, and is so saddened by it that she falls ill again.

Miaozhen attends upon her grandmother assiduously, seeks many remedies, and prays and beseeches the gods for help, but to no avail. When Miaozhen falls asleep from fatigue at her grandmother's bedside one night, a deity [*daozhe* 道者 (223); *shenren* 神人 (226)] appears in her dream, and informs her that a broth made with a piece of her liver would cure her grandmother. Miaozhen cuts open part of her left abdomen as instructed, but cannot find her liver. Only after she kneels down several times to Heaven to request help, vowing to become a nun to repay heavenly kindness, does her liver protrude into view. She cuts off a piece of her liver, minces it, and cooks it in the medicinal broth. Her grandmother indeed recovers after drinking the broth, and is able to live three more years.

When her grandmother finally dies, the devastated Miaozhen builds a little hut on the grave and dwells in the hut for three years to mourn her grandmother. Refusing a marriage proposal, Miaozhen becomes a nun and moves into a nunnery. Upon noticing that the abbess is avaricious, Miaozhen moves to a second nunnery—only to discover that the second abbess, though ostensibly pure, is actually lustful. After leaving the second nunnery, Miaozhen resides alone in a thatched hut beside her grandmother's tomb and continues to practice Buddhist self-cultivation.

One day over a dozen years later, Miaozhen thanks her neighbors for their help, returns to her hut, and passes away while sitting in meditation. People build a stūpa for her and call it "The Tomb of the Filial Girl" [*xiaonü zhong* 孝女冢] or "The Stūpa of the Divine Nun" [*shenni ta* 神尼塔] (237).

Although Lu Renlong's story is highly fictionalized, its heroine, Chen Miaozhen, appears to be based on a historical figure from Lishui in Zhejiang province. A famous scholar-official and a native of Zhejiang, Song Lian 宋濂 (1310-1381), wrote a biography of Chen Miaozhen 陳妙珍 entitled "Lishui Chenxiaonü zhuanbei" 麗水陳孝女傳碑 [The Biography of Filial Girl Chen, Inscribed on a Stela] (hereafter "Lishui Chenxiaonü"). We also find a reference to Chen Miaozhen 陳妙真 in an entry entitled "Chenshinü" 陳氏女 [The Girl Surnamed Chen] in the "guixiaobu" 閨孝部 [Section of Filial Women] of the Yuan dynasty in the early 18th-century voluminous collectanea, *Gujin tushu jicheng* 古今圖書集成 [Complete Collection of Ancient and Contemporary Books and Illustrations].[5]

The brief account in "Chenshinü" states that its information comes from *Chuzhou fuzhi* 處州府志 [Chuzhou Prefecture Gazetteer]. The end of the account mentions that Song Lian wrote a biography of the girl. However, there is a significant difference between these two narratives. In "Lishui Chenxiaonü," Song Lian not only wrote about the girl's act of *gegu*, but also greatly elaborated upon her act of *gegan*, specifically mentioning that she dreamed of the *daozhe* one night in the fourth month of the year 1344. In contrast, neither of these acts is referred to in "Chenshinü," and Miaozhen is said to have saved her ailing grandmother and extended the latter's life span for three more years simply by "tearfully pleading with Heaven for help, pledging to die in her grandmother's place" [*yuanyi shendai* 願以身代, "willing to substitute her own body for her grandmother's body"].[6] Lu Renlong's story obviously expands upon Song Lian's biography when detailing Miaozhen's acts of *gegu* and *gegan*.

In addition to her bodily self-sacrifice, Miaozhen's vow to never to marry and her asceticism also distinguish "Cunxin yuange shenming." The two antecedents again differ on this point. In "Chenshinü," "as soon as Miaozhen came of age, she vowed to support her grandmother and not to marry for the rest of her life." By way of contrast, in Song Lian's "Lishui Chenxiaonü," it was only after Miaozhen "cut off a piece of her liver and put it on the table" that she "vowed if her grandmother would be saved, she would take the Bodhisattva's oath of abstinence and never marry for the rest of her life." Similar to Song Lian's version, "Cunxin yuange shenming" also places Miaozhen's vow in the context of attempting to save her ailing grandmother's life by sacrificing part of her liver. In Song Lian's biographical account, Miaozhen's vow is intended to move the gods so they will ensure the efficacy of her liver-medicine. In "Cunxin yuange shenming," however, the timing and emphasis differ slightly: after cutting open the red line on her abdomen, as instructed by a deity, Miaozhen still cannot find her liver; and so she prays to Heaven for guidance, and vows to become a nun and serve Heaven in return for its kindness (Lu 224).

We find primarily Confucian discourse on filial piety in "Chenshinü." By contrast, both Song Lian and Lu Renlong incorporated Buddho-Daoist references into their works, though some of the motifs they use vary.

Filial Piety in Confucian and Buddhist Contexts

Filial piety [*xiao* 孝] is one of the most fundamental virtues in Confucianism. In *The Analects* [*Lunyu* 論語], Confucius emphasizes that to be truly filial, one must show "reverence" [*jing* 敬] in serving one's parents, rather than merely providing for [*yang* 養] one's parents.[7] Chapter 10 of *Xiaojing* 孝經 [*The Classic of Filial Piety*] underscores the importance of sincerity and reverence in caring for one's parents when they are alive, sick, or dead: "Filial children in serving parents in their daily lives show them real respect [*jing*], in tending to their needs and wants strive to bring them enjoyment [*le*], in caring for them in sickness reveal their apprehension, in mourning for them express their grief, and in sacrificing to them show true veneration" (Rosemont and Ames 111).

However, of the many passages discussing filial piety in these two Confucian canons, none advocates extreme acts of self-mutilation or asceticism. Instead, we find implied suggestion that one should take good care of oneself in order to spare one's parents from worry.[8] Chapter 1 of *Xiaojing* stresses a filial child's responsibility in caring for the body: "Your body, hair, and skin are bequeathed by your parents. Not daring to let your body be injured or destroyed is the beginning of filial devotion" [*shenti fafu, shouzhi fumu, bugan huishang, xiaozhi shiye* 身體髮膚，受之父母，不敢毀傷，孝之始也].[9] This includes safeguarding one's body from penal mutilation, thereby not bringing disgrace to one's parents (Wang Shoukuan 5).

Yet another quote relevant to our discussion comes from the Confucian classic *Mencius*: "Of the three situations in which one is unfilial, the worst is having no heir" [*buxiao you san, wuhou wei da* 不孝有三，無後為大].[10] Just as one should keep one's body intact (because it is an extension of one's parents and ancestors), so is one expected to marry and produce heirs in order to continue the family line and ancestor worship.

When Buddhism was first introduced to China, it was "attacked as unfilial" (Ch'en 15-16). For example, the requirements for monks to shave their heads, leave their families and not to marry contradict Confucian teachings about keeping one's body intact, serving one's parents, and producing heirs to continue ancestor worship. Some early Chinese Buddhists felt compelled to defend this foreign religion from attack. In *Mouzi lihuolun* 牟子理惑論 [Mouzi's Refutation of Errors], Mouzi 牟子 (c. 170 -?) cites many examples and passages from Confucian and Daoist classics to refute the criticism of Buddhism, contending that Buddhism in fact shares similar fundamental values with the two indigenous doctrines.[11]

As Kenneth Ch'en observes, to make Buddhism "acceptable to the Chinese," the Buddhists pointed out "the numerous sutras" that "stress filial piety," and forged "apocryphal literature which emphasizes piety." Furthermore, they contended that "the Buddhist concept of filial piety was superior to that of the Confucians in that it aimed at universal salvation (this would include all previous ancestors in different forms), while the Confucian piety was limited to just one family" (Ch'en 18, 42-43). One could be filial by becoming a Buddhist to pray for the redemption of the parents and ancestors, converting the parents to Buddhism, and bringing glory to the family through universal salvation. Based on this argument, Chinese Buddhism also underscores filial piety, though the conception and manifestations of filial piety may differ in these two doctrines. Despite these arguments, many Confucians continued to criticize the Buddhist practice of renouncing one's family and parents as unfilial.

Gegu and Buddhist Bodily Sacrifice

Based on historical records, the earliest known example of *gegu liaoqin* dates from the mid-7th century (Chiu 1997, 25-26). It has been suggested that *gegu* originated from the legends about "offering up one's body as a sacrifice" [*sheshen gongyang* 舍身供養] and the medical lore in ancient Indian Buddhist parables (Jin 31, 38, 43). The famous anti-Buddhist scholar-official Han Yu (768-824) condemned the practice of *gegu* in his "Huren dui" 鄠人對 [Responding to the People of Hu]. He appeared to associate *gegu* with Buddhist practices of "burning the head or fingers" and "cutting off an arm or slicing flesh off one's body" as an "offering" [*gongyang* 供養] (Wu 2008, 420).

Stories of bodily sacrifice abound in *jātaka* tales that recount the Buddha's former births and lives and reveal the connection between past causes and current situations. For a religion that opposes killing and promotes celibacy and a vegetarian diet, such accounts about the offering and eating of flesh and blood might seem incongruous. Yet when examined "within the context of a larger Buddhist discourse on giving [*dāna*], these gift-of-the-body accounts not only make sense but also serve the purposes of enlightenment (Ohnuma 59).

In *The Lotus Sutra*, the bodhisattva Medicine King in his past life made an offering of his own body to the Buddha through self-immolation, earning great praise from all the Buddhas (281-282). On another occasion, he made an offering to the relics of the Buddha by burning his own arms; upon making a vow, however, his two arms "reappeared" (284-285). According to this sutra, offering a gift of the body is regarded as the most generous act, and the best way to attain the enlightenment of a Buddha.

Although such gift-of-the-body tales differ significantly from *gegu* accounts, they may still have indirectly inspired the practice of *gegu*. While a number of the gift-of-the-body tales in *The Sutra of the Wise and the Foolish* (10-11, 14-15, 111-114) seem to have little connection with *gegu*, we find one, "Prince Swasti," that eulogizes filial devotion through extreme bodily sacrifice (29-32).[12] To escape from an evil minister, a king goes into exile with his wife and young son. When they run out of provisions, the king decides to kill the queen and eat her flesh. Beseeching the king not to kill the queen, the boy-prince offers an alternative: "Father, without killing me, cut off my flesh bit by bit and feed the three of us." Following his suggestion, his parents feed on his flesh and bone marrow, and later abandon him and move on (31). As the boy-prince is one of the many former births of the Buddha, the tale implies that the Buddha also approves of filial devotion as well as bodily sacrifice to one's parents in extremis.

In addition, there are some Buddhist stories in which human parts are used for "medicinal purposes" or even for saving one's parent from illness (Yü 2001: 316-317). Chün-fang Yü finds one such story in the sutra, *Dafangbian Fo baoenjing*大方便佛報恩經 [Sutra of the Buddha's Repaying Kindness with Great Skillful

Means], which contains many stories about the Buddha performing filial acts in previous lives. In the story, the ailing king can only be cured by a medicine concocted with "the bone marrow and eyes of someone who is free of anger." Prince Patience donates his eyes and bone marrow, and dies. The king then ordered a *stūpa* erected for worshipping him (316). This story may have provided an inspiration for the Chinese legend of Princess Miaoshan 妙善公主, who was a previous reincarnation of the Bodhisattva Guanyin 觀音, a.k.a. Kuan-yin, the Goddess of Mercy).

As indicated by Chün-fang Yü in her expert study of the cult of Guanyin, the similarity between the story of Prince Patience and that of Princess Miaoshan is striking (316). Princess Miaoshan, the third daughter of King Miaozhuang 妙莊王, grew up to be a devout Buddhist. Her refusal to get married offended the king so much that he punished her and had her executed. Miaoshan was able to return to the world and attain enlightenment through meditation. Later the king fell ill and somehow could not be cured. Miaoshan offered her eyes and hands to be made into a medicine that eventually cured the king. Upon discovering the truth, the king repented, and along with all of his family, converted to Buddhism. When Miaoshan died, a pagoda was built to house her relics (Yü 2001: 293-294; Dudbridge 1978).

In the legend of Princess Miaoshan, the Buddhist motif of bodily sacrifice combines with the notion of filial piety and the belief in the medicinal function of certain body parts. This legend was already known in the Song dynasty, and was further developed in various genres during the Ming and Qing (Yü 298). It may have provided a clear Buddhist justification for the practice of *gegu*. It may also have served as one of the inspirations in the representation of Chen Miaozhen in "Cunxin yuange shenming."

An Ethical Irony or Dilemma

Chiu Chung-lin, the scholar who wrote a social history of *gegu liaoqin*, terms this practice "unfilial filial piety" [*buxiao zhi xiao* 不孝之孝] (1995). This term encapsulates the ethical irony or dilemma inherent in the practice of *gegu*. The people who perform acts of *gegu* in order to save their parents or grandparents should be regarded as "filial." However, if they die from such self-mutilation and become unable to serve their parents or prolong the family line, then they are in effect "unfilial" by Confucian standards. Furthermore, if these people perform the acts out of a secret desire to be praised or rewarded by the society or government, then the ostensibly self-sacrificing acts become hypocritical and unethical. Therefore, the practice of *gegu* can present ambivalences, dilemmas, and ironies in the ethic of filial piety.

Beginning in the Tang, a number of scholars and officials debated this controversial topic. Han Yu's "Huren dui," an extremely anti-*gegu* essay, argues that people can be severely injured or die from practicing *gegu*, and this could be most "unfilial"; that some people perform *gegu* in order to obtain official recognition and material rewards; and that the government should severely punish—not reward—those who perform *gegu* so as to discourage this practice (493).

In contrast with such anti-*gegu* discourse, we find some more moderate and sympathetic views about *gegu*. While agreeing with Han Yu to some extent, the literatus-historian Song Qi 宋祈 (998-1061) still commended some of those who performed *gegu* as exemplars of filial piety in his *Xin Tangshu* 新唐書 [New Tang History]. He particularly noted that these people came from the lower classes and did not receive much education in propriety and morals, yet they still performed *gegu* out of "sincere mind/heart" [*chengxin* 誠心]. Apparently Song did not suspect them of having ulterior motives.

On the other end of the spectrum is the discourse in defense of *gegu*. I would not categorize the defense of *gegu* as "pro-*gegu*" discourse, however. These instances of defending *gegu* were primarily intended to justify those who performed *gegu* as "filial" and worthy of recognition, rather than to actively promote the practice of *gegu*.

Among those literati who defended the practice of *gegu*, the philosopher Huang Zhen 黃震 (1213-1280) of Zhejiang was perhaps the most outspoken. Arguing against Han Yu's "Huren dui," Huang believed that such a bigoted piece could not have been written by the eminent scholar-official Han Yu. Huang contended that when a filial son performed *gegu* under desperate circumstances, he could not be intending to seek official rewards. Believing that gods would "pity the sincerity" of the filial children and protect them, Huang was convinced that these children would not feel pain or be hurt when performing *gegu*, and their ailing parents would surely be cured (Huang, "Huren dui"; Chiu 1997: 162). Huang also declared that "filial piety is like loyalty to the sovereign" [*xiao you zhong* 孝猶忠], and a filial son would bring honor to his family (Huang, "Huren dui").

Huang Zhen's overly sanguine defense of *gegu* affected a number of later writers, including Song Lian and Lu Renlong. At the end of his "Lishui Chenxiaonü," Song Lian cites Huang Zhen's argument about Han Yu not being the author of the anti-*gegu* piece, as well as Huang's equating "filial piety" with "loyalty," in order to justify Song's own commendation of Chen Miaozhen's acts of *gegu* and *gegan*. When writing the story "Cunxin yuange shenming," as we will see later, Lu Renlong was inspired by Huang Zhen's arguments in defense of *gegu*, though he did not mention the issue of skepticism about Han Yu's authorship of "Huren dui."

Throughout China's imperial history since the Tang, various rulers held different attitudes toward the practice of *gegu*. I would only mention one example that is relevant to our discussion. As T'ien Ju-K'ang points out, in 1394 the founding emperor of the Ming dynasty rewarded three ordinary people who performed *gegu*, yet in 1395 he "suddenly forbade" *gegu* and other "excessive filial activities" (158). As a result, in the *Mingshi* [Ming History], no more than a few cases of *gegu* were recorded. T'ien observes, "The main expression of virtue then shifted from *ko-ku* [*gegu*] to *lu-mo* [*lumu* 廬墓]—to dwell in a hut by the grave of a parent" (159).

However, after checking many local chronicles, T'ien Ju-K'ang discovered that from mid- to late-Ming, most provincial and county officials still approved of *gegu* (T'ien 160). By checking into 166 sources, he also found that only three places had a "significant number of devotees of this kind." Wenzhou prefecture in Zhejiang province was one of the three (160). Conceivably, Wenzhou's local officials and gentry might have supported the practice of *gegu*–or at the very least, not have forbidden it.

Therefore, historically and geographically speaking, *gegu* was practiced—and not entirely uncommonly—in Lu Renlong's period and region. Still, the debate on *gegu* continued. Even Wang Gen 王艮 (1483-1541), a well-known philosopher who emphasized filial piety in his teaching, clearly objected to the act of *gegu liaoqin* in his essay "Mingzhe baoshenlun" 明哲保身論 [Discourse on How the

Enlightened Wise Man Protects His Body Whole]. He argued, "If I cannot protect my own body, how can I protect my sovereign or father?" (Chaves 412). Nevertheless, Wang Gen's objections did not prevent Lu Renlong from writing an elaborate story about Chen Miaozhen's *gegu*. Instead, the anti-*gegu* discourse seemed to provide an impetus for Lu's writing.[13]

Positive Portrayal of *Gegu liaoqin*

In the discursive remarks prefacing his dramatization of Chen Miaozhen's life, Lu Renlong demonstrates his keen awareness of the imperial government's injunction against *gegu*, the debates on *gegu*, and *gegu*'s potential ethical ironies. Lu nevertheless justifies the motivation of those who perform *gegu* as truly sincere and filial, rather than greedy for rewards:

> However, *gegu* arises from children's utmost sincerity [*zhicheng* 至誠]. If they do not even care about their own bodies and lives, why would they care about official honors? Extremely filial people would perform *gegu* even if they were not to be granted any official honors. In contrast, unfilial people would cherish their own bodies even if official honors were to be conferred daily on those who performed *gegu* (206).

In underscoring children's utmost sincerity, Lu may have been influenced by Wang Yangming 王陽明 (1472-1529), the eminent scholar-official and philosopher who championed the School of the Mind and emphasized innate goodness.

Fully conscious of the notion from *Xiaojing* that a person's body is received from the parents and thus is something that should never be intentionally injured, Lu Renlong appears to suggest that instead of being bound by the canonic passage, we should be flexible in interpreting it. He states, "Some pedantic people argue that the act of *gegu* injures the person's body which was bequeathed by that person's parents. They do not realize that if people can save their parents' lives, even if by doing so they injure their own bodies, it is the same as keeping their bodies whole" (206). Instead of rigidly adhering to the text in *Xiaojing*, Lu seems to try to re-define this particular principle of filial piety. Apparently regarding a person's body as a part of the parent's body (the ur-body, the root) rather than as a completely separate entity, Lu suggests that we look at the effect on the ur-body rather than the temporary injury of the part. Even though *gegu* can be seen ostensibly as injuring the child's own body, as long as it helps to revive a dying parent—thereby making the parent's body whole—then the person's injured body can also be perceived as having become whole. A shift in perspective can thus cause one to perceive *gegu* as making a minor injury to part of the child's body and yet saving the parent's whole ur-body, and so in turn the injured part of the child's body would also be made whole and healthy again. In other words, the benefits would outweigh the costs.

Like Huang Zhen and Song Lian, Lu Renlong also draws a parallel between filial piety and loyalty to the sovereign in his argument. In the Confucian context, officials who die on the battlefield or from remonstrating with errant rulers are praised for their loyalty, patriotism, and martyrdom. Lu poses a rhetorical question: if we adopt the pedantic view—which regards injury to one's body as being unfilial—would we say that these officials should not have sacrificed their bodies for a higher aim? (206) While justifying the injury made to the body through the filial act of *gegu*, Lu also equates minor bodily sacrifice for one's parent with major bodily sacrifice for one's ruler and country, thereby elevating those performing *gegu* to a lofty martyrdom.

Lu Renlong was cognizant of the fact that *gegu* did not always achieve a win-win effect, and could be a precarious undertaking. Before introducing how extraordinary Miaozhen's act of *gegan* is, Lu mentions two examples from the Ming: in one, the daughter who performed *gegan* not only saved her mother, but also survived the injury; in the other (which reportedly happened in Lu's own city Hangzhou), the son who sliced off a piece of his heart not only failed to save his father, but also died from his self-inflicted wound (207). The knowledge of the risks involved enhances the suspense and dramatic effect of the story—as well as the reader's appreciation for the 13-year-old girl's courage.

Turning to the lengthy dramatization of Chen Miaozhen's life, I shall discuss only a few of the many interesting issues in the account and its representation. Rather than showing Miaozhen's act of *gegu* as arising from a mere sense of moral duty, Lu Renlong emphasizes sincerity, affection, and spontaneous reciprocation of parental kindness. Miaozhen's father died when she was less than two years old. Her mother could not take her along when remarrying three years later. Miaozhen could have been an abandoned orphan at five had her paternal grandmother, neé Lin, not volunteered to keep and raise her. Lu tells about how "Miaozhen regarded her grandmother as her mother," while Lin "treated her granddaughter like a jewel" because she was the only descendant left in the family line (217-218). Lin's love and care for Miaozhen led to the mutual affection and strong bonding between the two.

In terms of Miaozhen's moral upbringing, Lu Renlong depicts it not so much as a case of being compelled to obey or inculcated through studying books, but rather a case of spontaneous learning by example and oral transmission. In specially mentioning that Lin "originally hailed from a Confucian family" (218), the author implies that Lin had received moral education and was brought up to be ethical and chaste. As depicted in the story, Lin is also knowledgeable and well-informed; and as Lin cooks, sews, and does household chores together with Miaozhen, Lin would tell her stories and examples of virtuous conduct from the ancient times to the contemporary period (218). Lu suggests that Lin is a woman of integrity who instructs by setting an example, and Miaozhen, by living with her grandmother day in and day out, internalizes the old woman's values by example. Miaozhen also acquires and internalizes moral knowledge through listening to Lin's tales and anecdotes. Thus Miaozhen, already sincere and kind by nature, is further nurtured by the moral influence and environment that Lin provides.

The mutual love between Miaozhen and her grandmother is delineated as a key trigger to Miaozhen's first act of *gegu*. When Lin falls very ill at an old age, Miaozhen works very hard to serve her and to search for possible cures. Lu Renlong shows that even when seriously ill, Lin worries only about Miaozhen's future rather than being selfishly engrossed with her own illness and mortality. Saying that it is time for herself to die, Lin apologizes for not yet having found a husband for Miaozhen to depend upon (219). Conceivably, Lin's love induces in Miaozhen a desire to reciprocate. When none of the medicines Miaozhen obtains can cure Lin, she "remembered that Grandmother once mentioned an example of *gegu jiuqin* [slicing off flesh from one's thigh to save one's parent]" (219), and so decides to imitate the example. Had there been little mutual affection between Lin and Miaozhen, even if Miaozhen had known about examples of *gegu*, she would not have been willing to follow this practice.

Ironically, however, it is due to Lin's love for Miaozhen that the miraculous curative effect Miaozhen's flesh has on Lin disappears. A few days after recovering from the illness, Lin happens to hear the neighbor Mrs. Zou asking about Miaozhen's arm, and so discovers that Miaozhen performed *gegu* for her sake. Remarking plaintively, "I thought you were already so fatigued from attending upon me—why would you even want to cut out your flesh for me, too?" Lin cried, fainted, and later fell ill again (222).

To portray *gegu* positively, Lu Renlong incorporates Buddho-Daoist themes of the supernatural into the story. He delineates Miaozhen's filial devotion to be so extraordinarily strong that it moves the gods and triggers their response, help, and protection. A deity instructs Miaozhen to use a slice of her liver as medicine, guides her through the process, and teaches her how to heal her wound. As a result of the divine intervention, not only does Miaozhen's grandmother recover and live three more years, but Miaozhen also feels no pain from the injury, and her body becomes whole again soon afterwards. It is also possibly due to the vow Miaozhen makes that her body becomes whole again—thus echoing a theme in some of the gift-of-the-body tales.

While in his biography of Miaozhen, Song Lian recounts that the government conferred honors upon her and provided her with a monthly grain stipend until her death, Lu Renlong gives a different version in this regard. In Lu's story, when hearing that Miaozhen slices a piece of her liver to save her grandmother, all her neighbors want to report her extraordinary filial act to officialdom for commendation. Yet Miaozhen adamantly urges her neighbors to refrain from publicizing her filial devotion, claiming that her act came from her desire to save her grandmother, not from a desire to "invite fame" (226). Such a representation further strengthens Lu Renlong's positive argument about the respectable motivations of those performing *gegu*. Miaozhen performs *gegu* and *gegan* without any ulterior motives, and she refuses to be honored and rewarded by officials. That she becomes famous is entirely due to the local community that spontaneously spreads the extraordinary news of her filial conduct.

Asceticism and Filial Piety

In conventional Confucian thinking, failing to marry and produce heirs to continue the family line is unfilial. While the duty of continuing the family line in general fell more on the son's side than on the daughter's, a woman was still expected to marry and bear children. In contrast, Buddhism idealizes asceticism as a way to enlightenment. The two doctrines' conflict—and possible resolution—in this issue can be seen in the legend about Princess Miaoshan. We may recall that Miaoshan at first angers her father when she disobeys his wishes for her to be married. In that context, her refusal to marry and bear a son can be perceived by the society as being unfilial. As Chün-fang Yü argues, Miaoshan's "breach in familial and cosmic harmony could only be mended by having herself reincorporated by her father through the latter's eating of her flesh" (2001: 341). As the goddess Guanyin is worshiped throughout China, Miaoshan may have become an inspirational model for female lay Buddhists who refuse to marry.

Scholars have discussed the lay Buddhist movement and "the syncretizing of Three Teachings" in the late Ming. Instead of arguing about ideological differences in Confucianism, Daoism, and Buddhism, a number of thinkers and religious leaders pointed to the common emphasis on moral virtues and filial piety in all three doctrines (Greenblatt). The eminent monk Zhuhong 袾宏 (1535-1615) could succeed in attracting huge numbers of lay followers—many of them belonging to the gentry class—because he accepted and preached such Confucian virtues as filial piety and loyalty (Greenblatt 115-116).

This kind of crossing and fusion of divergent philosophies might have ignited fresh re-thinking and possible shifting of existing paradigms. Such a cultural milieu certainly produced the extraordinary female visionary, religious teacher, and controversial figure Tanyangzi 曇陽子 (1558-1580) (Waltner). Though born of a scholar-official family, Tanyangzi began worshipping Guanyin since childhood. Uninterested in marriage, Tanyangzi chose to live as a "widow" after the early death of her betrothed (Waltner 43). She thus utilized the widow chastity sanctioned by Confucianism to practice the asceticism she needed for Buddho-Daoist transcendence. We might note that she did not enter the monastic order or live in a nunnery.

Lu Renlong does not depict Miaozhen as coming from the elite class like Princess Miaoshan or Tanyangzi, or as a controversial public figure or a widely worshipped goddess. Instead, Miaozhen is portrayed as an ordinary girl from a humble background in a village. Unlike Princess Miaoshan and Tanyangzi, Miaozhen is neither already a devout Buddhist nor a resister to marriage since early childhood. It is her filial love and desperation to cure her grandmother that drive her to seek help from Buddho-Daoist deities and to eventually become a lay Buddhist or nun.

The circumstances surrounding Miaozhen's resistance to marriage thus differ substantially from those of Princess Miaoshan and Tanyangzi. With the spreading of the news of Miaozhen's act of liver-slicing, many gentry or wealthy families in town vie with one another to propose marriage to her. They apparently believe that such a filial girl will surely make for a virtuous wife and a model daughter-in-law. This provides a rare opportunity for an impoverished and poorly educated girl like Miaozhen to marry into a prominent and wealthy family and to enjoy a comfortable and affluent life. Yet Miaozhen declines all the offers, claiming that she already vowed to Heaven that she would not marry. When her grandmother repeatedly urges her to consider marriage, she says, "If I marry, I can no longer serve you," and she reiterates the need to fulfill her vow (226-227). Unlike Princess Miaoshan's father, Miaozhen's grandmother does not keep pressuring her or punish her for her disobedience in this regard. The lack of control by a male in the household thus gives Miaozhen the freedom to decide.

Instead of being prompted by a religious calling, Miaozhen's decision not to marry comes primarily from her innate devotion to her grandmother and the desire to keep her grandmother company in life and in death. The vow to become a nun, which Miaozhen wants to keep in order to repay Heavenly kindness, was also made out of her fervent wish to save her grandmother. It is Miaozhen's filial piety that leads to her decision and vow not to marry. Rather than being compelled to keep chaste, she thus embraces chastity on the basis of her own free will.

Using Miaozhen's case, the author illustrates that under certain circumstances, celibacy is indispensable for a filial child to be able to perform the more intense acts of devotion as she wishes to. Precisely because Miaozhen is unmarried and not burdened with the onerous duties of being a wife, daughter-in-law, or even a mother with a family of her own, she can focus all of her effort on taking care of her grandmother (especially when the latter becomes bedridden and needs intensive care). Moreover, because Miaozhen and her comings and goings are not under the control of a husband or his family, she has the freedom to live in a tiny thatched hut on her grandmother's grave for three years to accompany and nourish the spirit of the departed (227). Later, because a scholar in town persists in pressuring Miaozhen with marriage offers, the young woman shaves her head and enters a nunnery (227-228). There, unencumbered by marital solicitations, she can freely engage in Buddhist practices and pray for the redemption of her grandparents and parents (228). After a brief sojourn in two nunneries—which she later discovers to be corrupt—Miaozhen chooses to build a little nunnery of her own near her grandmother's grave (235). She continues with her ascetic mode of existence for over a dozen years until her death. Only because she is unmarried can she devote so many years to performing the extremely filial act of *lumu*—living austerely in a little hut near the parent's grave—and spend so much time in self-cultivation and praying so as to bring salvation to her ancestors' souls.

Lu Renlong defends Miaozhen's asceticism as being filial, rather than unfilial, by depicting it as having arisen from her filial piety and free choice, and as having yielded positive results. I should point out that despite his praise for exemplars of Confucian morality, Lu does not come across as a stickler for widow chastity. Lu depicts Miaozhen's mother very sympathetically, dramatizing in detail the bleak life and harsh living conditions confronting her as a widow, the pressures from her brother to remarry, and her sadness due to her inability to take Miaozhen along to her new husband's home (208-217). On the one hand, Lu reveals the complex realities that prevent Miaozhen's mother from remaining a chaste widow, and implies that she obtains financial support by remarrying. On the other hand, Lu also informs us that after remarrying, she dies from childbirth when Miaozhen is ten years old, and Miaozhen mourns her for three years (218-219). This detail informs us of Miaozhen's innate filial piety, while also disclosing the possibly lethal risks of marriage for a woman. By comparison, Miaozhen's ascetic life is simple and impoverished but peaceful and stress-free, and she lives a relatively full life-span.

Unlike a hagiography, this story contains vivid and sometimes even humorous slices of life, exhibiting the foibles of ordinary folks. For example, Miaozhen's kind neighbor, old Mrs. Zou, loudly complains about her unfilial son who would scold and beat her, but would not gather firewood or buy a piece of tofu for her, let alone performing *gegu* for her (220, 221). This example of an unfilial son contrasts so sharply with a filial granddaughter like Miaozhen as to enhance the uniqueness of her atypical filial piety.

The depravity in the two nunneries, perceived through Miaozhen's point of view, demonstrates not only that greed and lasciviousness are common weaknesses, but also that true virtue is hard to find even in sacred places. Furthermore, the account of how the abbesses and nuns in the two nunneries are punished by the government for their crimes, defrocked and driven out, exposes monastic Buddhism's potential abuses and harm to the secular community (235-236). By contrast, as a stay-at-home ascetic, Miaozhen keeps herself pure, fulfills her filial devotion, and attains enlightenment.

Although not writing a hagiography, Lu Renlong borrows some Buddho-Daoist motifs to depict Miaozhen as having become a saint through her filial and religious asceticism. When she lives in a little hut near her grandmother's grave, many wild beasts from the mountains roam around the hut but do not enter it. We also find symbols of auspiciousness such as magic mushrooms growing on the grave and a white magpie nesting on the pine tree near the grave (227). These signs reveal the gods' response to her filial piety and their protection and blessing of her. Moreover, Miaozhen's attainment of enlightenment is demonstrated in her full awareness of when her mortal life will come to an end. On that day, she visits and thanks all her neighbors for their help, and then returns to her hut and passes away while sitting in meditation (236-237). The locals are amazed to see how alive she looks when dead. When they set fire to the hut to cremate her, over a hundred bone relics spew forth from the flame. The locals store the relics in a bottle and build a *stūpa* at the site for worship (237). Such a miracle implies that Miaozhen has been sanctified. Her sanctification is also illustrated by the name given to the *stūpa*—"The *Stūpa* of the Divine Nun" (237).

By sanctifying Miaozhen, Lu Renlong also expresses his ideas about two different types of asceticism—with or without filial piety:

> In thousands of classics and canons, filial piety and rightness [*xiaoyi* 孝義] are most prominent. If people are truly filial, would they not become Buddhas? Yet if people abandon their parents at home and cannot provide for the elders, even if they read sutras, pray, and repent every day, I'm afraid Avichi Hell is designed specifically for them. Isn't this a case in which a man is morally inferior to a woman? (237-238)

In Lu's view, a truly filial lay nun can attain sainthood, while a monk who renounces his parents and lives in a monastery might eventually go to hell. Furthermore, Lu suggests to his readers that though in general men are regarded as superior to women, an ordinary but filial girl can in fact be superior to an unfilial man.

Conclusion

This story exhibits influences from Confucianism and Buddhism, while also expressing reactions to some of the doctrines' teachings. Viewed from the perspective of traditional Confucianism, injury to one's body and failing to produce an heir are unfilial. In this context, the act of *gegu*—injuring one's body in order to save one's parent—becomes an ethical irony or dilemma. Emphasizing sincerity and spontaneous innate love, Lu Renlong defends Miaozhen's act of *gegu* as filial and without ulterior motives. Borrowing Buddho-Daoist themes, Lu portrays Miaozhen's bodily sacrifice positively, and so resolves the dilemma. In addition, Miaozhen's asceticism is shown to arise from her filial devotion and free choice, and to be essential for her to carry out the more intense act of filial devotion that she desires. Such representations thus challenge the stereotypical traditional definition of filial piety, while suggesting a flexible extension of the range of acceptable behaviors for Confucian filial piety to embrace—even such extreme and controversial acts as *gegu* and asceticism. Finally, Lu also challenges the monastic Buddhist asceticism that requires the renunciation of one's parents. He uses

Miaozhen's example to demonstrate that a lay Buddhist can both perform acts of filial piety and practice asceticism at home, and still attain enlightenment.

Endnotes

¹Lu Yunlong probably wrote most of the short prefaces and brief comments to the stories in *Xingshiyan* (Chan 5). An alternative English rendering of *Xingshiyan* is *Words to Establish Models for the World*. Its author's home province is Zhejiang.

²The Korean scholar Park Jae-yeon 樸在淵 also contributed to the rediscovery of *Xingshiyan* (Miao 2010).

³The three forty-piece collections compiled by Feng Menglong are *Yushi mingyan* 喻世明言 [Clear Words to Instruct the World], originally titled *Gujin xiaoshuo* 古今小說 [Stories Old and New], 1620; *Jingshi tongyan* 警世通言 [Common Words to Warn the World], 1624; and *Xingshi hengyan* 醒世恆言 [Constant Words to Awaken the World], 1627.

⁴For example, Wei Wenzhe condemns the work's promotion of such moral values of "feudal society" as loyalty to one's sovereign, filial piety, widow chastity, and the like (188). Another scholar, Chen Liao, proposes that *Xingshiyan* offers a "realistic history" of the period from late-Yuan to late-Ming (3-5). See also Quan 2.

⁵*Gujin tushu jicheng*, juan 32, "Liezhuan" 1, p. 337. Note the sinograph for *zhen* in the name Chen Miaozhen in "Chenshinü" is 真, not 珍.

⁶I have discussed Song Lian's "Lishui Chenxiaonü zhuanbei" in more detail in Wu 2008: 425-430.

⁷See *Lunyu* 論語 II.7 (*Analects* 64).

⁸*Lunyu* 論語 II.6. However, this sentence may be interpreted differently.

⁹Wang Shoukuan 汪受寬, trans. and annotated, *Xiaojing yizhu* 孝经译注 2.

¹⁰*Mengzi* 孟子 IV.A.26. Cf. Mencius 127. In its original context, this quote can be interpreted differently, but such discussion is outside the scope of this chapter.

¹¹See Ch'en 17-19; Ren Jiyu 1981.1: 186-227; and de Bary 130-131.

¹²See *The Sutra of the Wise and the Foolish* 1981. Stanley Frye translated this sūtra from Mongolian into English. This sūtra was first

translated into Chinese in 445 (Mair 1). In his study of the linguistic and textual antecedents of this sūtra, Victor H. Mair concludes that although it was "compiled by Chinese monks from materials collected in Khotan and pronounced with a Khotanese accent, it is primarily an Indian text" (18).

[13] I have no space to discuss the medicinal aspect or the various types of publications that might have influenced Lu Renlong's to write about *gegu*. For example, Lu was likely influenced by Ming educational manuals for women, which typically include some accounts and illustrations of *gegu*. See also Wu 2000 for a number of other literary works that portray *gegu*.

Works Cited

The Analects. D. C. Lau, trans. Harmondsworth: Penguin Books, 1979.

Chan Hing-ho 陳慶浩 [Chen Qinghao]. "Daoyan: yibu yishile sibaiduonian de duanpian xiaoshuoji *Xingshiyan* de faxian he yanjiu" 導言：一部佚失了四百多年的短篇小說集《型世言》的發現和研究 [Introduction: the Discovery and Studies of the Short Story Collection Which had Been Lost for Over 400 Years, *Exemplary Stories for the World*]. In Lu Renlong 陸人龍. *Xingshiyan* 型世言. 3 vols. Taipei: Zhongyang yanjiuyuan Zhongguo wenzhe yanjiusuo, 1992. Vol. 1. Pp. 1-42.

Chaves, Jonathan. "Moral Action in the Poetry of Wu Chia-chi (1618-84)." *Harvard Journal of Asiatic Studies* 46.2 (1986): 387-469.

Ch'en, Kenneth K.S. *The Chinese Transformation of Buddhism*. Princeton: Princeton University Press, 1973.

Chen Liao 陳遼. "*Xingshiyan* xinlun" 型世言新論 [A New Study of *Exemplary Stories for the World*]. *Neijiang shifan xueyuan xuebao* 内江師範學院學報 29.3 (2014): 1-5.

Chen, Thomas S.N. and Peter S.Y. Chen. "Medical Cannibalism in China: The Case of *Ko-ku*." *The Pharos* 62 (Spring 1998): 23-25.

Chiu, Chung-lin 邱仲麟. "Buxiao zhi xiao – Sui Tang yilai gegu liaoqin xianxiang de shehuishi kaocha" 不孝之孝——隋唐以來割股療親現象的社會史考察 [Unfilial Filial Piety—a Socio-historical Investigation into the Phenomenon of *gegu liaoqin*

Since the Sui and Tang Dynasties]. Dissertation. National Taiwan University, 1997.

---.. "Buxiao zhi xiao—Tang yilai gegu liaoqin xianxiang de shehuishi chutan" 不孝之孝—唐以來割股療親現象的社會史初探 [Unfilial Filial Piety—A Socio-historical Exploration into the Phenomenon of *gegu liaoqin* Since the Tang Dynasty]. *Xinshixue* 新史學 6.1 (1995): 49-94.

Chong, Key Ray. *Cannibalism in China*. Wakefield, NH: Longwood Academic, 1990.

De Bary, Wm. Theodore, ed. *The Buddhist Tradition in India, China and Japan*. New York: Vintage Books, 1972.

Dudbridge, Glen. *The Legend of Miao-shan*. London: Ithaca Press for the Board of the Faculty of Oriental Studies, Oxford University, 1978.

Greenblatt, Kristin Yü. "Chu-hung and Lay Buddhism in the Late Ming." In *The Unfolding of Neo-Confucianism*. Wm. Theodore de Bary, ed. New York: Columbia University Press, 1975. Pp. 93-140.

Gujin tushu jicheng 古今圖書集成 [Complete Collection of Ancient and Contemporary Books and Illustrations]. Chen Menglei 陳夢雷, comp., Jiang Tingxi 蔣廷錫, ed. Chengdu: Bashu shushe, 1985.

Han Yu 韓愈. "Huren dui" 鄠人對 [Responding to the People of Hu]. In Han Yu, *Han Changli quanji* 韓昌黎全集 [Complete Works of Han Yu]. *Wenyuange Siku quanshu dianziban* 文淵閣四庫全書電子版. Hong Kong: Dizhi wenhua chuban, 2005.

---. "Lun fogu biao" 論佛骨表 [Remonstration Against Buddha's Relic]. In Han Yu, *Han Changli quanji* 韓昌黎全集 [Complete Works of Han Yu]. *Wenyuange Siku quanshu dianziban* 文淵閣四庫全書電子版. Hong Kong: Dizhi wenhua chuban, 2005.

Huang Zhen 黃震. "Huren dui" 鄠人對 [Responding to the People of Hu]. In *Huangshi richao* 黃氏日抄 [Daily Notes of Huang Zhen], *juan* 59. *Wenyuange Siku quanshu dianziban* 文淵閣四庫全書電子版. Hong Kong: Dizhi wenhua chuban, 2005.

Jin Baoxiang 金寶祥. "He Yindu fojiao yuyan youguande liangjian Tangdai fengsu" 和印度佛教寓言有關的兩件唐代風俗 [Two Tang-dynasty Customs Connected with Indian Buddhist Allegories]. In Jin, *Tang Song lunwenji* 唐宋論文集 [Collected Essays on the Tang and Song Dynasties]. Lanzhou: Gansu renmin chubanshe, 1982. Pp. 31-52.

The Lotus Sutra. Burton Watson, trans. New York: Columbia Univ. Press, 1993.

Lu Renlong 陸人龍. "Cunxin yuange shenming, piangan dunsu zumu" 寸心遠格神明，片肝頓蘇祖母 [An Inch of Heart Reaches the Deities from Afar; a Sliver of Liver Revives Grandma Instantly]. In Lu, *Xingshiyan* 型世言 [Exemplary Stories for the World]. Vol 1. Taipei: Zhongyan yanjiuyuan Zhongguo wenzhe yanjiusuo, 1992. Pp. 203-238.

---. *Xingshiyan* 型世言 [Exemplary Stories for the World]. 3 vols. Taipei: Zhongyan yanjiuyuan Zhongguo wenzhe yanjiusuo, 1992.

Mair, Victor H. "The Linguistic and Textual Antecedents of The Sūtra of the Wise and the Foolish." *Sino-Platonic Papers*, no. 38 (April 1993). Philadelphia : Dept. of Asian and Middle Eastern Studies, University of Pennsylvania, 1993.

Mencius. D. C. Lau, trans. Harmondsworth: Penguin Books, 1970.

Miao Huaiming 苗懷明. "Pu Zaiyuan he Zhongguo xiaoshuo wenxian yanjiu" 樸在淵和中國小說文獻研究 [Park Jae-yeon and the Study of the Sources on Chinese Fiction]. Originally published in *Zhongguo shehui kexue bao* 中國社會科學報, 26 October 2010. See http://www.literature.org.cn/Article.aspx?id=58459. Accessed 23 November 2014.

Ohnuma, Reiko. *Head, Eye, Flesh, and Blood: Giving Away the Body in Indian Buddhist Literature*. New York: Columbia University Press, 2007.

Quan Ning'ai 權寧愛. *Xingshiyan yanjiu* 型世言研究 [A Study of *Exemplary Stories for the World*]. Taipei: Fuji wenhua tushu gongsi, 1993.

Ren Jiyu 任繼愈, ed. *Zhongguo fojiaoshi* 中國佛教史 [A History of Chinese Buddhism]. Vol. 1. Beijing: Zhongguo shehui kexue chubanshe, 1981.

Rosemont, Henry, Jr. and Roger T. Ames. *The Chinese Classic of Family Reverence: A Philosophical Translation of the Xiaojing*. Honolulu: University of Hawai'i Press, 2009.

Song Lian 宋濂. "Lishui Chenxiaonü zhuanbei" 麗水陳孝女傳碑 [The Biography of Filial Girl Chen, Inscribed on a Stela]. In *Songwenxiangong quanji* 宋文憲公全集 [Complete Works of Song Lian], *juan* 16. *Wenyuange Siku quanshu dianziban* 文淵閣四庫全書電子版. Hong Kong: Dizhi wenhua chuban, 2005.

Song Qi 宋祁. "Xiaoyou" 孝友 [Filial Exemplars]. In *Xinjiaoben Xin Tangshu* 新校本新唐書 [Newly Edited New Tang History], *juan* 195, "Liezhuan" 列傳 [Biographies], 120, "Xiaoyou" 孝友 [Filial Exemplars]. *Zhongyang yanjiuyuan Hanji dianzi wenxian* 中央研究院漢籍電子文獻, *Ershiwushi* 二十五史. http://www.sinica.edu.tw.

The Sutra of the Wise and the Foolish (Mdo bdzaṅs blun) or The Ocean of Narratives (Üliger-ün dalai). Stanley Frye, trans. Dharamsala, Distt. Kangra, H.P., India: Library of Tibetan Works & Archives, 1981.

T'ien, Ju-k'ang. *Male Anxiety and Female Chastity: A Comparative Study of Chinese Ethical Values in Ming-Ch'ing Times*. Leiden: E. J. Brill, 1988.

Waltner, Ann. "Learning from a Woman: Ming Literati Responses to Tanyangzi." *International Journal of Social Education* 6.1 (Spring 1991): 42-59.

Wang Shoukuan 汪受寬, trans. *Xiaojing yizhu* 孝經譯注 [*The Classic of Filial Piety*, Translated and Annotated]. Shanghai: Shanghai guji chubanshe, 1998.

Wei Wenzhe 魏文哲. "*Xingshiyan*: fengjian lijiao de youyimian jingzi" 型世言: 封建禮教的又一面鏡子 [*Exemplary Stories for the World*: Yet Another Mirror of Feudal Morality].

Wu, Yenna. "Moral Ambivalence in the Portrayals of *Gegu* in Late Imperial Chinese Literature." In *Ming Qing wenhua xinlun* 明清文化新論 [New Studies of Ming Qing Culture]. Chenmian Wang 王成勉, ed. Taipei: Wen-chin Publishing Co., 2000. Pp. 247-274.

---吳燕娜. "Lijiao, qinggan, he zongjiao zhi hudong: fenxi bijiao *Xingshiyan* disihui he 'Lishui Chen xiaonü zhuan bei' dui gegu liaoqin de chengxian" 禮教、情感、和宗教之互動: 分析比較《型世言》第四回和 "麗水陳孝女傳碑" 對割股療親的呈現 [Interactions Between Emotion, Religion, and the Confucian Ethical Code: Analyzing and Comparing Representations of *Gegu liaoqin* in the Fourth Story of *Xingshiyan* and "Lishui Chen xiaonü zhuan bei"]. *Wen yu zhe* 文與哲 [Literature and Philosophy] 12 (2008): 413-454.

Yü, Chün-fang. "The Cult of Kuan-yin in Ming-Ch'ing China: A Case of Confucianization of Buddhism?" In *Meeting of Minds: Intellectual and Religious Interaction in East Asian Traditions of*

Thought. Irene Bloom and Joshua A. Fogel, eds. New York: Columbia University Press, 1997. Pp. 144-174.

---. *Kuan-yin: The Chinese Transformation of Avalokiteśvara*. New York: Columbia University Press, 2001.

Photo Courtesy of Andrea Augé

6

Thinking of Burton Watson

Robert E. Hegel

My years at Columbia as a graduate student (1965 to 1970) were intellectually exciting and yet emotionally draining. Many factors contributed to the latter situation, but among them was my lack of rapport with faculty. Except, of course, for Burton Watson.

Watson saw himself—and his students saw him—as different from the other faculty members; most were aloof and self-absorbed; he was not. If he had a private office like the others, he did not use it; instead he hung out in a common space used as well by the graduate teaching assistants. He welcomed students to come by and chat in the afternoon—about anything, ranging from poetry, of course, to politics, living in the City, Japan, and languages. He seemed to take us seriously while maintaining a dry sense of humor and a willingness to tease us if we took ourselves too seriously.

The spring of 1968 clarified just what Watson stood for. With the campus in turmoil, police everywhere, and all classes cancelled, Watson generously invited us over to his apartment to continue our studies. We sat on the furniture and sat on the floor to discuss Tang poetry, as we drank his tea and looked around his house. He had a splendid piece of calligraphy hanging on the wall. It was written in a very fast and abstract style, and not one of my classmates (none of us being native speakers of Chinese) was able to read it. Neither could he, Watson admitted, but of course he knew what it was because the calligrapher had inscribed this famous literary text in his honor.

Consequently, Burt could tell us what it said. Yet it heartened me, and I'm sure others there as well, that our famous professor could so easily admit his own limitations.

During one class someone asked him why his *Early Chinese Literature* (1962) stopped at the Han. By the Han there was too much to read, he replied; he had read every relevant piece of writing produced up to that point in order to write this magnificent little study. We took him at his word, and indeed, his publications all reveal that indeed he did read everything relevant before writing. His comments inspired us all to new levels of commitment to our work.

Several years later, Burt gave me a place to stay for a couple of days at his apartment in Japan. I was still a graduate student, but his hospitality seemed boundless: we talked half the night about my work, about his, about living in Japan versus living in Taiwan (as I had been). In short, he treated me like an old friend, without making any reference to his being so clearly my academic superior.

This was precisely how he taught as well. All subjects were worthwhile unless proven otherwise; all opinions and analyses were to be considered until someone had a better idea. We worked together with him: he lectured from his forthcoming publications, *Chinese Lyricism* (1971) and *Chinese Rhyme-Prose* (1972), noting his hesitations over his analyses even when we found them inspired. We discussed poems he had addressed, seeking ever more nuanced interpretations as we tried out our own ideas.

It was only long after taking up my own teaching career that I came to realize what it means to be a humanist, and to be genuinely interested, as a scholar, in human existence both in general and in particular. I realized that my own approach to learning was indebted in significant ways to the model Burt had presented. And perhaps to an even greater extent I have come to recognize that my successes as a teacher have stemmed in large part from following Watson's model of enthusiasm in seeing his students make progress on their own. His interest and his support were always unwavering, and for that I (and my students) will always be grateful.

7

Pipings of Heaven—Ink on Paper

Stephen Addiss

Of the many marvelous translations by Burton Watson, the one that has meant the most to me for many years is his *Chuang Tzu* [*Zhuang Zi* 莊子], and above all the passage on "The Pipings of Heaven" so radiantly translated:

> The Great Clod belches out breath and its name is wind.
> So long as it doesn't come forth, nothing happens.
> But when it does, then ten thousand hollows begin
> crying wildly. Can't you hear them, long drawn out?
> In the mountain forests that lash and sway,
> there are huge trees a hundred spans around with hollows
> and openings like noses, like mouths, like ears, like jugs,
> like cups, like mortars, like rifts, like ruts. They
> roar like waves, whistle like arrows, scratch, gasp, cry,
> wail, moan, and howl, those
> in the lead calling out yeee!, those behind calling
> out yuuu! In a gentle breeze they answer
> faintly, but in a full gale the chorus is gigantic.
> And when the fierce wind has passed on, then all the
> hollows are empty again. Have you never
> seen the tossing and tumbling that goes on? (pp. 31-32)

8
Translation and Translucence in the Work of Burton Watson

Lucas Klein

Teaching from Eliot Weinberger's *Nineteen Ways of Looking at Wang Wei*, I pointed the class to Burton Watson's translation of Wang Wei's "Deer Fence" (Weinberger and Paz 1987):

> Empty hills, no one in sight,
> only the sound of someone talking;
> late sunlight enters the deep wood,
> shining over the green moss again (Watson 1971: 12).

One student, a young woman from Shanghai exposed to translation theory and a traditionalist sense of poetry in English, scoffed: "That's it?"[1]
    I remember a college professor of mine relating how her graduate advisor, a meticulous philologist whose translations overflow with annotation, also disparaged Watson's translations, saying he probably typed up his first drafts and sent them to his publisher without looking at them again. But I also remember William Butler Yeats, from "Adam's Curse":

> ... A line will take us hours maybe;
> Yet if it does not seem a moment's thought,
> Our stitching and unstitching has been naught.

For all the work it takes, Yeats says, to be a poet is still to be "thought an idler by the noisy set / Of bankers, schoolmasters, and clergymen / The martyrs call the world" (Yeats 80–81). Throw certain readers of translation into that noisy set, for the fact is that beneath the surface simplicity of Burton Watson's lines hides not only years of accumulated scholarly expertise, but the internalized discipline of the contemporary American idiom as well.

Since Chinese poetry started being translated into English, poets and sinologists have presented poetry and sinology as if they were locked in eternal conflict. Amy Lowell described this conflict in 1921: "Chinese is so difficult that it is a life-work in itself; so is the study of poetry. A Sinologue has no time to learn how to write poetry; a poet has no time to learn how to read Chinese" (Lowell v). In a similar vein but from a Sinologist's perspective, George Kennedy later criticized the semantic errors that flowed from Ezra Pound's "ideogrammic method" of translating Chinese poetry: "Undoubtedly this is fine poetry. Undoubtedly it is bad translation" (Kennedy 1964: 462). Drawing a distinction between the "poet-translator" and "critic-translator," James J.Y. Liu wrote in 1982 that while the latter's "primary aim is to show what the original poem is like, as a part of his interpretation," the former "is a poet or poet *manqué* whose native Muse is temporarily or permanently absent and who uses translation as a way to recharge his own creative battery and write a good poem in English based on his understanding or misunderstanding of a Chinese poem, however he may have arrived at this" (Liu 37). Finally, against those who "believe that translations should consist of word-for-word cribs in which syntax, grammar, and form are all maintained, and in which the translator is merely a facilitator who allows the original poem to speak for itself in a new language," Tony Barnstone posited in 2004 that the "literary translator is like the musician who catalyzes the otherwise inert score that embodies Mozart's genius ... *Fidelity*, true fidelity, comes from a musician's deeper understanding of the music" (Barnstone 2). The genius of Burton Watson's translations is that they reconcile the rift between poetry and scholarship.

As Weinberger points out in *Nineteen Ways*, Watson was "the first scholar whose work displayed an affinity with the modernist revolution in American poetry: absolute precision, concision, and the use of everyday speech," particularly impressive at a time when most Anglophone "scholars of Chinese ignored, or were actively hostile to modern poetry... Many still are" (Weinberger and Paz 25). That precision, concision, and everyday speech deepened what T.S. Eliot called Ezra Pound's invention "of Chinese poetry for our time." Though Eliot acknowledged it to be an illusion ("an illusion which is not altogether an illusion either"), he explained that when "a foreign poet is successfully done into the idiom of our own language and our own time, we believe that he has been 'translated'; we believe that through this translation we really at last get the original ... His translations seem to be—and that is the test of excellence—translucencies" (Eliot 367). This is the quality that compelled my student, expecting more audible poetic devices, to scoff; but she should know that this quality is itself a poetic device, honed from Watson's own attentive readings in the entwined lineage of American and Chinese poetry, particularly as seen in Ezra Pound and Kenneth Rexroth. Pay attention, and you can hear it in the echoing *ohs* and whispering *esses* that turn "only the sound of someone talking," above, into something like onomatopoeia. Watson is perhaps the only translator of Chinese one could possibly imagine writing to a literary journal's editor to say, "I can't tell you how honored I am to be in the same magazine as Charles Reznikoff"; he sent Pound some of his earliest poetry translations (Pound wrote back, but made no comment on the versions), and he had drafts edited by Joanne Kyger, Cid Corman, Gary Snyder, and Allen Ginsberg.[2]

Watson is not the sort of poet-translator who is largely ignorant of Chinese, as both Pound and Rexroth were. Watson has lived mostly in Japan since the 1970s; at the present age of ninety, he still spends hours each morning and evening on translation work. Born in 1925, he was first exposed to Asian languages while growing up in New Rochelle, NY, when workers at the laundry where his father was a regular customer sometimes gave him litchi nuts, jasmine tea, and illustrated Chinese magazines. After dropping out of high school and joining the Navy, he was stationed in the South Pacific, where he learned enough basic Japanese to get around while on shore leave. Following his departure from the military he studied at Columbia University, both as an undergraduate and for his PhD (completed in 1956), under L. Carrington Goodrich and Chi-chen Wang. He later became a faculty member there as a departmental colleague of C.T. Hsia. As a scholar, Watson is known for broad cartographies such as *Early Chinese Literature* (1962), ranging from the eleventh century B.C.E. to the third century C.E., and *Chinese Lyricism: Shih Poetry from the Second to the Twelfth Century* (1971). These books are authoritative and insightful as overviews and introductions from an era in which few students studied Chinese and even fewer had access to it as a living language, yet they are still useable in or out of the classroom today. Nor is their authoritativeness authoritarian; Watson acknowledges his subjectivity when speaking of translation: "The reader should perhaps be reminded that when he reads these early Chinese works in translation, he is at many points reading not an incontrovertible rendering of the meaning of the original, but only one of a variety of tentative interpretations" (Watson 1962: 12). In this way, he acknowledges the illusoriness of his translations' translucency.

His translations, appropriately, also aim at readers looking for an introduction to Chinese literature, rather than at specialists who want to test a fellow academic's mettle via footnotes and bibliographies. Yet even as the scholar in him acknowledges that he can offer nothing but "one of a variety of tentative interpretations," the translator in him nevertheless finds ways to make us, in Eliot's words, "believe that through this translation we really at last get the original." Of his many translations of classical Chinese philosophy, history, and religion—including the *Records of the Grand Historian of China* (1961), the *Complete Works of Chuang Tzu* (1968), *The Tso Chuan: Selections from China's Oldest Narrative History* (1989), and *The Lotus Sutra* (1993)—he says his "aim was to make the most famous and influential passages of these texts available in easily readable form so that they could be read by English readers as one reads Herodotus, Thucydides, Polybius, or Livy." About "Deer Fence," Weinberger notes: "His presentation is as direct as the Chinese. There are 24 English words (six per line) for the Chinese 20, yet every word of the Chinese has been translated without indulging, as others have done, in a telegraphic minimalism" (Weinberger and Paz 25). Furthermore, Watson's translation hints at Wang Wei's prosody: a five-character Chinese line contains a caesura after the second word; "Empty hills, no one in sight" replays that with a comma, using the Chinese rhythm as the basis for his English free verse.

In another translation, that of Du Fu's "Spring Prospect," Watson does something similar:

The nation shattered, mountains and rivers remain;
city in spring, grass and trees burgeoning.
Feeling the times, blossoms draw tears;
hating separation, birds alarm the heart.
Beacon fires three months in succession,
a letter from home worth ten thousand in gold.
White hairs, fewer for the scratching,
soon too few to hold a hairpin up (Watson 2002: 30).

Du Fu (712-770) was of a generation with Wang Wei (699-759) and Li Bai (701-762); in Chinese he is considered the greatest of the three—indeed, the greatest lyric poet of the tradition. But while Wang Wei and Li Bai have been translated repeatedly and successfully, Du Fu in English has proven harder—Watson has said that Du Fu is the most difficult Chinese poet to translate. I find Watson's renderings of Du Fu among the best.

As with Wang Wei and other pre-modern poets, a pause breaks Du Fu's five-character line after the second syllable, which, again, Watson implies with the comma in the first line—and, in fact, five of the poem's eight lines. Gary Snyder inserts a visible caesura into his translation with extra spaces, so that "The nation is ruined, but mountains and rivers remain / This spring the city   is deep in weeds and brush" (Weinberger 2004: 100). But the form of Snyder's rendition of this poem is not equivalent to the form of Wang Wei's quatrain, above, which Watson makes implicit in the punctuation of his end-stopped lines: in "Spring Prospect," each couplet forms one sentence, whereas in "Deer Fence" one sentence carries through the entire quatrain. The form is "regulated verse," itself the result of medieval translations from Sanskrit, in which the central two couplets in the eight-line poem must observe a strict semantic and prosodic parallelism (Mair and Mei 1991).

Du Fu was a radical in the history of regulated verse's development. Following its origins in Sanskrit, the language of *sūtras* and *gāthās*, an association with Buddhism developed for regulated verse. But Du Fu was one of the first to nativize, or domesticate, the form and write in it for local and historical topics, such as this poem's mourning over bodies politic and physical in deterioration (though canonized as of a generation after his death, he was not highly regarded as a poet while alive; perhaps this is part of the reason why). Watson explains it this way in *Chinese Lyricism*: before Du Fu, regulated verse "had been mainly for displays of verbal dexterity," whereas Du Fu brought it "to full maturity" and established the form "as a vehicle for serious poetic statement." He "packed the utmost amount of skill and significance into the parallel couplets, using them not, as earlier writers had done, to display a series of essentially static tableaux, but to propel the poem forward by putting it through a succession of highly disciplined maneuvers" (Watson 1971: 153–154).

Here, the parallelism requisite in regulated verse's middle couplets is softened by American English's historical inattention to the convention, but it emerges nonetheless: a gerund, a conceptual noun, a comma, a noun from nature, a verb, a noun of emotion define both lines in "Feeling the times, blossoms draw tears; / hating separation, birds alarm the heart." Watson's following couplet, "Beacon fires three months in succession, / a letter from home worth ten thousand in gold," portrays perhaps a subtler artistry. The "beacon fires" [*fenghuo* 峰火] and "a letter from home" [*jiashu* 家書] are parallel in the Chinese, as are the numerical values and elemental metonymy of "three months" [*san yue* 三月] and "ten thousand in gold" [*wan jin* 萬金]. "Month" and "gold" are parallel because they are abstractions of the "Seven Luminaries," or the sun and moon plus the five planets visible to the naked eye, themselves named after the five elements: "gold" is metal, or the planet Venus, and "month," of course, is the moon. In Japanese, the Seven Luminaries also name the days of the week: *moon*, as in English, is Monday, while *metal* is Friday, named in Latin *dies Veneris* [day of Venus]. Yet Du Fu anchors the components in a central verb in each line, "to link" [*lian* 連] in the first case and "to be worth" [*di* 抵] in the second. Perhaps emphasizing the timelessness many English readers wish to see in Chinese's lack of tense distinction, Watson's sentence omits verbs; instead, the parallelism of the lines comes in presenting both images as encapsulated—"three months *in succession*," and "ten thousand *in gold*."

Watson's methods for signifying the regulated verse form in his translation also represent the incisiveness of his revisions; in the translation published in the earlier *Columbia Book of Chinese Poetry*, among other differences, sentences do not correspond with couplets, and line five ends "three months running," not yet parallel with "ten thousand in gold—" in the following line (Watson 1984: 225). But these are implicit formalizations. At the head of the poem, Watson makes the form of the poem explicit with a parenthetical "(5-ch. regulated verse; written early in 757 when Du Fu was still a captive in Chang'an)." Such comments by the translator remind readers that they are reading a translation and, as such, a work of scholarship, distinct from, yet related to, contemporary poetry originally composed in English. Yet these, too, extend the poem's poetic effects: regulated verse's association with Buddhism was embodied in a tendency toward transcendental timelessness in the middle couplets' parallel imagery, or what Watson called the "essentially static tableaux," emerging from the immediate scene set and resolved in the first and final couplets respectively (even when, as in "The nation shattered, mountains and rivers remain; / city in spring, grass and trees burgeoning," the first couplet observes parallelism, too). Coming before and after the translation, Watson's annotations extend the immediate scene of Du Fu's capital Chang'an into the context of the translation, rising in the middle but rooted at its extremities in the realities facing the poet and, in his paratexts, the translator.

Ascent and grounding describe as well Watson's reconciliation of the scholarly and poetic demands of translation: the solidity of his knowledge of classical Chinese finds expression in a style of English that calls attention to itself primarily in how it barely calls attention to itself. It is an extension of the overall architecture of the regulated verse form, down to the "succession of highly disciplined maneuvers" that define the antithetical parallelism of their middle couplets at their best. Where others have presented poetry and translation as forever at odds, Watson's work sees this conflict as its own static tableau and reduces it to a productive part of his own translational poetics.

According to Weinberger, "Most translators are capable of translating only a few writers in their lifetimes. The rest is rote" (Weinberger 1992: 60).[3] Clearly an exception to this rule, Watson has explained that "one should not be too fussy about what sort of material one is required to translate. Any type of translating is good experience in both the language one is translating out of and into." Burton Watson's translations never read as rote. Effortless, translucent, yes. And beneath these illusions, which are not altogether illusions either, Watson gives us what Yeats called the stitching and unstitching, the parallelism of scholarship and poetry, within one simple act, which is never simple: translation.

Endnotes

[1] An earlier version of this article was published in *World Literature Today* 88.3 (August 2014): 1-9.

[2] Details of Watson's life come from personal correspondence with Eliot Weinberger, Gary Snyder, Joanne Kyger, and Jesse Glass, as well as from Watson's interview with John Balcom. Otherwise unattributed quotations are from the Balcom interview.

Snyder writes that he and his then wife Kyger "spent time with Burton, and though I don't remember which book it was, we talked with him at length about his translations of poems from the Chinese and described the effort of contemporary American-language poets to be vernacular, thrifty, precise, and vivid. Joanne in particular talked one on one with Watson several times at length. I think he learned a lot from her, and it was reflected in subsequent volumes of translation."

Kyger writes, "When I spent a little time speaking with him about his translations, as far as I can recall, it had to do with William Carlos Williams's concept of scoring the page for the voice, including empty space for breath pauses, or commas; making line breaks at the end of a breath phrase, and generally simplifying the language. I was also very much into Charles Olson's *projective verse*, as a way to translate the dynamics and energy of the breath and voice to the page."

Glass, publisher of Ahadada Books, writes that Watson "doesn't particularly like the very latest of experimental poetry—in fact we have a joke about that—it's an 'ahadada' poem for an ahadada book … The last time we were looking at books together I picked up Thomas Pynchon's *V.*, and he promised he'd give Pynchon a try. I suggested *Gravity's Rainbow*, but if I recall correctly, he walked away with the original 1922 version of *Ulysses* tucked away in a blue Maruzen bag."

For more on his Charles Reznikoff reference, see Klein 165–166. Reznikoff pays tribute to Chinese poetry in an interview, quoting Wei Tai 魏泰 (fl. 11th cent.) from the epigram to A.C. Graham's *Poems of the Late T'ang*: "Poetry presents the thing in order to convey the feeling. It should be precise about the thing and reticent about the feeling"; see Dembo 193 and Graham 7.

[3]In an interview with Jeffrey Errington many years later, Weinberger walked this back: "I've translated some things—most of them many years ago—but just as there are pianists and people who play the piano, there are translators and those who translate. Burton Watson is a translator; I'm a dilettante" (Errington 2011).

Works Cited

Balcom, John. "An Interview with Burton Watson." *Translation Review* 70.1 (2005): 7–12.

Barnstone, Tony. "The Poem behind the Poem: Literary Translation as American Poetry." *The Poem behind the Poem: Translating Asian Poetry*. Frank Stewart, ed. Port Townsend, WA: Copper Canyon Press, 2004. Pp. 1–11.

Dembo, L. S. "The 'Objectivist' Poet: Four Interviews [Charles Reznikoff]." *Contemporary Literature* 10.2 (1969): 193–202.

Eliot, T. S. "Introduction: 1928." *New Selected Poems and Translations*. Richard Sieburth, ed. Second Edition. New York: New Directions, 2010. Pp. 361–372.

Errington, Jeffrey. "The Eliot Weinberger Interview." *The Quarterly Conversation* 6 June 2011. http://quarterlyconversation.com/the-eliot-weinberger-interview.

Glass, Jesse. Personal Communication. 5 Feb. 2014.

Graham, A. C. *Poems of the Late T'ang*. London: Penguin, 1965.

Kennedy, George A. "Fenollosa, Pound and the Chinese Character." *Selected Works of George A. Kennedy*. Tien-yi Li, ed. New Haven: Far Eastern Publications, Yale University, 1964. Pp. 443–462.

Klein, Lucas. "The Self Is That Which Gets Lost in Translation: A Sociolinguistic View of Chinese Poetry Translation through Modernity & Parataxis." *Forum For World Literature Studies* 4.1 (2012): 165–185.

Kyger, Joanne. Personal Communication. 28 Jan. 2014.

Liu, James J. Y. "The Critic as Translator." *The Interlingual Critic: Interpreting Chinese Poetry*. Bloomington: Indiana University

Press, 1982. Pp. 37–49.
Lowell, Amy. "Preface." *Fir-Flower Tablets: Poems Translated from the Chinese.* Boston: Houghton Mifflin, 1921. v–x.
Mair, Victor, and Tsu-Lin Mei. "The Sanskrit Origins of Recent Style Prosody." *Harvard Journal of Asiatic Studies* 51.2 (1991): 375–470.
Snyder, Gary. Personal Communication. 22 Jan. 2014.
Watson, Burton. *Chinese Lyricism: Shih Poetry from the Second to the Twelfth Century.* New York: Columbia University Press, 1971.
---. *Early Chinese Literature.* New York: Columbia University Press, 1962.
---, ed. *The Columbia Book of Chinese Poetry: From Early Times to the Thirteenth Century.* Burton Watson, trans. New York: Columbia University Press, 1984.
---, trans. *The Selected Poems of Du Fu.* New York: Columbia University Press, 2002.
Weinberger, Eliot. *Outside Stories, 1987-1991.* New York: New Directions, 1992.
---. Personal Communication. 24 Nov. 2010.
---, ed. *The New Directions Anthology of Classical Chinese Poetry.* William Carlos Williams et al., trans. New York: New Directions, 2004.
Weinberger, Eliot, and Octavio Paz. *19 Ways of Looking at Wang Wei: How a Chinese Poem Is Translated.* Kingston, RI: Moyer Bell Limited, 1987.
Yeats, William Butler. *The Collected Poems of W. B. Yeats.* Richard J. Finneran, ed. New York: Scribner, 1996.

9
The Kindly Scholar: Burton Watson

Hiroaki Sato

The evening Burton Watson invited me to his apartment to go over my Miyazawa Kenji translations remains unforgettable. From time to time he would ask if I would like some more beer, lift himself up on his long legs from the Japanese-style low table where both of us sat—the apartment was one Donald Keene let him use while in Japan, he said, as I recall—and, across the room that seemed vast and bare, return with two cans of beer from the other end where the refrigerator was. He had written out his suggestions and errors for my translations on a yellow pad, and there were many of them. It took him several trips before we finished.

By the time Mr. Watson walked me down the stairs to the street and helped me get a taxi, I was drunk—on *beer*! I'd tell anybody who cared to listen. It must have been in late 1972 or early 1973, though if there was anything wintry outside, I do not remember it. If it was in early 1973, it was my fifth year in New York. Mimicking my New York friends, such as the poet Michael O'Brien who had meticulously gone over the same translations with wit and humor, I had become quite an imbiber, but my favorite liquor was Jack Daniel's bourbon. I seldom touched beer except for a boilermaker.

It was a mystery as to why a famous scholar like Burton Watson was so kind and considerate to me. First of all, I didn't even know him. I had studied English in Kyoto. (He had also studied there a dozen years earlier, but his subject was classical Chinese, and he had studied at the prestigious University of Kyoto.) Worse, I was new to the field of translation, and I was translating into an acquired language besides. Some years later, Mr. Watson told me that he had once been happy to serve as the campus escort of a Japanese visitor to Columbia University. In spite of being an academic specialist in Shakespeare, the visitor could not speak much English. But then Mr. Watson couldn't speak much Chinese, either, even though he was a translator of classical Chinese. In fact, he was approaching the end of his fifth Zodiacal cycle before he managed to visit China.

Mr. Watson wrote an introduction to my Miyazawa translations. It was a model of its kind, breezily knowledgeable and generous to a fault. The book came out in 1973 under the title of *Spring & Asura: Poems of Kenji Miyazawa* (Sato 1973). As it happened, it was the first of what Chicago Review Press, which published it, planned as a series of modern poets in my translation, and Mr. Watson also wrote introductions to the second and the fourth, *Mutsuo Takahashi: Poems of a Penisist* (Sato 1975), and *See You Soon: Poems of Taeko Tomioka* (Sato 1979). Of these two contemporary poets, Tomioka would later become a prominent critic of how Japanese male writers depicted women in their novels and stories. Yet at that time she appeared to disdain anything with so much as a whiff of "feminism." This must have been clear to Mr. Watson, for he described Tomioka as a person of "the big city dweller's savvy and refusal to be awed by affectation or cant" (Sato 1979: 12).

By the time *See You Soon* came out, Mr. Watson had agreed to work with me on a large anthology of Japanese poetry from ancient to modern times. The result was *From the Country of Eight Islands* (Sato and Watson 1981); "The Nation of Eight Islands"八島国 is one of the original names of the Japanese archipelago. Mr. Watson suggested the eye-catching title, where, imagining I was current with the fad of the day, I had thought up one of bare-bone simplicity, "Japanese Poetry: An Anthology." I'm happy he did. It became a distinct, unforgettable title. The anthology won the PEN American translation prize in 1982. That might not have happened without Mr. Watson's generous help and great reputation.

With that naming in mind, a dozen years later when I began work on a large anthology of women poets, I thought long and hard about its title and eventually came up with what I thought would be an enticing one. But when the manuscript was ready and I found a publisher for it, M.E. Sharpe, its sales department objected, arguing that the title had to be generic and general. So the titular reverse, as it were, occurred. The sales department's choice was *Japanese Women Poets: An Anthology* (Sato 2008). The title I had decided on was "White Dew, Dreams, and This World." It is the first part of Lady Izumi's tanka lamenting how short-lived "love" can be in comparison with Buddhist metaphors for the transience of all phenomena: しらつゆも夢もこの世もまぼろしもたとへていへばひさしかりけり[White dew, dreams, this world, illusions: all these last for eternities for comparison] (Sato 2008: 75).

Dismayed by the sales department's alternative, I took a poll among my friends who are poets and writers, and showed the publisher the result—more than a dozen respondents said the title I recommended would be far more attractive and appealing, while only two expressed reservations. Yet it was to no avail.

For all the kind things Mr. Watson did for me, one thing I cannot recollect is how it all began: how he came to do what he did—compare my Miyazawa translations against the original and write an introduction to the book. Was it Andrea Miller, who ran the Asian Literature Program at the Asia Society and most likely knew him, that suggested him for the work? Or was it Alexander Besher, who recently told me that he had known Mr. Watson in Japan during the late 1960s, that asked him to write an introduction?

I do know Ms. Miller had sent all my translations to Mr. Besher—my "translator's note" says so—and at that time Mr. Besher and Curt Matthews were student co-editors of *Chicago Review.* The two of them accepted most of my translations and devoted an entire issue of the magazine to them. Then they went a step further and started their own publishing house, naming it Chicago Review Press. An important part of their plan was to start a series of Japanese poets in my translation, as noted earlier. But how did Mr. Watson come to be involved in my Miyazawa project in the first place?

In any event, the dozen years or more from then on would prove to be a Golden Age for modern Japanese poetry in English translation. It was as if I could find a publisher for any poet I translated.

The strong interest worldwide in Japanese poetry began to wane around 1990, the year when the bubble in Japan's economy burst. I was reminded of this recently while preparing to write this piece when I retrieved from my shelves some of Mr. Watson's books he'd given me over the years—and spotted *The Rainbow World* (Watson 1990). It is a collection of his essays first published in Japan in 1984, and reissued six years later in a new edition by a new publisher in Seattle. A couple, both Microsoft employees, founded a publishing house there called Broken Moon Press, apparently deciding to devote some of their ample salaries to a worthy literary cause. They wanted to do a series on Japanese poetry with me, as Chicago Review Press had previously done. I planned the series with excitement. But alas, the couple's publishing venture fizzled out even before they could bring forth a single volume of mine.

Among Mr. Watson's many books, his two-volume *Japanese Literature in Chinese* was a particular revelation to me (Watson 1975, 1976). A negligent student of *kanshi* 漢詩 and *kanbun* 漢文 in high school, I had not expected to read works in Chinese by the statesman Sugawara no Michizane (845-903), the monk Ryōkan (1758-1831), and the historian and poet Rai San'yō (1780-1832), let alone those by the novelist Natsume Sōseki (1867-1913). When Arthur Waley's translation of *The Tale of Genji* came out, the novelist and literary critic Masamune Hakuchō (1879-1962) is known to have confessed that it was easier for him to read it than Lady Murasaki's nebulous original (Sato 2002; Murasaki 2010). For me to say something like that in regard to *kanshi* and *kanbun* would be a gross understatement. I can barely read them.

I later learned that for Japanese literati, writing in Chinese was even more important than doing so in their mother tongue—at least until the country fully opened itself to world commerce and diplomacy during the second half of the nineteenth century. But the relative status began to shift soon enough, and the importance of writing in Chinese quickly receded both in practice and in retrospect in favor of writing in Japanese. When I bought the English professor and scholar Hinatsu Kōnosuke's three-volume history of poetry of Meiji and Taishō Eras, originally published in 1929, I was surprised to see that *kanshi* were written and freely cited without *yomikudashi* 読み下し [Japanese renderings of *kanbun* phrases] well into the Taishō Era.

Thus Sōseki wrote in *kanbun*, in Mr. Watson's translation:

When I was a boy I memorized thousands of T'ang and Sung works and loved to compose in Chinese. Sometimes I strained my ingenuity, polishing and refining and spending ten days to get one piece into shape; at other times the words just came tumbling out of my mouth, and I was sure I had achieved a fine flavor of naturalness and simplicity (Watson 1976: 174).

No wonder Sōseki was able to cite ancient and at times obscure Chinese phrases at will in the first novel that won him fame, *Wagahai wa neko de aru* 吾輩は猫である [I Am a Cat] (Natsume 2002). I recently had the pleasure of rereading it for the first time in probably five decades—this time in an edition with French-fold binding.

More than a dozen years after publishing *Japanese Literature in Chinese*, Mr. Watson came out with what I think was his fourth *kanshi* volume, under the title *Kanshi: The Poetry of Ishikawa Jōzan and other Edo-period Poets* (Watson 1990b). This book highlights writings by Ichikawa Jōzan (1583-1672), the samurai who built what has been for some time now a favorite tourist spot for those inclined to quietude, *Shisendō* 詩仙堂 [The Hall of the Poetic Immortals]. Mr. Watson honored me by dedicating the book to me.

I remember Mr. Watson once noted that there was no reason to make a fuss over the general inability of the Japanese language to clarify whether a noun is singular or plural, which is something you can easily do in English with the mere addition of "s" or "es." When I later bought his *Chinese Lyricism*, I found he had made an entertaining argument about this (Watson 1971). It took the form of a rebuttal to what James J.Y. Liu called the "strength" of Chinese on account of the fact that it is "a completely uninflected language" that is "not burdened with Cases, Genders, Moods, Tenses, etc." (Liu 1962: 40). This can result in ambiguity, admitted the scholar who had been born in Peking (so spelled at the time) and educated in England. Yet in poetry "the gain is on the whole greater than the loss," he went on, "for, as Aristotle observed, the poet is concerned with the universal rather than the particular" (Liu 40). To the Chinese poet, Liu added, "it is of no consequence whether 'mountain,' 'bird,' and 'valley' are singular or plural" (Liu 40).

"Such an assertion of the superiority of the generalized over the particular might have gladdened a reader of English poetry at the time of Dryden and Pope," Mr. Watson wrote (1971: 7). "But the twentieth-century reader, influenced as he is by Imagism, by demands for real toads in his imaginary garden or declaration that there are 'no ideas but in things,' is hardly likely to give such ready assent" (1971: 7).

"To be sure," Mr. Watson continued, "English, by distinguishing so importantly between 'one' and 'more than one,' and then leaving us in the dark as to how many more, presents almost as fuzzy a picture" (1971: 7). But such arguments are silly, he suggested, for "we must by the same reasoning claim that English nouns are more poetic than those of, say, French or Italians because they lack gender, a claim that few Frenchmen or Italians are likely to allow" (1971: 8).

Incidentally, the phrase "imaginary gardens with real toads" comes from Marianne Moore's famous poem, "Poetry" (Moore 1972: 452). In most of her many revisions of the poem, Moore is known to have put that particular phrase in single or double quotation marks, but if there was a source, it has yet to be found, or so I gather.

The phrase, "no ideas but in things," comes from William Carlos Williams. Some say he wrote it down first in *Paterson* in 1927, though the publication of his "epic" on the industrial town where he worked as a pediatrician did not get underway until 1946. However, by the late 1920s, he certainly was talking about "the bastardy of the simile," asserting in *The Descent of Winter* (1928), for example, that "That thing, the vividness which is poetry by itself, makes the poem," and noting at one point, "10.28 born, September 15, 1927, 2nd child, wt. 6 lbs. 2 ozs. The hero is Dolores Marie Pischak" (Schott 1971: 241).

As far as his published books are concerned, it may well be in The Wedge (1944) that the oft-quoted phrase appeared in full, in the poem, "A Sort of a Song," though the poet put it in parentheses for some reason (Ball 2013). In the published *Paterson*, in any case, he repeated it like a mantra, beginning with "for the poet there are no ideas but in things" in the Author's Note (Williams 1963). Here is the passage from Book I:

—Say it, no ideas but in things—
nothing but the blank faces of the houses
and cylindrical trees
bent (Williams 14-15).

The poem Mr. Watson chose for Liu's "ambiguity" is the famous one by "the T'ang nature poet" Wang Wei 王維 (699-759).

Empty hills, no one in sight,
only the sound of someone talking:
late sunlight enters the deep wood,
shining over the green moss again. (Watson 1971: 12)

空山不見人
但聞人語響
返景入深林
復照青苔上

I once used this passage in a talk at Brown University.

I'd like to add one more thing to the making of *Spring & Asura: Poems of Kenji Miyazawa*, for which Gary Snyder wrote a gracious blurb. I was one lucky fellow. But lazy as I was, I didn't know Mr. Snyder had translated eighteen of Miyazawa's poems until I read Mr. Watson's introduction. So, again, I wonder which of the two, Andrea Miller—a daughter of Mitch Miller of *Sing Along with Mitch*, the TV program I used to watch in the 1950s—or Alexander Besher turned to the poet for words of praise.

I did not learn that Mr. Watson had become friends with Mr. Snyder in Kyoto in the mid-1950s until I bought a book about Gary Snyder published in the 1990s (Halper 1991). In Mr. Watson's "Kyoto in the Fifties," he recalls that one of the anthologies of new American verse that Mr. Snyder gave him or lent him was "a revelation" to him (Allen 1960). He added, "Thereafter I read as much modern American poetry as I could get hold of, a fact that I hope is reflected in my translations" (Halper 1991: 57).

Gary Snyder is a big-hearted man. A few years after *Spring & Asura* appeared, he came from Kitkitdizze in Nevada City, California, to New York to give a reading at the 92nd Street Y. As he announced he would read some Miyazawa poems, he stood straight at the center of the stage, and read—not his own but my translation. He wrote another blurb when North Point Press did *A Future of Ice*, my second and expanded translation of Miyazawa (Miyazawa 1989). In the late 1970s or in the early 1980s, I stumbled upon a poetry anthology (Howard 1974), and was happy to find Mr. Snyder quoting Mr. Watson's translation in the "past" part. It is a poem by Su Dongpo 蘇東坡 (1037-1101), the first line of which Japanese students used to memorize—maybe they still do—as if it were an old saying to treasure.

> Spring night—one hour worth a thousand gold coins.
> Clear scent of flowers, shadowy moon.
> Songs and flutes upstairs—threads of sound;
> In the garden, a swing, where night is deep and still. (Su 1977: 24)

春宵一刻直千金
花有清香月有陰
歌管楼臺聲細細
鞦韆院落夜沈沈

This comes from a collection of Mr. Watson's translated verse of Su Dongpo, and he appends a note to it: "To convey the stillness of the night, the poet avoids a single verb of action" (Su 24). Some say that the poem describes a scene in a pleasure house, a drinking establishment. That reminds me of an anecdote Mr. Watson related to me about his translation of short stories by an early 20th-century Japanese writer (Oda 1990). Having already lived in Osaka for some years, Mr. Watson would drop in at his favorite eateries after going to the public bathhouse and query what some of the truly delicious snacks Ryūkichi finds for Chōko in particularly "dirty" eateries in the story "Meoto Zenzai" 夫婦善哉 [Hurray for Marriage, or Sweet Beans for Two!] were made of and how—so he might have a better idea in rendering them in English (Oda 1990).

Speaking of such things, I fondly remember Mr. Watson telling me what Yoshikawa Kōjirō, the redoubtable scholar of Chinese classics and one of his professors at the University of Kyoto, was like. Once, when a drunk student cracked a raw egg on the professor's head while he was drinking with his students in an *aka-*

chōchin or *izakaya*, the redoubtable scholar, smiling, returned the favor by doing the same to the student.

For one reason or another, I did not have a chance to go out to drink with Mr. Watson. But I have no doubts that he is a gentle and fun drinking companion like Yoshikawa Kōjirō.

Works Cited

Allen, Donald, ed. *The New American Poetry*, 1945-1960. New York: Grove Press, 1960.

Ball, Sally. "Saxifrage: 'A Sort of a Song' for 2013" (2013). http://www.thevolta.org/ewc27-sball-p1.html

Halper, Jon. *Gary Snyder: Dimensions of a Life*. New York: Random House, 1991.

Howard, Richard, ed. *Preferences: 51 American Poets Choose Poems from Their Own Work and from the Past*. New York: Viking, 1974.

Liu, James J.Y. *The Art of Chinese Poetry*. Chicago: University of Chicago Press, 1962.

Miyazawa Kenji. *A Future of Ice: Poems and Stories of a Japanese Buddhist*. Hiroaki Sato, trans. New York: North Point Press, 1989.

Moore, Marianne. "Poetry." In *Poetry and its Conventions: An Anthology Examining Poetic Forms and Themes*. John T. Shawcross and Frederick R. Lapides, eds. New York: Free Press, 1972. P. 452.

Murasaki Shikibu. *The Tale of Genji*. Arthur Waley, trans. 1933. North Clarendon, VT: Tuttle Publishing, 2010.

Natsume Sōseki. *I Am a Cat*. Aiko Ito and Graeme Wilson, trans. North Clarendon, VT: Tuttle Publishing, 2002.

Oda Sakunosuke. *Stories of Osaka Life*. Burton Watson, trans. New York: Columbia University Press, 1990.

Sato, Hiroaki. "'Genji': the Long and the Shorter of it." *The Japan Times* 10 March 2002. http://www.japantimes.co.jp/culture/2002/03/10/books/book-reviews/genji-the-long-and-the-shorter-of-it/#.VRk3GJPF9XY

Sato, Hiroaki, trans. *Japanese Women Poets: An Anthology*. Armonk, NY: M.E. Sharpe, 2008.

---. *Mutsuo Takahashi: Poems of a Penisist*. Chicago: Chicago Review Press, 1975.

---. *See You Soon: Poems of Taeko Tomioka*. Chicago: Chicago Review

Press, 1979.

---. *Spring & Asura: Poems of Kenji Miyazawa*. Chicago: Chicago Review Press, 1973.

Sato, Hiroaki and Burton Watson, eds. *From the Country of Eight Islands: An Anthology of Japanese Poetry*. Garden City, NY: Anchor Press, 1981.

Schott, Webster, ed. *Imaginations: William Carlos Williams*. New York: New Directions, 1971.

Su Dongpo (Su Tung-p'o). *Su Tung-p'o: Selections from a Sung Dynasty Poet*. Burton Watson, trans. New York: Columbia University Press, 1977.

Watson, Burton. *Chinese Lyricism: Shih Poetry from Second to the Twelfth Centuries*. New York: Columbia University Press, 1971.

---. *Rainbow World: Japan in Essays and Translations*. Seattle: Broken Moon Press, 1990a.

Watson, Burton, trans. *Japanese Literature in Chinese*. 2 vols. New York: Columbia University Press, 1975, 1976.

---. *Kanshi:The Poetry of Ishikawa Jōzan and other Edo-period Poets*. New York: North Point Press, 1990b.

Williams, William Carlos. *Paterson*. New York: New Directions, 1963.

10

Linked Verse

Yoko Danno

"Heaped with snow
bamboos in the garden
bend and topple —"

                        Saigyō 95

Only yesterday the branching river
was young, rushing between rocks

                        Yoko

"Ice wedged fast
in the crevice of the rock
this morning begins to melt —"

                        Saigyō 19

Fertilized eggs rest under thin ice
ready to be born into unseen oceans

                        Yoko

"I'll forget the trail…,
go searching for blossoms
in directions I've never been before"

      Saigyō 35

Your unknown features are seen
through a cast-off skin of yourself

      Yoko

"Even in a person
most times indifferent
to things around him"

      Saigyō 67

A smile escapes from tight lips
when silver peaks glow at sunset

      Yoko

Work Cited

Saigyō. *Poems of a Mountain Home.* Burton Watson, trans. New York: Columbia University Press, 1991.

11

Hagiwara Sakutarō's Arcane "Harmful Creatures"

Robert Epp

Introduction

It is hard to challenge the claim that Hagiwara Sakutarō (1886–1942) made compelling contributions to Japanese free verse.[1] Often considered the progenitor of early modern Japanese poetry, he greatly expanded the themes and images available to his fellow poets. Like Baudelaire before him, Sakutarō showed how a writer might express with decadent artifice the dark, ugly, and unpleasant aspects of man's inner self. That led Sakutarō to pioneer a psychological mode of Japanese verse that transformed his spiritual chaos into literary documents exposing the luckless, superfluous, and splintered modern non-person he felt himself to be. These aspects of his work testify to the sharp break his writing makes with traditional Japanese lyricism.

   Many poems published between 1913 and 1923 demonstrate how Sakutarō's contributions went beyond a mere mastery of the free verse form. From the outset, he hoped to create a new style of verse with fresh figures of speech and unprecedented content. He also believed that poetry must deal with the underside of existence, not just the appealing wonders of nature. If poetry is to reflect the human heart, it should engage depressions, depravities, and nightmares, as well as joys, graces, and dreams. That explains why from early on Sakutarō pushed beyond simply resisting certain old-fashioned aspects of Japanese poetry's ten-century weight of convention. He became absorbed in communicating something akin to what William Butler Yeats called a "Vision of Evil" (Meihuizen 1998: 25). Unveiling the primordial dreads of the soul, Sakutarō envisioned a poetics rooted in the modern urban era. Together with that vision he made clear his mission to revivify, perhaps even to reinvent, the traditional Japanese emphasis on human feelings.

These objectives sometimes produced difficult verse. Many readers have been especially baffled by the dismaying opacity and manic leaps in his notable 1915 poem "Yūgai naru dōbutsu" 有害なる動物 [Harmful Creatures] (Hagiwara 1975.1: 236). This unique portrait of a feral man may also disincline all but the intensely curious from trying to grasp its mélange of enigmatic imagery—the likes of which I doubt exist in premodern Japanese verse. This poem's obscurantism, disconnected lines, cryptic surfaces, and lack of the slightest hint of narrative or connectivity combine to make "Harmful Creatures" one of Sakutarō's most impenetrably hermetic works. That forces us to read between and beyond the lines so we can "collaborate" with the poet in making sense of this challenging work. The interiority and disjunctive symbolic figures in "Harmful Creatures" are far too daunting to approach this work as though it were a typical lyric poem. Certainly, no Sakutarō piece indicates better than "Harmful Creatures" the degree to which the buried internal meanings of a poem can prove far more challenging than its vocabulary, syntax, and grammar.

The Poem and Its Focus on Animals

"Harmful Creatures"

Since dog-like creatures howl,
since goose-like creatures are freaks of Nature,
since fox-like creatures luminesce at night,
since turtle-like creatures congeal into crystal,
all the more since wolf-like creatures sprint with sickening speed
—— every one is harmful to our bodies.

有害なる動物

犬のごときものは吠えることにより
鷲鳥のごときものは畸形兒なることにより
狐のごときものは夜間に於て發光することにより
龜のごときものは凝晶することにより
狼のごときものは疾行することによりてさらに甚だしく
すべて此等のものは人身の健康に有害なり。

    Sakutarō's focus on animals presents its own problems. He loved the pleasures of the metropolis, but when he dealt with penitential acts or prayer, he often preferred a natural rather than an urban framework. Dealing with animals also reflects the long-standing East Asian belief that nature has the power to purify and heal. Most ancients uniformly paid less attention to plant life than to animals, who were related not only to the gods but to themselves. Of course, it is easier to develop a relationship with a horse or dog, living creatures with complex behavior patterns, than with flowers, fruit, or vegetables. Moreover, primitive folk everywhere imagined that the attributes of beasts remained constant while those of human beings did not. They believed, too, that critters' names transcended being simple nouns, for the animals themselves were far more than static "objects." From very early on, animal names implied activities, concepts, and values. Folk also held that animals symbolize the self and mankind's instinctive nature, a notion that inspired identity with the perceived qualities or characteristics they ascribed to beasts. Those who read this poem must keep all this in mind.

The Beasts of the Zodiac

Legends about the source of the Chinese zodiac (from the Greek word for "beast") abound. According to one tale, the Buddha once invited all of the world's animals to pay him a visit on the New Year; he promised to name a year after each animal that showed up. Only twelve animals came, namely the rat, ox, tiger, rabbit, dragon, snake, horse, sheep, monkey, chicken, dog, and pig—in that order.
    Over the centuries, each of these creatures acquired a list of human attributes said to characterize individuals born during that year. How likely are people born in the same year to have similar

characteristics? The Western zodiac at least deals with much smaller segments of time. First, it breaks each year into twelve signs of the zodiac from Aries the Ram through Pisces the Fish. Astrologers then fine-tune their readings in terms of the location of various heavenly bodies at the hour of one's birth. Note, however, that both Western and Asian zodiac cycles assume qualitative existential connections between people and stars or people and animals. Scholars label the latter "animatism," which ascribes personal qualities to living creatures or assumes that animals possess the same qualities as humans, or vice versa. This conceit resembles the way Western astrologers correlate human attributes with inanimate heavenly constellations represented by our twelve zodiac signs.

From an early age, Sakutarō showed an awareness of having been born in the Year of the Dog (Chiba 1965: 26). Fearing a witch might transform him into a puppy, he was terrified as a boy that his mother might fail to recognize him and shoo him out of the yard. Zodiac animal characteristics connect with a person's *being*. Even a superficial knowledge of his character makes us wonder where he was when the gods distributed the "dog" traits. His most obvious human qualities rather resemble those ascribed to people born in the Year of the Horse, who have a weakness for members of the opposite sex, love to wear showy clothes, are excessively independent, and detest listening to advice. Although Sakutarō was ever mindful of his "dogness," several poems reveal his affinity to "horse people" (Epp 1999: 108, 135, 160; Epp and Iida 2005: 166, 124).

As broad and as imprecise as they may be, correlations between human traits and animals have some significance. After all, from the beginning of recorded time folk have insisted on regarding animals as "vehicles of cosmic meaning" that mirror humankind and the soul's depravities. That belief favored incorporating beasts into zodiacs or mythologies. Furthermore, the existential roots of the connections between beasts and *being* have penetrated the English language, as the vocable "animal" attests. "Animal" associates with *anima*, the individual's soul or inner self. For Jung, animals represent the realm of subhuman instincts and the unconscious areas of the psyche; moreover, "The *anima* is a personification of all feminine psychological tendencies in a man's psyche...." (Jung and Franz 1964: 177).[2] As the individual's true inner self, *anima* contrasts with the external aspects of one's personality.

In commenting on these five creatures, Sakutarō intuitively perceives the "animal mind" dimension of the human psyche, which represents a primitive layer of *being*—one generally associated with instinctive behaviors that can menace our serenity. Stressing these creatures' metaphoric aspects explains why the animals in "Harmful Creatures" differ noticeably from those with the same names that we view with the naked eye. Note, too, how Sakutarō insists on saying, "dog-*like*," "goose-*like*," "fox-*like*," "turtle-*like*," and "wolf-*like*." While the names may be the same, his animals are broad categories only approximating those that resemble real dogs, geese, foxes, turtles, or wolves. This causes the reader not only to regard these creatures symbolically but to see one's self in them. After looking through—or more precisely *beyond*—their physical shapes and characteristics, Sakutarō creatively disassembles what he takes to be the essence of each of these five creatures so that with his inner eye he is able to observe the attributes giving birth to those traits that plague him.

By deciding to perceive these creatures either as aspects of his deepest self or as symbols inhabiting his psyche, Sakutarō encourages us to confront them in a unique way—one that allows us to see how the self becomes an aspect of what it observes. This suggests a modern psychological approach: distortions like those in "Harmful Creatures" force readers to look at the animals through another lens and so gain a new perspective on them. I believe Sakutarō wants us to engage this work in particular, and all his verse in general, in a fresh way—less in terms of descriptive content than of how substance gets formed from the inside out, existentially and psychologically. In accepting the mental processes that created "Harmful Creatures," and by trying to get on the poet's wavelength, we can condition ourselves to his point of view. Once we manage that, we can see something of what he saw and better appreciate his radical modernity.

How might one make Sakutarō's fears palpable? Japanese never had many beasts of prey to contend with, so they had no reason to become hunters of trophy animals. Nor, for almost a millennium, has the populace needed to defend itself against dangerous beasts. Moreover, Japanese for the most part have regarded wild flesh as "unclean," and thus have been reluctant to consume it. Buddhist strictures against killing living creatures (except for fish) were also inhibiting. There may have been a reason to avoid certain animals, but few incentives to regard them as harmful to one's health. Sakutarō's fantasy created his own rationale. That is why one early step in making this work intelligible is to uncover how the poem holds together. Along the way, we will find that the unity of "Harmful Creatures" derives from Sakutarō's intense concerns with *being* and libido. Another step is making sure we read his work through the various framing notions he provides: psychological, spatial, temporal, and textual.

Doing that argues for considering Sakutarō's concerns when he wrote the poem. This includes the predictable scenario: data from his life, the context of the section, and the works before and after the piece under consideration. Learning to read Sakutarō in a sense resembles listening to a symphony. One listens both diachronically and synchronically—that is, both to the development of figures or melodies played over time, and to the harmony of notes played at the same moment. Reading "Harmful Creatures" that way not only encourages an interpretive, hermeneutic, and heuristic encounter with the text, but also urges us to delve into the poet's inner self. That will make our reading of "Harmful Creatures" an encounter, first with the poet's *being*, and then with our own, thus allowing us make sense of this somewhat exasperating poem.

Biographical Background of the Poem

Several weeks before composing "Harmful Creatures" near the end of 1914, Sakutarō wrote a Tokyo *tanka*-poet friend about the need to wash away his sinful dissipations. Doing that required quiet prayer and purgation, which is why he wrote confessional verse. Sakutarō also wished to purge the personal inhibitions that got in the way of achieving a stronger authenticity in his poetry. He later boasted to a friend that he composed his best verse after wasting his body, claiming that he could write great poetry even on the day after a drunken binge when he was virtually cadaverous. He implied that letting his subconscious generate the verse made it more psychological and consequently more authentic.

Late in November 1914, Sakutarō wrote his mentor Hakushū about visions he could not put to paper. The sins that he felt God was punishing him for also continued to anguish him. He felt torn between panic and fright, perplexities and bafflements—none of which he could resolve or share with others. He also informed Hakushū that he had come down with the flu and had contracted gonorrhea. He added that he also suffered from neurosis, which his father Dr. Hagiwara had diagnosed as a nervous breakdown.

Frames in the Collection

Sakutarō placed "Harmful Creatures" in the "Glowing on the Pine" section of his *Dreaming Butterflies* collection. A work's position in a collection represents the poet's conscious decision, often based on principles beyond his awareness. Sakutarō calculatingly set "Harmful Creatures" in an environment meant to influence our reading and understanding of the work. He named the "Glowing on the Pine" section in *Dreaming Butterflies* after the second poem in this part, "Glowing Pine Needles." This piece depicts a human corpse hung on a burning pine tree: the man had been executed for his *tsumi* [sins/crimes] against his *being*. The third work after "Evening Bar" in this section, "Harmful Creatures" —directly before "My Solitary Self" and "Lover of Love"—follows "Moonlit Night" and "Invisible Brigand."

In depicting an "orphaned" or alienated fellow crying out for a friend, "My Solitary Self" offers several hints about the "secret sins" that afflict the persona. Perceiving himself "aflame in a withering blur of searing lusts," the persona "shudders with dread" as he laments:

> This most solitary self
> resoundingly howls for a nameless friend
> ... my perverse, my puzzling self,
> wretched as a crow,
> shivers on the edge of this forsaken winter bench. (Epp 1999: 137)

"My Solitary Self" centers on the persona's thirst for relationship. He perceives that his *being*, which molders in winter's lonely wither, is in crisis. However, he has no idea how he can resolve his predicament. Testosterone so dominates him that he appears unable to relate to others in a wholesome way. No wonder he feels "wretched as a crow"—who would dream of associating with a crow, that messenger of death and ultimate emblem of rejection and alienation?

In "Lover of Love," Sakutarō depicts a sex-starved male who transforms himself into the object of his desires. Japanese censors banned this poem, fearing that it would "corrupt public morals." The persona, dressed in drag, affects a blend between a geisha and a European courtesan. Counterfeiting the coquetry of a nubile maiden looking for love, he then "romances" a tall white birch. Since such behavior cannot mitigate the poet's thirst for a woman, we imagine he will end up far more frustrated than he was before he began "flirting" with that birch (symbol of a phallus) "in a stand of dazzling trees / on this fragrant May-time field" (Epp and Iida 2005: 68).

We see, then, that Sakutarō inserted "Harmful Creatures" between works dealing with sinfulness, self-punishment, a reluctance to reform, overpowering loneliness, estrangement and guilt, not to mention insatiable yet unsatisfied sexual desires. The persona's recognition that his behavior is perverse and puzzling lurks in the background. Context implies the persona's need for self-examination to clarify the reasons for his perversity and puzzlement. When we bring together these diverse elements we may discern how the animal imagery dominating "Harmful Creatures" might relate to the themes of sexual desire and sin, pain and punishment, alienation and lasciviousness, and guilt and penitence. What more effectively violates indigenous poetic conventions than Sakutarō's commitment to such existential issues? Then, too, by sneezing at middle-class inhibitions toward sexual themes, he points to his modernity and the paradigm shift that, by the end of 1914, he had begun to fashion.

The Poem's Title, "Harmful Creatures"

Literally, the Japanese title means "animals that are baneful," that is, bad, detrimental, harmful, injurious, or noxious. I somehow feel more comfortable using "creatures," simply living beings instead of "animals," which are often considered beings with a soul. However, the English term "baneful" contains a hint of something deadly, even sinister, which may slightly misrepresent Sakutarō's intent with *yūgai*. *Yūgai* is probably best rendered as "harmful," for the creatures he portrays embody something pernicious, injurious, or damaging in both a psychological and a physical sense.

A prose essay published four months after "Harmful

Creatures" shows how Sakutarō's dread of animals relates to the psyche. He confesses that watching animals—he lists cats, clams, dogs, and geese —"conversing" with each other fills him with dread. He felt they were "discussing" covert topics that only instinct and intuition can apprehend.

> Possessing special sensory organs that humans do not have, animals observe animate things that humans cannot see. They hear things humans cannot hear. They are aware of natural disasters that will occur in the future. And they are constantly communicating with each other about secrets of the world hidden from us. I turn pale and tremble with uncanny dread whenever I see more than two animals standing face-to-face for an extended time (Hagiwara 1975-1978.3: 184).

Sakutarō believed these creatures were sharing their observations about realms beyond the reach of our limited human senses. We know that dogs can sometimes sense a human's impending epileptic fit, for example, and that elephants can sometimes detect a distant *tsunami*. Other animal-human correspondences exist as well. Darwin noticed that the same anti-depressant medications that humans use can reduce a dog's high-pitched wail when left alone or lessen depression in young monkeys that have been separated from a parent. Sakutarō's view of animal capabilities, by contrast, appears to border on paranoia. He presumably feared that animals observing us from a dimension on the other side of the mirror might smash the glass, invade our reality, and threaten our well-being.

Line-by-line Close Readings

The average reader may wonder whether Sakutarō truly imagined that his readers would or could understand this work—or even imagine that it made sense. "Harmful Creatures" shows that he by no means felt compelled to produce "readerly" texts. Note the lack of transitions. Each of the five animals stands isolated in its own line—a wall of silence invites us to make up or imagine our own connectives. The burden lies entirely on the reader. Having compacted these lines to an extreme degree, Sakutarō dares us to unpack them and refashion connectives that might merge them into an organic whole. That requires more effort than most readers are prepared to invest. "Harmful Creatures" might hardly seem worth the effort. Admittedly, we cannot expect Sakutarō to create a Hallmark greeting card, especially when he is in the process of exposing his troubled self. Yet it would have been nice if he had not avoided clarity, omitted connectives or referents, and concealed clues to his meaning. Many serious readers will conclude that some of Sakutarō's works—and certainly this one—border on artistic perversity.

Japanese readers are no doubt more likely than most Westerners to appreciate being forced to participate in the writing process. This is why they often enjoy "writerly" texts and find great charm in obscurity, for it gives them the impression they are taking part in the poem's creation. For many Japanese, a "good" poem resembles a dream that they help unravel. Whatever one may think of "Harmful Creatures," it does boast "writerly" lines that impel readers to recreate the text. We must rewrite, reorganize, parse, and clarify the poem. Far more consistently than authors in the West, average Japanese writers choose not to be held accountable to their readers. While that is also the intrinsic nature of poets as contrasted to novelists or essayists, in "Harmful Creatures" Sakutarō goes a step beyond and drives us to new heights of reader responsibility. "Harmful Creatures" illustrates the reader-accountable qualities of Sakutarō's most challenging verse. Strictly speaking, it is not as though he never offers readers any clues; he does provide helpful hints, if sometimes in surprising places. The most important hints to his meaning he buries in the settings—in the frames and contexts—of each work. The primary task for the reader and critic, then, is easily stated: bring that setting to light.

Line 1: Since dog-like creatures howl

What aspects of the simple fact that "dog-like creatures howl" might possibly be considered "harmful to our bodies"?[3] What drove Sakutarō to arrive at this conclusion? Could the question center simply on the cliché that an animal's instinctive sensitivities are far more finely-tuned than those of humans? Because he was born in the Year of the Dog, could Sakutarō's conclusions relate to his identifying with either the dog or his queasy feelings, cited earlier, vis-à-vis the considerable lode of "knowledge" animals possess that we do not?

One well-known work reveals Sakutarō's cheerless self-concern as he projects himself onto the sickly, "unfamiliar" dog that hounds him like his shadow:

> Yes, this stray hound dogs my path,
> never ever letting up.
> Shuffling over the grimy ground,
> this sickly pooch follows me, dragging one hind leg. (Epp 1999: 141)

Sakutarō did not just identify with this animal; he saw himself a spiritually crippled mongrel. This dog thus symbolizes the fate that shadowed his life and the way the townspeople, even relatives, treated him at times like an alien. In his outlandish getups and Turkish fez, he did at times look like "a man from Mars." "Since dread chalks the dogs' hearts, / they howl endlessly on that night-shrouded road" (Epp 164). Submissive to primal dreads and instinct, both poets and dogs feel driven to bay at the moon. Moon symbolism points to the psyche and the feminine or maternal principle (*yin*), which may explain one source of the hound's dread. Another reason this gloomy poet readily identified with hounds was because he knew that a dog was the companion of Melancholy, the black-bile aspect of the four temperaments.

Instinctual drives lie at the root of the howling of the dog, and Sakutarō by extension. In the poet's case, howling is rooted in a sex drive beyond his control, determination, intentions, or logic.

> The path of lust.
> The path of a troubled and sentimental twilight
> transforming dogs and beasts into silver
> and choking that street with the trolley tracks.... (Epp 97)

Sakutarō's path connects with lasciviousness. Twilight ignites his lustfulness by transforming "dogs and beasts," not to mention poets, into silver—his code for the libido that symbolizes the life force. This innocent image of a dog or poet responding to nature becomes not only a metaphor of Sakutarō's *being* but an epidemiological insight into "what ails him." Internally and externally oppressed, he imagines that the world is closing in on him ... the way his hometown of Maebashi's dreary buildings seem to strangle its streetcar tracks, those universal symbols of escape.

In Sakutarō's view, a dog yelping at the moon stands for a man so thirsty and so anxious for a woman that he finds himself hurling poems at the moon. This figure provides a tentative explanation of why he thinks the dog's howling harms humans. A baying hound not only keeps others from sleep, but its howling may also remind us of the unpleasant truth that—more often than we care to admit—instinctual drives rather than rationality govern much of our behavior. To acknowledge that truth can be depressing and thus detrimental to our physical and mental health.

Line 2: since goose-like creatures are freaks of Nature

How can Sakutarō consider geese "harmful to our bodies" just because they are "freaks of Nature"?[4] Actually, that may not be too far-fetched. The term Sakutarō uses for "freak," which can also mean a monster or monstrosity, usually refers simply to something ill-formed or crippled. In a society dominated by people who treasure uniformity and believe in karma, the mere hint of physical deformity can result in exclusion from one's primary group. After all, a deformed member constitutes a karmic judgment—visible punishment for bad behavior or evil thoughts. Families consequently concealed a crippled member to prevent negative judgments about possible amoral conduct. Being excluded from the polity is exceptionally cruel and unusual punishment for anyone who lives in an organic society.

However, there is much more to geese than freakishness. Their symbolic associations would not only be of interest to Sakutarō, but allow him to identify with (or avoid) this bird. A tubular phallic neck and roundish feminine body have long made geese a sacred emblem of ardor. Geese have also customarily been connected with the realm of women and the household; in many cultures geese thus serve as symbols of love. That alone is more than enough to inspire Sakutarō to believe they could be injurious to his health. Connections with love explain why geese also relate to female sexuality: creation, fertility, and maternity; the "goose month" in medieval England referred to the month when mothers were confined following childbirth.

    A goose was not only an attribute of the goddess of love—Venus or Aphrodite, who is often depicted riding a goose—but connects, as well, with a phallic fertility god and Cupid or Eros. Thus for ages folk have considered the bird's dark meat an aphrodisiac. In folklore and in ancient Rome, "goose" could moreover refer to a prostitute. In Shakespeare's writings, geese generally have sexual import. People in his time even associated geese with bitterness, disease, infection, or plague; a "goose" can likewise refer to a syphilitic swelling. The fact that Sakutarō had a social disease when he wrote this piece offers a rationale for finding these freakish birds "harmful to our bodies." Consequently, a goose-like creature might be injurious to Sakutarō's health simply because of its long-standing connections with sexuality.

    Sakutarō could not conceivably have been familiar with all, or even most, of this data. It is nonetheless surprising to find how many of these details seem to agree with the poem's content. There is no way that Sakutarō was not at least minimally aware of the sexual nature of the goose image. In fact, given his prurient orientation, it is odd that he did not refer more often to this bird (Epp and Iida 50).

    Its flocking instinct and the territorially aggressive gander suggest the goose's sociability and lack of passivity (Theroux 2006: 41). The term "goose" has incidentally served in Japan as argot for a breed of human being whom Sakutarō deeply detested and tried to avoid: the bullying martinet or fussy supervisor. Given the symbolism and the carnal connotations long associated with this bird, however, we imagine that Sakutarō may have found geese harmful to his health mainly because of their psychological and symbolic associations—particularly those relating to authority, birth, and sex.

Line 3: since fox-like creatures luminesce at night

What could Sakutarō have had in mind by claiming that "fox-like creatures" are harmful simply because they luminesce or radiate light?[5] Nor, unless actual cancer-causing radiation is involved, is it immediately clear how luminescence in itself might adversely affect our bodies. The "mystery" lessens considerably once we understand the framework of this image.

    Of course, real foxes do not glow in the dark. Nonetheless,

ancient Japanese connected the fox with the phosphorescence that flits eerily over swampy ground at night. They called it "fox-fire" [*kitsunebi*], which we designate "will-o'-the-wisp," "friar's lantern," or *ignis fatuus*. The spontaneous combustion of gases emitted by rotting organic matter causes this natural phenomenon. Will-o'-the-wisp implies delusive hopes or the illusory, but ascribing fluorescence to foxes transports us well beyond associations with the "will-o'-the-wisp." To Sakutarō, fluorescence connects with both the gleam of radium and the "glow" of libido, either of which he regarded extremely threatening, even perilous. Keep in mind that he saw a firefly's luminescence, which he believed resembled radioactive rays, as a symbol of sensual love. That alone makes foxes or fox-fire potentially harmful, as he wrote in early 1915:

> The fluorescence or radium-like emissions of diseased plants and even of animal spines—consider how harmful they are to our health. Scientists need fresh discoveries to prevent new-born humans from being pitifully ravaged. (Epp 109)

In a work written a month before "Harmful Creatures," Sakutarō laments "hands that glow in space" and "metallic wrists" whose gleams blind him and rend his flesh: "pale radium sickens my hands/ and agonizes my fingers…." (Epp 100). Harmful to human health indeed!

    The word "fox" has other notable sexual connotations. For example, it is a long-standing argot designation of a prostitute registered with the government. This term derived from the fact that girls who were kidnapped and then sold into prostitution were given the slang appellation *Inari*, the name of the god of the rice harvest or the fox deity. Potential customers have always regarded "foxes" as considerably "safer" than streetwalkers because the government regularly screened and treated them for sexually-transmitted diseases. Officials insisted that those who turned up positive for a "social affliction" get treatment before being allowed to continue plying their trade. No doubt Sakutarō had been warned when he visited Tokyo to patronize "foxes" rather than unregistered whores. He still managed to contract a case of gonorrhea, though it is far from clear whether he contracted it in the capital or back home in Maebashi.

As erotic symbols in East Asia, foxes have for centuries been associated with the *yin* or feminine principle. Several Chinese references to foxes, some of which Sakutarō certainly knew, contain weighty sensual implications that could make them potentially harmful to his well-being. Foxes are, to begin, symbols of seduction. The ancient Chinese, who saw foxes as extremely lecherous, often believed that a man could not find a better aphrodisiac than to drink ground-up fox testicles in his wine. It was common for a Chinese man to imagine that wearing a fox tail on his arm would sexually arouse a woman and make her susceptible to his advances. Presumably, Chinese often believed as well that after the fox lived a thousand years, it developed unimaginable powers of seduction. These "fox women" creatures are irresistibly sensuous and have ravenous sexual appetites. In truth, they make such insatiable sexual demands on a man under their spell that they endanger him by depleting his vital life force.

Because this creature represents fertility, folktales invariably connect foxes with women. Or these tales depict foxes as sly beasts full of cunning and wiles, flattery and sexuality—like women. *Vulpus*, Latin for fox, can suggest "voluptuous." The vixen, a female fox, refers to a woman regarded as malicious, quarrelsome, shrewish, spiteful, or surly. Throughout history, people in the West have often depicted foxes as the Devil, the ace trickster, because a fox's red fur matches the imagined color of Satan's skin. And in Japan foxes have long been regarded as supernatural beings able to transform themselves into men or women capable of bewitching others. Could Sakutarō have known the story in Judges 15:4-5— his Old Testament text was full of underlinings and penned-in reactions—that tells how Samson burned down the grain fields of the Philistines by releasing 300 foxes with lit firebrands tied to their tails? This act mimicked a folk fertility rite, providing another ancient link between foxes and sexuality.

Creatures with such sexual potential who also luminesce like radium must surely pose a threat to human health, but especially to Sakutarō's libido. Remember, too, that foxes have a long history of being connected with superstition—far longer than any other animal in Japan (Piggott 1983: 109).

Line 4: since turtle-like creatures congeal into crystal

To make sense of this line, we need to grasp the reasoning of the assertion that turtles "congeal into crystal"[6] Assuming that a turtle could metamorphose into crystal, we then have to ask how that transformation might become "harmful to our bodies" (i.e., health). From the outset, we should realize that without a basic understanding of Sakutarō's perception of the tortoise, it is unreasonable to expect cogent answers even to such sensible questions. He wrote this terse but memorable poem around the same time as "Harmful Creatures":

> I sense the weight of a pure-gold turtle
> resting silently in my hand.
> Bearing Nature's wretched pains,
> this gleaming turtle
> burrows into my beating heart,
> sinks into the depths of the blue. (Epp and Iida 38)

Sakutarō offers two primary frames that provide important contextual clues to "Turtle." The first is chronological and consists of at least a dozen poems written during December 1914 and mostly published in January 2015. Two that have thematic connections with and are chronologically close to "Turtle" are "Flute" and "Winter." The second set of frames consists of Sakutarō's placement of this poem in the context of the collection in which it appeared. In *Howling at the Moon* (1917), "Turtle" appears in the "Bamboo and its Pathos" section between "Rancid Chrysanthemum" and "Flute." In *Dreaming Butterflies* (1923), he inserted "Turtle" between "Pilgrimage" and "White Night" in the "Glowing on the Pine" section. These environments provide instructive clues regarding what Sakutarō took to be the meaning and import of the turtle image.

Pain and anticipation of punishment are common to each of the framing works. "Rancid Chrysanthemum" features a flower (a masculine image) that serves as the Imperial crest. Mums symbolize wealth, the sun, or regal beauty and imply cheerfulness and optimism, long life and happiness. Japanese consider it a September flower, so by early November—the poem's setting—mums should be "turning sour / ... [and] oozing pain." In fact, the poet identifies with the sickened mum that "throbs with agony" (Epp and Iida 36). "Flute" describes a penitent wholeheartedly grieving over his sinfulness (Epp 102). The persona in "Pilgrimage" confesses that his "secrets, [all] sexual," dangle from his arms and are "more terrifying than death." He masochistically thrashes himself as he sets off on a pilgrimage to heaven, anticipating the trials and temptations that Christian experienced in *A Pilgrim's Progress*. "White Night" describes a paranoid experience featuring an anticipated attack by an adversary wielding "a silver weapon ... / frozen in the darkness" (Epp 98). In both collections containing "Turtle," Sakutarō painstakingly framed the poem in an environment of guilt feelings, fear of punishment, and the need for penitence.

"Turtle" simply exists; like "Harmful Creatures," its existence conveys a jumble of impressions that Sakutarō expects readers to absorb. Perhaps this brief and enigmatic work has no specific interpretation. Mentioning possible meanings embedded in or suggested by the opening lines of the poem may nonetheless spur thought or nourish intuitions. Folk generally regard woods and forests as sites of potential peril: the playground of both dangerous animals and snakes as well as dreaded supernatural beings like witches, werewolves, and spooks. A marsh brings to mind the will-o'-the-wisp and eerie night-time glowing, which contains erotic significance for Sakutarō. Clear blue skies are associated with autumn, the time to contemplate life's meaning and the future. A golden turtle will neither rust nor turn dull, but gleams like radium. Precious metals like gold not only signify for this poet the life force or libido, but suggest density and weight as well.

A "pure-gold turtle" can only be artificial or symbolic. "Nature's wretched pains" may refer to genes or Sakutarō's sex drive. Lust cannot be satisfied short of maintaining an erection, which requires a heart pumping blood. The word "beating" differentiates the abstract "heart" [*kokoro*] from the muscular pumping organ [*shinzō*]. The turtle, or its symbolic significance, "burrows into" the persona's heart, which if it actually occurred would mean certain death. This "tunneling" turtle echoes bamboo roots—symbols of Sakutarō's sin-guiltiness that punish him by boring steadily through his thorax to jeopardize his life. The turtle's carapace stands for the sky's arc, so Sakutarō easily imagines it merging with the azure dome. However, he turns the image around by having the creature *sink* into what lies above it—a case of inverted values? In the last two lines the persona's "beating heart" and the "depths of the blue" converge into a single figure. In many cultures, blue stands for calmness, dimension, harmony, the heavens, openness, perfection, space, or truth—i. e., for certain fundamental hopes of the human heart. Little wonder, then, that for Jung the color blue indicates spiritual process, or that ancient Egyptians painted mummies blue—the hue of life, rebirth, and immortality—to indicate that the corpse had been united with the "soul of Truth."

One critic claims the reptile in "Turtle" has neither symbolic import nor profound meaning. That may apply to the tortoise in "Harmful Creatures," but can it square with the fact that in "Bamboo and its Pathos" Sakutarō placed the poem in a section dealing with the agonies of guilt? Several works written and published at the same time relate to that theme. In "Winter," the persona claims that "Testimony to my sinfulness [is] evident in the heavens, / evident on piled-up snow." All Nature tries to convince him of his need for penance (Epp 103). "Eggs" suggests that "It's time now for this sinner to pray" (Epp 102). "Strung Up in the Sky" describes the remorse of the persona "suspended in the posture of prayer" as, begging forgiveness, he hangs himself on a pine tree. How could "Turtle" be devoid of "profound meaning"? More importantly, Sakutarō claimed that in writing "Turtle" he "had staked his life to state the truth" (Hagiwara 1975-1978.13: 71). His penchant for histrionics aside, this claim provides a cogent incentive to take this poem seriously.

Turtles in East Asia have for millennia symbolized stability, long life, happiness, and good fortune. Thus killing a tortoise guaranteed bad luck. Ancient Chinese typically identified turtles with the feminine. A phallic head with a roundish womanly body and copious eggs imply fertility, no doubt encouraging some to regard the turtle an image of the female genitals. Jung considered this creature a symbol of the self in dreams, where it may imply covert hostility or frustrated cravings—good matches with Sakutarō's mental state in those days. Recall that a turtle's mound-like back is said to stand for heaven, its flat plastron below for the earth. Its protective shell implies a secure universal order that guarantees safety and security. All of this infuses turtles with an existential dimension. Because turtles represent material existence rather than transcendence, alchemists believed that they stand for "highly concentrated materialism."

As a hoary figure of old age, the tortoise is associated with longevity and the future. It could thus stand for the seer's crystal ball into which the poet gazes for hints of the future. In this sense, then, the turtle could "congeal into crystal," a substance that contains an intriguing number of significant symbols. Crystal might stand for spirit and the intellect, purity, intuitive knowledge, or immortality, just as it can function as a talisman against the evil eye. Simultaneously, its transparency functions as an object of contemplation; transparent crystal might even be considered matter that exists as though it did not exist. Crystal is associated, moreover, with crystal balls, crystal gazing, and divination. Ancients believed that crystal contains the life force and that crystallomancy or scrying—seeing the future through a crystal ball—revealed the path to the center of reality. That is why crystal can symbolize the self. Some Jungian psychologists think that a person's nuclear self appears in dreams as crystal, which represents the spiritual in corporeal form. Could that explain why Sakutarō associates the turtle with gleaming transparency and with bearing "Nature's wretched pains" of ageing, decay, and genes? The turtle image is truly charged with profound significance.

Sakutarō regards as harmful the fact that turtles "solidify into crystal."[7] As suggested, this mineral has a far deeper symbolic relation with turtles than most casual observers might conceivably imagine. Since crystal's purity and transparency allow a glance into the future and imply wisdom, it relates to eyes with the special characteristics of clarity and intuition—eagerly coveted by poets. Or might Sakutarō mean to suggest that as the turtle's longevity makes it a symbol of immortality, excessive concern about long life and the future may be unhealthy? The severity of his psychic and physical miseries made him most unlikely to be interested in living long, which meant suffering long. His new paradigm rather required him to turn inward and penetrate the core of his existence, an attribute of crystal, instead of becoming concerned about the future. Or could he imply that exploring the psyche is perilous and so might jeopardize his health? Fleeing life's contamination and illusions by probing one's innermost self could conceivably unhinge his psychic stability.

In a hallucinatory state experienced when he was ill or

drunk, Sakutarô reports he could do the following:

> ... see chrysanthemums gleaming like candles, and yes the anguish
> of genital juices trickling down one's fingers.
> I see turtles turning into platinum and antipyrin snowing from the sky.
> All of these harmful to health. All glow with the acidic gleam of precious metals. (Epp 118)

Notice that the turtle appears in the wake of "genital juices trickling down one's fingers." That certainly would include semen. Undoubtedly, Sakutarō links the turtle to the erotic. Beyond the words "turtles turning into platinum," he mentions "the acidic gleam/ of precious metals." Recall that this gleaming is associated with concentrated cosmic energy and symbolizes libido, forever Sakutarō's bane. And what about antipyrin? In the early 20th century, Japanese used it like aspirin to treat pain, headaches, and fever; it also functioned as a mild sedative. Based on the elements considered to this point, we can surmise that Sakutarō believed whatever relates to sexual matters, to the deep center of the self, or to the future has the potential to threaten a human's well-being.

Line 5: since wolf-like creatures sprint with sickening speed

This line challenges readers to determine how a sprinting wolf harms human health merely because of its swiftness.[8] One problem is the impossibility of isolating the wolf's speed from its basic nature—and from the intricate web of symbolism that causes Sakutarō to invest this animal with such terror. "Sprint with sickening speed" renders the compound "to rush fast." The first graph in this two-character term means to be in a hurry or to be sickly, ashamed, or have a guilty conscience. "Sickening speed" may not register the best nuance of this uncommon compound, which defies a one-word translation, but may nonetheless resonate both with the pathology of the poet's sexuality and with this work's theme of critters that are injurious to our well-being. Most ideas about the "wolf" are negative or contain a sexual dimension.

Dictionaries describe a wolf as a man "given to paying unwanted sexual attention to women." The wolf for Sakutarō reflects similar threats from man's lower or sexual nature. In an early unpublished work describing how humans mature, he writes that we begin as fish, turn into birds, which then become snakes that change into lions. Following that is the final transformation:

> the lion becomes a wolf
> saying it wants to devour a woman's gory body. Her breasts, her heart.
> Becomes a wolf with the lethal weapon of a carnal appetite.
> Thus do human children evolve; thus do they mature. (Epp 164)

The acme of a man's maturation results in runaway testosterone: the flowering of an often insatiable sexual appetite. The supreme level of human development is not higher intelligence but honed carnality! In the poem "Wolf," the animal's image elicits the chaotic, the destructive, and the untamed. That is a potent reason why the creature's approach terrifies the poet as he nears Tokyo's largest red-light district. He evidently finds it impossible to escape his lasciviousness.

The wolf's "sickening speed" means that we can't escape this animal or our lusts. Are we then fated to succumb to its powers? No wonder Sakutarō dreams of killing "this wolf with its reflection [in a mirror] … to halt his fearful dash at me" (Epp 108). Aside from vanity, mirrors serve as an amulet against evil. Ancient folk beliefs held that incarnations like the devil or the wolf will die if they see their own image in a mirror—a collector of light. A wolf relates not only to darkness and lust, but feeds on carrion and implies melancholia or black bile. In folklore, this animal symbolizes a host of forces. In the external realm, the wolf stands for whatever is asocial and devouring. In the realm of our inner capacities, it represents subconscious powers ready to feast on us. Sakutarō believes he must try to protect himself from those powers and the influences this animal represents. Wolves terrorized him; his dread leaves a spoor to his psyche.

Sakutarō also viewed the wolf and the dog as lonely beasts that respond instinctively (like him) to deep primordial urges. This reflects how folk have long regarded the lone wolf—one that has left or been driven out of the pack and lives on its own. Lone wolves must fend for themselves, so they tend to be stronger and more aggressive than pack wolves. That is why people regard them as far more dangerous than any average wolf. Moreover, a lone wolf could not by itself bring down a larger animal like an antelope, so it generally hunts smaller critters and turns to scavenging. Wolves depicted in fables and folklore tend to reflect the characteristics of those most likely to come into contact with humans and their domain: the lone wolf.

Other negative characteristics stem from how wolves in the Middle Ages of the West symbolized heresy or gluttony. Wolves are leery of allowing strangers into their pack; the presence of an alien wolf may make the pack either fiercely aggressive or meekly passive. Perceiving himself as an "alien wolf," Sakutarō had reason to fear how the beast dashing at him might regard him because, in psychic terms, a wolf represents the lower instincts that endanger or menace man's humane nature or better angels. Besides, who wants to be overtaken by something with such "sickening speed"?

Line 6: ⎯⎯ every one, harmful to our bodies.

"Our bodies" renders *jinshin*, which means, "the human body." *Jinshin* also stands for *"corpus"* in the Japanese translation of *habeas corpus*, for "slave" in "slave trade," for "human" in "human trafficking" and "human sacrifice," as well as for "personal" in "personal attack." Symbolic connections with sexual themes epitomize the pernicious effects that every single one of these animals might conceivably exert on Sakutarō's physical and psychic well-being.

Conclusion

"Harmful Creatures" invites us to visit or revisit several issues regarding Sakutarō's concerted attempts to modernize indigenous verse. In the context of two major aspects of customary views on this topic, he asks, "How do humans relate to nature?" The first is that Japanese have long believed in an intimate relationship between man and the gods or man and nature. It is so immediate, in fact, that at death Japanese become either a Buddha (if they are Buddhist) or a "god" (if they are Shintō).

    The second is that the traditional view of nature leans toward the positive and the optimistic. Japanese customarily regard nature and everything natural in benevolent terms. In fact, traditional East Asian thought holds that returning to nature can heal a troubled soul. In "Harmful Creatures," Sakutarō not only takes issue with the notion that nature restores, he urges an opposing view. To begin with, he perceives nature as charged with potential perils—many of them erotic— capable of exerting a negative impact on his psyche. "Harmful Creatures" portrays Sakutarō as a saboteur dedicated to undermining conventional values. He also agrees with psychiatrists who believe our animal natures, particularly our "beast-level" values, can imperil our physical and mental "health"—a modern idea not found in classical verse.

    Throughout "Harmful Creatures," Sakutarō probes the symbolic significance of these five erotic creatures. It is less a matter of the beasts without than the beasts within that concerns him; his focus remains on the psyche. Until a human becomes attuned to his innermost self, he will neither confront nor humanize his animal mind. Consequently, he will fail to develop good relationships with the self and nature. Because libido's urges affect the psyche, they can't help but relate to wellness. Those who achieve psychic equilibrium will no doubt manage to come to terms with and discipline their sexual fantasies and behavior. That's what Sakutarō fixes his attention on. Each of these five creatures displays some degree of eroticism, symbolic or actual. There is, in any case, no more private or secretive area of an individual's life than sexual desires and intimacy—experiences that permeate modern poetry and form the basis of Sakutarō's paradigm shift to what is clearly an existential issue.

    Another issue connects with the urge to deal with our innermost being by confronting it directly. The five creatures described in this poem—mere observed realities external to the poet and his self—exist, in a sense, only in Sakutarō's mind, and only on the surface of "Harmful Creatures." After isolating each living thing in separate lines, Sakutarō urges us to consider their interior realities—just as he hopes his readers will move beyond surfaces to confront their private selves. From early on, he felt quite uncomfortable dealing blandly with the "out-there" world, preferring instead to focus on and expose what lay within. Along the way, he thought his psyche resonated with the qualities of creatures generally considered harmless to our mental and physical health. Unlike most of what exists in nature, always *out there* and thus insulated from us, these animals can potentially imperil our psyches. Unpredictable behaviors intimidate because animals conform to instincts that logic cannot fathom. However carefully we observe beasts extracted from the wildness of nature, whether they are domesticated or confined to a zoo, we cannot predict with certainty how they might react to us. Regardless of how much we project our anxieties onto them or extrapolate their behavior based on our own, we can never feel certain of our path through the jungles of animal instinct.

What might "Harmful Creatures" imply about Sakutarō's views of his fellow Japanese? We already know that he believed tradition-bound individuals, especially village farmers, were condemned to live an animal existence. Sakutarō believed that all those chained to the earth and to the past and its hoary practices were little more than beasts. In his opinion, most people in Japan existed in a state of forced domestication or captivity, precisely like creatures in a zoo. He personally rebelled at the very thought of being cooped up or limited, and so he lamented that many of his countrymen were such willing thralls to culture or convention, the family system or the nation-state (as he was to sex and liquor). Sakutarō identifies himself in several works with a caged animal (Epp and Iida 300, 304). However, the five creatures in this poem hint at how libido actually holds him hostage like a village farmer— enslaved not only by convention but by animal values. Once we grasp his sexual "take," we can see why Sakutarō thought these creatures are potentially harmful to human—specifically to *his*— well-being.

The content of "Harmful Creatures" overlaps, as well, with the way modern poets treat the most alien areas of the psyche: our animal and reptilian selves, which reflect Sakutarō's new paradigm. Moreover, there are subtle parallels with the Garden of Eden myth where humans are described as being but one step above the animals. Once Adam ate the fruit of the "Tree of Knowledge of Good and Evil," neither he nor any other human could continue to reside in Eden as an unthinking creature. The irony is that he could participate wholly in his humanity only after he had become aware of the choice between obedience and freedom—only after he had tasted independence and knowledge.

Sakutarō's "discovery" of his psyche reflects the Edenic experience that awoke Adam and Eve. Once aware of their *selves*, they could not remain obedient; the self-aware cannot tolerate the comfortable darkness of Plato's cave. Similarly, Sakutarō knows he must brave the light and reject every yearning for the days of his youth when he was ignorant of distinctions between light and darkness, animal and human. On its most subtle level, "Harmful Creatures" can lead readers to see how irrational and subconscious animal drives cloud our vision. When we nuzzle up to ignorance, we return to the primordial animality of Eden, to the "ineradicable darkness" of sex, instinct, and bigotry—sneering perils that would control us all.

Perhaps readers should be less concerned about demanding what each expression in "Harmful Creatures" *means*, in any objective sense, than to ask what these lines and images suggest or imply to oneself as a reader. The answer might be nothing or an absence of personal significance. In that case, what might Sakutarō want the figures and symbols to imply about his inner life, or the inner life of people in general? Could he be implying that he finds his animal nature teeming with peril, and perhaps extends this parlous state to people in general?

Furthermore, "Harmful Creatures" suggests that an absence of transitions or a center is disturbing enough to force readers to invest extraordinary energy in probing the work. These five creatures reflect an aspect of the poet's psyche or character that can in some way threaten or discomfort him. On the one hand, the poet ascribes certain human qualities to animals. Doing that blurs the gap between sentient beings and beasts (an instance of animatism, as stated). On the other hand, Sakutarō projects aspects of his feral animal and reptilian behavior—the deepest and least "civilized" layers of the mind—onto creatures long associated with attributes and behavior that we may at times imagine echo our own.

The fact is that most poetry lovers expect poets to exhibit the primary mark of creative artistry: to solve tensions between inspiration and form and thus resolve chaos. After all, we expect the act of creation to result in cohesiveness or unity and some degree of concentration, whether of thought or feelings. "Harmful Creatures" challenges such expectations. Sakutarō perversely introduces elements of implausibility and ambivalence, not to mention antithetical juxtapositions. These features not only convey the essence of this seven-line work; they also demonstrate how feelings can conceal themselves behind a bulwark of emblems and enigmas. The moment the symbols in the poem generate the slightest reader reaction, the psyche can open like a flower to sunlight. Perhaps it may have been Sakutarō's hope to reshape the real world beyond his self by perceiving it in new ways—that is, in ways that are metaphorical or symbolic: ways where the analysis consumes more space and requires a far more commodious and lavish scale than the surface of the poem itself. To the extent that it epitomizes the chaos of the mind, "Harmful Creatures" surely qualifies as a persuasive example of Sakutarō's new paradigm.

Finally, we should not neglect the "numbers game." Including the poem's title, "Harmful Creatures" occupies exactly seven lines. The symbolism of seven, a fundamental number, appears several times in Sakutarō's early verse and merits comment.[9] A poem containing seven lines could offer a subtle hint about the "sense" of "Harmful Creatures." In the West, seven has often symbolized pain, "inverted holiness," evil, the deadly sins, as well as consecration. Yet East Asians have for centuries regarded the number seven as auspicious. Note the seven treasures, the seven spring and seven fall flowers, the seven gods of good luck, the seven sages, and the seven syllables in classical poetry, to mention but a few.

Notice also that this poem deals with five creatures, a number associated with both universals and the cardinal aspects of human existence. Aside from the five syllables of classical poetry, this number resonates with the five senses and the ancient theory of the Five Phases [*Gogyō*], which comprise the basic components of all matter. A five-pointed star implies the universe in miniature: man's four limbs and head. Five thus symbolizes humankind as well as health, the number of our sensory organs, and even love. In Buddhism, the number five represents the shape of the heart, the basic sins and virtues, as well as the essentials that the Five Phases symbolize. What could be more essential, more basic to existence than sexual reproduction? "Harmful Creatures" clearly deals with human existence. Hinting that this work contains a coherent symbolic structure, these correspondences expose the poet's mindset around the end of 1914 and the beginning of 1915 when he was striving to escape the disorder that his irresponsible behavior had made of his life.

"Harmful Creatures" gives us glimpses of Sakutarō's animal and reptilian nature to show what weight he puts on sex and libido—the psychic and emotional dynamism yoked to instinctive bodily drives. This chapter has demonstrated how his poetry is a living, dynamic study of the psyche.

Endnotes

[1] Like many other famous Japanese personages, this poet has been mostly referred to by his given name of Sakutarō instead of by his surname of Hagiwara. This chapter follows that convention in naming.

[2] The sense of *anima* cannot conceivably be recovered from the Japanese vocable for "animal," *dōbutsu*, which simply means "something that moves."

[3] Statements about the dog are based mainly on de Vries 1984:138–141, Biedermann 1992: 97–99, and Cirlot 1962: 80.

[4] The majority of data on geese comes from de Vries 221–222 and Biedermann 156.

[5] Most data on foxes derives from de Vries 202–204, Biedermann 143–144, and Cirlo 108.

[6] Practically all data on turtles comes from de Vries 471, 477; Biedermann 358; and Cirlo 334.

[7] Statements regarding crystal come from de Vries 121–122, Biedermann 85, Cirlo 771, and Evans 1989: 292.

[8] Data about wolves derives from de Vries 505–506, Biedermann 387–389, and Cirlo 355.

[9] Most numerological data on "seven" are adapted from de Vries 415–416, Biedermann 302–303, and Cirlo 223.

Works Cited

Biedermann, Hans. *Dictionary of Symbolism*. James Hulbert, trans. New York: Facts on File, 1992.

Chiba, Reiko. *The Japanese Fortune Calendar.* North Clarendon, VT: Tuttle Publishing, 1965.
Cirlo, J. E. *A Dictionary of Symbols.* Jack Sage, trans. New York: Philosophical Library, 1962.
De Vries, Ad. *Dictionary of Symbols and Imagery.* Amsterdam: North-Holland Publishing Co., 1984.
Epp, Robert. *Rats' Nests—the Poetry of Hagiwara Sakutarō.* 2nd edition. Paris: UNESCO Publishing, 1999.
Epp, Robert and Iida Gakuji. *His Psychic Spoor—One Hundred Fifty Annotated Hagiwara Sakutarō Poems.* Los Angeles: Yakusha, 2005.
Evans, Ivor H. Brewer's *Dictionary of Phrase and Fable.* New York: Harper & Row, 1989.
Hagiwara Sakutarō. *Hagiwara Sakutarō zenshū* [Complete Works of Hagiwara Sakutarō]. 15 vols. Tokyo: Chikuma Shobō, 1975-1978.
---. "Yūgai naru dōbutsu" [Harmful Creatures]. In *Hagiwara Sakutarō zenshū* [Complete Works of Hagiwara Sakutarō]. Vol. 1. Tokyo: Chikuma Shobō, 1975. P. 326.
Itō Shinkichi, Itō Sei, Inoue Yasushi, and Yamamoto Kenkichi, eds. *Hagiwara Sakutarō.* In *Nihon no shiika* [Japanese Poetry], vol. 14. Tokyo: Chūō Kōronsha, 1968.
Jung, Carl G., M. L. von Franz, et al. *Man and His Symbols.* New York: Doubleday & Company, Inc., 1964.
Kitagawa Fuyuhiko and Kubo Tadao. *Hagiwara Sakutarō-shū* [A Hagiwara Sakutarō Collection]. In *Nihon kindai bungaku taikei* [Outline of Modern Japanese Literature], vol. 37. Tokyo: Kadokawa Shoten, 1971.
Meihuizen, Nicholas. *Yeats and the Drama of Sacred Space.* Amsterdam: Rodopi Bv Editions, 1998.
Piggott, Juliet. *Japanese Mythology.* New York: Peter Bedrick Books, 1983.
Theroux, Paul. "Living with Geese." *Smithsonian* 37.9 (December 2006): 38-44.

12
Topicality and Arboreal Imagery in the *300 Tang Poems*

Philip F. Williams

Introduction

Courses and sourcebooks on non-literary subjects in Chinese culture such as philosophy and religious studies are often organized along topical lines. Even though this sometimes occurs in relatively specialized courses in Chinese literature such as graduate seminars on a particular poet or literary tendency, basic survey courses in Chinese literature tend to be structured either chronologically in dynastic terms or else typologically in terms of literary genre.[1] Although neither the dynastic background nor the generic affiliation of a given literary work is lacking in significance, and in many instances may be gainfully highlighted even in a general introduction or survey, might there be a more engaging way to provide an overall structure to the course or sourcebook—especially for the general reader or non-majoring student whose interest in the subject might wane amidst an overly technical or strictly academic approach to Chinese literature?

      Burton Watson's rigorous yet broadly accessible scholarship on Chinese literature may well provide faculty with a blueprint for making a survey course or sourcebook in traditional Chinese literature more topical in organization, and less beholden to either of the categories of literary genre or dynastic chronology. In particular, Watson's analysis of nature imagery within the famous yet anonymously edited anthology *300 Tang Poems* [*Tang shi sanbai shou* 唐詩三百首] in his classic *Chinese Lyricism* is suggestive of how a conceptual approach might be able to focus on various mainstream tendencies and conventions within the Chinese literary tradition, thereby preparing readers to venture fruitfully on their own in further reading and study (Watson 1971). This chapter will focus particularly upon a topical approach to arboreal imagery in the *300 Tang Poems*, for which I will be using a 1972 edition.

Frequently Recurring Botanical Images in Tang Dynasty Poetry

Watson prefaces his analysis of nature imagery from *The Three Hundred Tang Poems* with some succinct characterizations of this type of imagery in the Zhou dynasty *Classic of Poetry* [*Shi jing* 詩經] and some other key pre-Tang collections of verse. For instance, the oral and folk orientation in much of the *Shi jing*'s verse lends itself well to a barnyard-style naming of specific plant and animal species, instead of the more generalized or abstract types of nature imagery preferred by the Tang dynasty's scholar-official poets (Watson 1971: 122-123).[2] Moreover, the preference for naming particular species of plants and animals in Han dynasty rhyme-prose [*fu* 賦], marked by such enumerative descriptions as the various species of wild game killed during a royal hunt, forms another point of contrast with the less concrete imagery in Tang regulated verse [*shi* 詩]—this time due as much to generic contrasts as to differences in dynastic or historical background (Watson 1971: 127).[3] Before moving into discussion of the topic at hand, namely Tang verse's typical approach to nature imagery, Watson has thus provided helpful contextual information about the historical background and generic dynamics of this literary phenomenon, just as an effective classroom presentation would often begin with an introduction of the historical or generic background of the topic under discussion.

A topical approach to Tang poetry would likely include sections on such widespread themes as partings with friends and relatives, particularly in the context of scholar-officials being rotated among postings that are always removed from their hometowns;[4] such officials' refreshingly bucolic interludes in forested hillside hideaways; utopian idylls of exemplary harmony and virtue, especially refreshing to scholar-official readers who are weary of societal conflict and the daily grind of *yamen* 衙門 goings-on; wistful musings on the evanescence and fragility of beauty; concerns about the well-being and livelihood of ordinary working people, especially those laboring on farms in the countryside; and thoughts on human mortality.

One can locate quite a bit of arboreal imagery in Tang verse that is specifically associated with each of the aforementioned topics. In tabulating the number of occasions when trees and other tall botanicals were mentioned in his Tang sample, Watson has found that they are mentioned in the abstract as "tree" [*mu/shu* 木/樹] (51 instances) or "forest" [*lin* 林] (26 occasions) considerably more frequently than as a specific variety of tree, such as willow [*yang/liu* 楊/柳] (29 instances) or pine [*song* 松] (24 occasions). Nevertheless, Watson has discovered that the willow and pine were far more frequently mentioned than other specific arboreal specimens, such as the next most frequent types of bamboo [*zhu* 竹] (12 instances), peach [*tao* 桃] (10 occasions), mulberry [*sang* 桑] (7 instances), and cypress [*bai* 柏] (6 occasions) (Watson 1971: 130).[5] The Tang poets' usual mentioning of these select few arboreal species—largely to the exclusion of other existing tree species—suggests that these botanical varieties are especially likely to carry symbolic or associational freight.

Willow branches were often broken off and presented to friends or relatives who were about to depart on a journey, and this type of tree has thus become associated with parting, one of the most frequent topics of Chinese poetry. Both landscape painting and poetry in China have often illustrated the joys of communing with nature in a bucolic hillside setting, and pine and bamboo are two types of woody plants that have been most closely associated with this type of rustic seclusion in China. The peach tree, in turn, has associations both with the sort of harmonious village utopia immortalized by Tao Yuanming's 陶淵明 fourth-century classical narrative essay "Peach Blossom Spring" [*Taohua yuan* 桃花源], as well as with the transitory nature of beautiful and delicate objects such as peach blossoms.[6] Mulberry trees provide the leaves that feed silkworms, and thus connote the material abundance that results from the common folk's toil in villages throughout the Chinese empire, especially in the warmer and wetter regions of southern and central China. Finally, cypress trees have long been associated with respect for the dead, and are commonly planted in and around Chinese cemeteries and other burial plots (Watson 1971: 130).

Parting or Separation and the Willow

Although Chinese poems that broach the theme of parting number at least in the tens of thousands, the commemoration of two lovers' parting that is certain to be permanent can be especially poignant. This is precisely the subject of Bo Juyi's 白居易 "Song of Everlasting Sorrow" [*Chang hen ge* 長恨歌], which suggests that the passionate vows between the Tang dynasty's Xuanzong 玄宗 emperor and his favorite consort Yang Guifei 楊貴妃 are immortal—destined to outlive even planet earth itself (*300 Poems* 242-259). Visions of willows adorn the Xuanzong emperor's forlorn recollections of having eternally parted with Yang Guifei: he recalls the "Weiyang Palace willows" [*Weiyang liu* 未央柳] as a prominent setting for their meetings and partings, and likens the delicate arch of Yang Guifei's eyebrows to willow leaves [*liu ru mei* 柳如眉] (*300 Poems* 251).

The image of the willow may similarly figure prominently in the melancholy of a person who misses an absent spouse or partner, as appears in Wang Changling's 王昌齡 poem "Boudoir Laments" [*Guiyuan* 閨怨]. When the young wife persona gazes down from an upper story of her home at the willows [*yangliu* 楊柳] growing along nearby lanes and paths, in her loneliness she sorely "regrets having persuaded my husband to venture afar in search of an official post" several months previously (*300 Poems* 373).

In other poems, the sense of parting or separation from friends or loved ones that is often implied by willows becomes generalized as the sojourner's longing for his homeland. In Du Shenyan's 杜審言 "Harmonizing Prime Minister Lu of Jinling's Poem on Gazing Afar during an Early Spring Outing" [*He Jinling Lu Chengxiang zaochun you wang* 和晉陵陸丞相早春遊望], the combination of the sight of willow trees and the sounds of a folk song from his homeland make the scholar-official persona so homesick as to shed tears (*300 Poems* 371). Yet the ability to express thoughts of homesickness is by no means limited to Han Chinese personae, for the tune of the forlorn Tartar soldier playing a flute in Wang Zhihuan's 王之渙 "Beyond the Border" [*Chu sai* 出賽] appears to be "lamenting the willows" [*yuan yangliu* 怨楊柳] (*300 Poems* 379). Again, a pensive figure far from home is thinking of willow trees while pondering his parting or separation from home—whether that is within China proper or in one of the neighboring states on China's borders.

None of this is to claim that willows invariably connote the melancholy of parting or separation in the poetry of the Tang or other dynasties. For instance, in Wang Wei's 王維 "Song of a Girl from Luoyang" [*Luoyang nü'er xing* 洛陽女兒行], there is no suggestion of separation or parting in the poem's reference to willows, which instead highlights the attractive pastel green or light-hued greenish color of willow foliage near the site of the song and dance (*300 Poems* 409-411). The poem features a singing and dancing girl from Luoyang whose patron and audiences both show appreciation for her talent, with the sole note of melancholy within the largely celebratory poem emerging in the final couplet, where a neglected young woman from the far southeast—possibly a would-be singsong girl who has yet to attract a local patron or audience—is forlornly washing silk at the riverbank (*300 Poems* 411). Overall, however, Tang poems that refer to willow trees frequently connote melancholic sentiments related to separation or parting from relatives or friends.

Upland Reclusion and the Pine

According to Watson, the pine is second only to the willow among frequent arboreal images in the *300 Tang Poems* (Watson 1971: 130). Along with bamboo and the cold-hardy flowering plum, the pine has long been known as one of the "three friends in winter" [*suihan sanyou*] 歲寒三友 that continue to grow and thrive even when most other plants are either dormant or dead from the cold. In Tang poetry, however, the pine is even more commonly associated with bucolic mountain landscapes and a spirit of reclusion; pines often stand as the serene sentinels of rustic temples or mountain lodges that are a world apart from the bustling crowds and dusty clamor of cities on the plain.

Pine trees often anchor a bucolic upland setting in Tang poetry, and may mark the pathways that connect buildings for collective religious worship such as Buddhist temples with private hermitages or lodges, as in Meng Haoran's 孟浩然 "Song of

Returning to Deer-gate Mountain in the Evening" [*Ye gui Lumen ge* 夜歸鹿門歌] (*300 Poems* 236-237). Some poems with pines figuring prominently in the setting deal solely with houses of worship, as is the case with Wang Wei's "Passing by the Temple of Heaped Incense" [*Guo Xiangjisi* 過香積寺]; other poems portray no buildings other than private hermitages, as in Wang Wei's "Composed in my Lodge at Wangchuan after a Soaking Rain" [*Ji yu Wangchuan zhuang zuo* 積雨輞川莊作] (*300 Poems* 392-393, 398-401).

In Tang poetry, the soughing of mountain breezes through pine tree branches frequently forms the aural counterpart of the pine's stately and serene visual presence in upland natural landscapes. The gentle sound of wind through pine branches outside the window of a mountain hermitage cleanses and delights the ears of the poetic speaker on a visit to his reclusive friend in Qiu Wei's 邱為 "Having Sought but not Found the West Mountain Recluse" [*Xun Xishan yinzhe bu yu* 尋西山隱者不遇] (*300 Poems* 28-29). In Li Bo's 李白 poem "Lodging and Feasting at the Home of the Rustic Hu Si After Having Descended Mount Zhongnan" [*Xia Zhongnanshan guo Hu Si shanren su zhijiu* 下終南山過斛斯山人宿置酒], the poetic speaker luckily finds his mountain-dwelling friend at home, where together they "sing at length to the tune of wind through the pines" [*chang ge yin song feng* 長歌吟松風] (*300 Poems* 114-115). The sonorous, musical quality of "cold winds blowing through pines" [*song feng han* 松風寒] in the mountains is similarly evoked when the poetic speaker listens raptly to a lute player strumming ancient tunes in Liu Changqing's 劉長卿 "Playing a Lute" [*Tan qin* 彈琴] (*300 Poems* 190-191). In each instance, pine trees tend to generate a mood of serenity at both the visual and aural levels, and are often associated with the joys of reclusion and occasional bucolic encounters with old friends in the mountains.

The Peach Tree's Associations with a Village Utopia and the Transience of Beauty

Since every existing human society can be found wanting in any number of ways, throughout the ages many poets have dreamed of a remote utopia that is delightfully unencumbered by the usual run of societal ills such as violence, tyranny, exploitation, and poverty. Due to the aforementioned *locus classicus* of this motif in Tao Yuanming's famous essay, "Peach Blossom Spring," references to the peach tree frequently evoke associations of a utopian sort. Pei Di's 裴迪 poetic speaker in his quatrain "Seeing off Cui Ninth" [*Song Cui Jiu* 送崔九] urges his friend Cui Ninth to tarry with him longer in the beautiful mountains and not be in such a hurry to return to the city. The speaker adds a cautionary note about how the Wuling武陵 fisherman who stumbled by accident upon the utopian village society of Peach Blossom Spring later came to sorely regret not having remained there longer, as his subsequent attempts to find his way back to the idyllic village all failed (*300 Poems* 238-239).

Wang Wei further elaborates the Peach Blossom Spring legend, originally in the form of a prose essay, by recasting it as a narrative poem in seven-character lines entitled "Ode to Peach Spring" [*Tao yuan xing* 桃源行] (*300 Poems* 416-419). Like Tao Yuanming, Wang Wei concludes his narrative by wistfully alluding to the frustration of the Wuling fisherman who could never find his way back to the elusive Peach Spring village utopia, no matter how carefully he tried to follow the landmarks he had previously made a mental note of during his departure from Peach Spring. Ideally, one or more such poems on this theme of what Lin Yutang 林語堂 has called China's "small utopia," as perhaps first envisioned in the eightieth chapter of Lao Zi's老子*Classic of the Way and its Virtue* [*Dao de jing* 道德經], would be assigned and read in conjunction with Tao Yuanming's prose essay.[7] One would thereby reveal the continuing interest in the ancient Chinese vision of a self-contained utopian society marked by peace, serenity, and rustic simplicity.

The Mulberry's Connections with the Chinese Homeland and Village Sericulture

One can hardly underestimate the importance of sericulture to China's traditionally agrarian society, at least in the rural areas where an overwhelming majority of the Chinese people lived prior to the 21st century. Images of the tree that produces the primary fodder of silkworms, mulberry leaves, have thus often carried warm connotations of a provincial homeland and even of the empire or civilization of China itself. For instance, the persona of the forlorn and neglected wife in Li Bo's "Spring Thoughts" [*Chun si* 春思] contrasts the lush and leafy branches of the many mulberry trees in her Chinese homeland with the shorter grasses that are dominant in the landscape and flora beyond China's northern borders, where her husband appears to be currently stationed to help ward off nomadic military incursions from the northwestern steppe (*300 Poems* 118-119).[8] As a signpost of Han Chinese civilization, the lush but fragile mulberry tree can barely withstand the climatic stresses of the relatively cold and arid regions in and around China's northwestern frontier. Wang Changling's "At the Border Outpost" [*Sai shang qu* 塞上曲] describes a small grove of bare-branched mulberry trees on the Chinese side of the border; these trees have already dropped all their leaves as early in autumn as August, thereby illustrating the harsh conditions that Han Chinese soldiers and officials must endure when posted to northern and northwestern border checkpoints. Heading just north or northwest of the frontier mountain pass, by August one finds "nothing but yellowing reeds and grasses everywhere" [*Chuchu huang lu cao* 處處黃蘆草], thus portending a lengthy and cold winter about to descend upon the northwestern borderlands (*300 Poems* 376-377).

  Sometimes accompanied by hemp [*ma* 麻] or other crops related to agricultural fiber production, mulberry trees frequently denote a decidedly rural or rustic milieu. After Lu Hongjian retires from official life and moves to the countryside, the path to his new rustic abode is lined with hemp and mulberries, as noted by the poetic speaker in Seng Jiaoran's 僧皎然 "Seeking but not Finding Lu Hongjian at Home" [*Xun Lu Hongjian bu yu* 尋陸鴻漸不遇] (*300 Poems* 270-271). The key fiber crops of mulberry and hemp become a central topic for convivial conversation between the poetic speaker and an old friend during a visit to the latter's rural home in Meng Haoran's "Stopping by an Old Friend's Farmhouse" [*Guo guren zhuang* 過故人莊] (*300 Poems* 226-227). On other occasions, the only part of the mulberry tree that we encounter are its leaves, sometimes in direct proximity to the silkworms that live upon and amidst these vital leaves before finally spinning their cocoons, as celebrated in Wang Wei's "A Wei River Farmhouse" [*Wei Chuan tianjia* 渭川田家] (*300 Poems* 406-407). Whether associated specifically with sericulture and village life or generally with China as a distinctive civilization, the mulberry tree is one of Tang poetry's leading arboreal images of an agriculturally-based society.

Cypresses and Showing Respect for the Dead

Commonly planted in Chinese graveyards and near ancestral temples, the cypress tree has long been associated with respect for the dead and bearing with feelings of loss. In some instances, the cypress's associations can extend to losses beyond that of death, as in Du Fu's 杜甫 "A Beautiful Woman" [*Jiaren* 佳人], whereby the poetic speaker has not only lost most of her natal family members as military fatalities, but has also been abandoned by her husband in favor of a younger paramour (*300 Poems* 326-327).

Cypresses tend to be especially noticeable near the ancestral temples of famous and celebrated personages such as the great third-century strategist and prime minister Zhuge Liang 諸葛亮, as can be observed in Du Fu's "The Prime Minister of the Shu Kingdom" [*Shu xiang* 蜀相] (*300 Poems* 312-313). Du Fu expands upon the role of the cypress in commemorating great individuals who have died by making this tree species the central subject of his poem "Song of an Ancient Cypress" [*Gu bo xing* 古柏行] (*300 Poems* 342-345). This poem also celebrates the life and deeds of Prime Minister Zhuge Liang, focusing upon a particularly old and majestic cypress tree near the latter's memorial shrine. This cypress tree had been reportedly planted by Zhuge Liang himself (McCraw 181). Just as Zhuge Liang achieved a magnificent stature in Chinese history, the ancient cypress tree next to his memorial shrine has been able to grow so tall precisely because it has grown such deep roots and made the best of the abilities that Heaven bestowed upon it. Yet like all other living things it is mortal, and cannot reveal all of its useful qualities until it is cut down for timber, just as Zhuge Liang's ability to inspire awe outlived the Prime Minister himself, with his reputation continuing to grow after his death. "Since ancient times," Du Fu concludes, "it has been difficult to make use of great timber" [*gulai cai da nan wei yong* 古來材大難為用] (*300 Poems* 345). In one of the finest Tang poems featuring arboreal imagery, Du Fu could at some level be referring in part to his own frustrated Confucian ambition to serve state and society amidst the chaos left in the wake of the An Lushan Rebellion. His use of cypress tree imagery helps to intensify the *gravitas* of the emotions he evokes in commemoration of Zhuge Liang.[9]

Conclusion

The time-honored method of structuring an anthology or survey course in traditional Chinese literature by dynasty or genre may well be optimal for specialists and advanced graduate students. However, this chapter proposes a topical approach to an anthology or survey course catering at least in part to non-majors and other generalists, who might be more interested in frequently encountered cultural symbols and literary associations than in a more technical or historical approach to Chinese literary studies. In Burton Watson's *Chinese Lyricism*, his thought-provoking analysis of nature imagery in the *300 Tang Poems* has provided the point of departure for this chapter's examination of patterns of arboreal imagery in that famous anthology.

A strikingly limited range of tree species receive a disproportionate level of attention in the *300 Tang Poems*, thereby leading the reader to infer that Tang poets tended to project a limited range of associations on specific varieties of trees and tree-like plants that they frequently mentioned. Willows often enter the scene in poems about parting or separation, while pines frequently accentuate an upland setting of reclusion in which communing with nature or Buddho-Daoist contemplation readily occur. References to peach trees may lead to associations with the Daoist "small utopia" immortalized by Tao Yuanming's famous essay, or more generalized motifs such as the evanescence of delicate beauty. Due to its role in the production of fiber in agricultural regions, the mulberry tree typically connotes a village or rural setting, and through generalization can also refer to the Chinese homeland itself, particularly in contrast with outlying regions populated mostly by steppe nomads or other foreigners. Finally, the frequent proximity of cypress trees to graveyards and ancestral temples underlines this tree's associations with commemorating the dead and keeping the memory of their virtues and achievements alive.

Endnotes

[1] Two highly regarded anthologies of Chinese literature represent these two main approaches to structuring a course or sourcebook in literature around either the chronologically-ordered progression of ruling dynasties or else a range of literary genres. Structuring an anthology along dynastic lines occurs in Owen 1996. A contrasting organization based largely on literary genres may be found in Mair 1994. Although both anthologies make use of various topical categories in sections of commentary from time to time, this is a relatively minor form of internal organization compared with the overarching structural emphasis on dynasty and genre, respectively.

[2] For example, in the *Classic of Poetry* XLVIII, "Amidst the Mulberries" [*sang zhong* 桑中], the *xing* 興 or opening evocative image names a specific botanical species: "Where did I pick the dodder?" [*yuan cai tang yi* 爱采唐矣], in which *tang* 唐 is an early reference to the long-stalked medicinal plant now known as *Cuscuta chinensis* or the "Chinese dodder" [*tusizi* 菟絲子]. See also Owen 1996: 55.

[3] For Burton Watson's translation of a famous Han composition of rhyme prose that names a wide range of specific botanical species, see Song Yu's 宋玉 "Rhapsody on the Wind," [*feng fu* 風賦] (Watson 1962: 260-262).

[4] Imperial China's rule of avoidance in official bureaucratic postings was a wise measure that generally prohibited any official from being centrally appointed to a governmental post in the vicinity of his hometown.

[5] Botanically, the bamboo is actually a variety of grass rather than a genuine tree, but due to its often impressive height and to literary convention, it can be discussed in literary or cultural terms as a tree, or at least a tree-like plant.

[6] For a translation of Tao Yuanming's prose narrative "Peach Blossom Spring," see Watson 1984: 142-143.

[7] Lao Zi's Daoist utopian vision is of a small state whose villagers are so content with their modest but comfortable subsistence and their folkways of rustic simplicity that even though they live within earshot of the barking dogs and crowing roosters that belong to residents in a neighboring district, over their entire lives these villagers would never be curious enough to bother with going over there for a look around. See also Lin 254.

[8]The poem does not refer to China directly, but instead to the region of the Yellow River valley around Shaanxi province that has long been considered a key cradle of Han Chinese civilization. This has become a sort of shorthand for China itself, as can be seen in Chen Kaige's 陳凱歌 1984 film *Yellow Earth* [*Huang tudi* 黃土地], about which see McDougall 1991.

[9]For a painterly vision of the cypress, see Ebrey 2010: 199.

Works Cited

Ebrey, Patricia B. *Cambridge Illustrated History of China, Second Edition*. Cambridge University Press, 2010.

Lin Yutang, ed. *The Wisdom of Laotse* [Laozi]. New York: Modern Library, 1948.

Mair, Victor, ed. *The Columbia Anthology of Traditional Chinese Literature*. New York: Columbia University Press, 1994.

McCraw, David R. *Du Fu's Laments from the South*. Honolulu: University of Hawai'i Press, 1992.

McDougall, Bonnie S. *The Yellow Earth, a Film by Chen Kaige with a Complete Translation of the Filmscript*. Hong Kong: Chinese University Press of Hong Kong, 1991.

Owen, Stephen. *An Anthology of Chinese Literature: Beginnings to 1911*. New York: W.W. Norton, 1996.

300 Tang Poems 唐詩三百首. Taipei: Imex Publishing, Ltd., 1972.

Watson, Burton. *Chinese Lyricism: Shih Poetry from the Second to the Twelfth Century*. New York: Columbia University Press, 1971.

---. *The Columbia Book of Chinese Poetry from Early Times to the Thirteenth Century*. New York: Columbia University Press, 1984.

---. *Early Chinese Literature*. New York: Columbia University Press, 1962.

13

An Acrostic Eulogy for Burton Watson

Jonathan
Chaves

Before Burt Watson, glimmerings of light
Unfurled their banners on the murky deep,
Reflected from the waters unexplored
That spread before us—ancient Chinese culture,
Ocean still awaiting galleons,
Not yet penetrated
        to the farthest shore.

When Watson put his hand to pen and paper,
At last the darkness lifted from the sea,
Thus mapping channels that might guide our ships
Straight towards the harbor at the far horizon
Of China's treasured past, her deepest heart
Never yet revealed
        with such full clarity.

Basic Writings: Chuang Tzu, Han Fei Tzu—
Untranslated, or badly done before—
Records of the Grand Historian,
Tso Chuan, and the Late Poems of Lu You,
Old Man Who Does as He Pleases, and Lin-chi—
No other scholar-translator
        ever gave us more!

Wild Goose by Ōgai, and then F*or*
***A**ll My Walking, Masaoka Shiki,*
Tu Fu, Kanshi, and the *Lotus Sutra,*
Ssu-ma Ch'ien, the Grand Historian. . .
On sinologists' and japanologists' desks
Now all lie handy, ready—
        treasured ever more.

Both *Cold Mountain* and *Grass Hill* will stand
Until the eschaton—*Vimalakirti,*
Rainbow World, and *Chinese Lyricism,*
Tales of the Heike, From the Country
Of Eight Islands, Japanese Literature—
Never done before!—
        'til these books—*in Chinese.*

We'll not forget the *Sources,* also *Saigyō*
And his *Poems of a Mountain Home.* Of course
There's more, much more, but the proverbial
Shelf of five-feet could not hold them all.
Ozymandias' image may have crumbled:
Nothing shall efface
        what Watson has inscribed.

14
Salutation to Burton Watson

Sam Hamill

So very much learned
from the feet of a master—
the fall of the Ch'in,
the rise of the T'ang and Sung,
tales from Masters Chuang and K'ung.

The long dusty roads
of the various poets
and monks, and sutras
chanted, the *sake* cups filled
with kinship and harmonies,

Hardships remembered.
It is December, the moon
full, snow turned to ice
on the frozen ground. I raise
a cup of good *Nihonshu*

To a master, a
lifetime's companionship in
wandering borders.
Through hard times and good, decade
by decade, when my heart yearned

For good company,
I always knew where to turn.
Tonight, just a cup
below Li Po's cold clear moon—
because it is impossible
to drink alone.

15

From Primer to Second-level Reader: David Hawkes and Du Fu

William H. Nienhauser, Jr.

What has always impressed readers about the scholarship of Professor David Hawkes (1923-2009) was his courage.[1] From what is generally known of his life, this seems also to have been the case. While many Westerners avoid the major works of Chinese literature, Hawkes plunged into the classics with his dissertation and subsequent book on the *Ch'u Tz'u: the Songs of the South* (1959), followed that up with his *Little Primer of Tu Fu* (1967),[2] turned next to four out of the total of five volumes of Cao Xueqin's *The Story of the Stone* (1974, 1977, 1981, 1982), and finally offered us *Liu Yi and the Dragon Princess* (Shang 2003). All are works of superb scholarship and literary sensitivity. I have consulted and read *Songs of the South* and the *Little Primer* regularly for well over thirty years.

  I first met Professor Hawkes in 1981 at a conference on *Honglou meng* [A Dream of Red Mansions] that Chow Tse-tsung organized.[3] Many of the major "Redologist" scholars were present in Madison—and since I was a young 38-year-old chair of the department, we had invited all the conference participants over for a reception. I recall that after several hours into the party, the more raucous participants had staked themselves out on the deck built atop our garage with lots of beer. When I started up the stairs to our second floor to check on them, I found Professor Hawkes sitting alone on the stairs, thinking of something that he was smiling about. I asked if he needed anything, and he said, "No, I'm fine."

This paper presents a close reading of a few of the poems Hawkes presented in his *Little Primer of Tu Fu*, which may have come out of his classes at Oxford (1967). Although I shall suggest revisions and additions to Hawkes' interpretations, I am merely, to borrow Han Yu's 韓愈 (768-824) critique of early critics of Du Fu, *pifu han dashu* 蚍蜉撼大樹 [an ant shaking a great tree] (Han Yu). In Hawkes' "Author's Introduction," he notes that the book was intended to teach the Western reader "something about Chinese poetry, and something about Tu Fu" (1967: ix).

Let us thus begin to learn something about Du Fu with Hawkes' discussion and translation of the fourth poem in the *Little Primer* entitled "Yue ye" 月夜 [Moonlight Night] (Hawkes 1967: 28-32). It is one of Du Fu's most famous poems. Hawkes gives the text of the poem along with the modern Mandarin pronunciation in *pinyin*. However, he does not note that this poem is variously titled "Dui yue" 對月 [Facing the Moon], "He shi" 何時 [When Will It Be Time], and "He dang" 何當 [When Will We] (Bian 2005: 33). Although this sort of detail is beyond the textbook Hawkes has envisioned, it is typical that Tang poems will have multiple titles, and particularly Du Fu's verse. Hawkes then provides the circumstances in which the poem was written, namely in the autumn of 756. During the previous summer, Du Fu had moved his family further away from the occupied capital of Chang'an to Fuzhou 鄜州, some two hundred miles distant. Du Fu then set out to join the new court of Emperor Suzong at Lingwu far to the northwest. Along the way, his path crossed with that of a band of rebels who forced Du Fu to return with them to the capital, probably as a porter. He must have been released when they reached Chang'an, but was unable for a time to return to his family. Hawkes notes that this poem was probably written during the *Zhongqiujie* 中秋節 [Mid-autumn festival].

Hawkes then briefly explains that the prosody of regulated verse is too complex to be reviewed for his purposes (a textbook), but does speak to the rhymes, noting that the rhymes *kàn* and *hán* in lines 2 and 6 were not level tones. The first couplet is then presented in what is called "Exegesis" as follows:

To-night Fu-chou moon
My-wife can-only alone watch

今夜鄜州月，閨中只獨看. (1967: 31)

There is an explanation of the metonymical *guizhong* 閨中 as "wife." And at the end of the exegesis we have Hawkes' translation: "Tonight in Fu-chou my wife will be watching this moon alone. I think with tenderness to understand about their father in Ch'ang-an" (1967: 32).

Here I would like to suggest the first emendation to Hawkes' presentation: the importance of the rhyme, which is here *han* 寒 [cold].[4] Thus 看 here should not be read as *kàn*, but as *kān*.[5] Although the meaning is not dramatically changed, *kan* means something more than just "watch." Du Fu uses *kān* in a similar fashion in his "Shihao li" 石壕吏 [The Official at Shihao] which begins: 暮投石壕村，有吏夜捉人。老翁逾牆走，老婦出門看。 吏呼一何怒，婦啼一何苦。In Eva Shan Chou's translation (1995), these lines read:

> At dusk I stopped at Shih-hao Village,
> An official came in the night to seize people.
> The old man fled over the wall,
> The old woman came out to answer the door.
> How angry were the shouts of the official,
> How broken the cries of the woman . . . . (Chou 1995: 91)

Kān in this poem, again used as the final word of a pentasyllabic line, means "to take care of" or "to look after"—or perhaps even "to take a look."[6] The same is true of Wang Jian's 王建 "Hanshi xing" 寒食行 [Lines on the Cold Food Festival Day], which begins with the lines:

> For the Cold Food Festival every family goes out of the old city,
> The old people take care of the houses, the young people go.
> 寒食家家出古城，老人看屋少年行。

Without arguing that the *kān* in "Moonlit Night" means "to take care of," I feel the word suggests something more responsible in Du Fu's wife. He watches the moon in Chang'an, knowing that she *can only be watching* with the concern that *kān* suggests.

The next couplet in "Moonlit Night," followed by Hawkes' word-for-word rendering, reads:

Distant sorry-for little sons-daughters / Not-yet understand remember Ch'ang-an
遙憐小兒女，未解憶長安。(Hawkes 1967: 31)

When fleshed out, this becomes "I think with tenderness of my far-away little ones, too young to understand about their father in Ch'ang-an" (1967: 32).

Although Hawkes translates *yi* 憶 in line 4 literally as "remember," it disappears in his final translation. In Du Fu's verse *yi* often means "to remember"; it can also mean "to miss, think of." Although some other translators have understood the line similarly,[7] I would argue that the subject of *yi* should be Du Fu's wife and that the lines read: "I think with tenderness of my distant little ones, who do not yet understand why she thinks of Chang'an [and me]." The early Qing-dynasty Du Fu scholars Huang Sheng 黃生 (b. 1622) and Bian Lianbao 邊連寶 (1700-1733) add support to such a reading in their comments. Huang opines: 閨中雖有兒女相伴，然兒女不解見月則憶長安。我知閨中遠憶長安，對月獨垂清淚 (1994: 116). Bian cites 先君子漁山翁 (Yuan Shouding 袁守定, 1705-1782), who argued 遙憐小兒女, "未解憶長安者," 未解其母之何以憶長安也 (Bian 33).

The third couplet reads 香霧雲鬟濕，清輝玉臂寒。Hawkes gives "Fragrant mist cloud-hair wet, / Clear light jade-arms cold" (32). The translation that evolves is "My wife's soft hair must be wet from the scented night-mist, / and her white arms chilled by the cold moonlight" (32). Both *shi* 濕 and *han* 寒 here suggest a process over time, suggesting a translation of "In the scented mist her piled-high hair grows wet, / In the clear moonlight her bare arms turn cold," a similar scene to that in Li Bo's "Yujie yuan" 玉階怨 [Lament on the Jade Steps]:

> On the jade steps, white dew forms,
> As the night lengthens, soaking her silk stockings.
> She turns within, lowers the crystal curtains and
> Gleaming continues to gaze at the autumn moon.
> 玉階生白露，夜久侵羅襪。卻下水晶簾，玲瓏望秋月。

A major difference is the respective personae in the two poems: Li Bo's persona is impersonal, possibly an allusion to a woman abandoned in the Han dynasty,[9] whereas Du Fu is speaking of his wife.

Moreover, there is a level of sensuality in Du Fu's lines that is lost in Hawkes' rendition of "my wife's soft hair must be wet from the scented night-mist, / and her white arms chilled by the cold moonlight," since it is his wife's hair (the cloudlike chignon or *yun huan* 雲鬟) that scents the night mist [*xiang wu* 香霧], not the other way around. This suggestiveness continues in Du Fu's view of his wife's bare, jade-like arms, once warm, now chilled by her exposure to watch "their moon."

The final couplet 何時倚虛幌，雙照淚痕幹, is nicely rendered by Hawkes as "When shall we lean on the open casement together and gaze at the moon until the tears on our cheeks are dry?" (1967: 32). However, some scholars would also suggest that it is either the reunited couple's warmth or the moonlight itself that dries their tears,[10] and that the *xu huang* 虛幌 indicates a window covered in light silk.

Finally, the whole poem may resonate with "Yue chu" 月出 (The Moon Appears), Mao #143 in the *Shijing*, the earliest poem metaphorically comparing a lover to the moonlight. The translation is that of Martin Kern, a rendition that brings out the full erotic connotations:

> The moon comes forth, how bright,
> The beautiful girl, how adorable!
> At leisure she is in her sensual allure–
> My toiled heart, how anxious.
>
> The moon comes forth, how brilliant,
> The beautiful girl, how lovely!
> At leisure she is in her beguiling charm–
> My toiled heart, how troubled.
>
> The moon comes forth, how radiant,
> The beautiful girl, how vibrant!
> At leisure she is in her enchanting appeal–
> My toiled heart, how haunted.
> 月出皎兮，佼人僚兮。舒窈糾兮，勞心悄兮。月出皓兮，佼人懰兮。舒懮受兮，勞心慅兮。月出照兮，佼人燎兮。 舒夭紹兮，勞心慘兮。(Kern 2010: 43)[11]

To conclude, the driving emotion of "Yue ye" in my reading is longing, both physical and emotional. On the other hand, Laurence Wong emphasizes the "tender lyricism" of the poem (2012: 79).

The second poem that I should like to discuss is "Ke zhi" 客至 [A Guest Arrives] (Hawkes 1967: 109-112). Translating the title of the poem as "The Guest," Hawkes follows the traditional dating of spring 760 in his introductory paragraph, pointing out that Du Fu's original note on the poem identifies the visitor as "Prefect Cui" 崔明府.[12] Cui was probably Du Fu's maternal uncle[13] and the poem likely written after his *Caotang* 草堂 [Thatched Hut] was completed that spring. This is of course but one of the several poems that Du Fu wrote about entertaining guests that spring; two less well-known poems on that theme are "You ke" 有客 and "Bin zhi" 賓至. Chengdu in the 760s must have been a refugee city, with officials from the Xuanzong emperor's government who had fled with the emperor in 756 still in residence–not unlike Taipei in the early 1950s.

In his note on the opening couplet Hawkes, reminds us that Du Fu is boasting about how remote a life he is living: 舍南舍北皆春水，但見群鷗日日來。His literal gloss reads: "House-south house-north both springtime water / Only see flock-gulls every-day come" (1967: 110). His translation expands this into "The waters of springtime flow north and south of my dwelling. / Only the flocks of gulls come daily to call on me" (111). Hawkes tells us that "to be a friend of the gulls is to be innocent and simple–a child of nature" (110). The *locus classicus* of the relationship between gulls and men is the *Lie Zi* 列子, a text which claims that gulls will visit only humans who are pure of heart (Yang 2004: 2.67-68; Graham 1960: 45-46). The isolation of the spring's high waters along with Du Fu's apparent intention to isolate himself in the "Thatched Hut" make the gulls [*ou* 鷗] only logical visitors. Whether they are actual gulls or allusive birds is debatable, although the frequency of the appearance of the gulls in the poet's verse and the inclusiveness of the *ou ke* 鷗科 within Chinese zoological terminology (reflected in the breadth of the term "gull" internationally), suggests they were an actual part of the scene.

The next couplet continues to depict the setting into which Prefect Cui has come: 花徑不曾緣客掃，　蓬門今始為君開。Hawkes glosses the lines as "flower-path not-have because-of-guest swept /

Wicker-gate now first-time for you open" (1967: 111), and translates the couplet adeptly as "I have not swept my flower-strewn path for a visitor, / and my wicker-gate opens the first time for you today" (111-112). Hawkes explains *hua-jing* as a path thick with the fallen petals of fruit trees during late spring. The "wicker gate" [*peng men* 蓬門] might also draw attention here, since it suggests not only poverty and reclusion,[14] but also another poet who was frequently visited in retirement by guests, namely Tao Qian (365-427). Tao referred to his residence as a *peng lu* 蓬盧 [wicker hut] in one poem and to himself as a *penglu shi* 蓬盧士 [gentleman of the wicker hut] in another. Du Fu may have been thinking of the first of these poems by Tao, "Da Pang Canjun" 答龐參軍 [A Reply to Adviser Pang], a poem that the preface tells us was also written when an official stopped by a poet's retirement residence, when he wrote "Ke zhi." The opening stanza of Tao's poem reads as follows:

Inside the rustic door	衡門之下，
I have cither and books.	有琴有書；
I pluck and sing aloud	載彈載詠，
And take my pleasure so.	爰得我娛。
Not that this is all I like,	豈無他好？
But retirement is my joy.	樂是幽居；
Mornings I water my garden	朝為灌園，
Evenings rest in my hut.	夕偃蓬廬。[15]

Tao's reference to himself as a "wicker-hut gentleman" occurs in "Jiuri xianju" 九日閒居 [The Double Ninth, In Retirement], a poem that echoes some typical concerns of Du Fu, aging, the rapid passing of time, and keeping a good stock of rice wine on hand:

Wine serves to exorcise all our concerns,	酒能祛百慮，
Chrysanthemums keep us from getting old.	菊解制頹齡，
But what is the wicker-hut gentleman to do	如何蓬廬士，
Who helplessly views time's revolutions?	空視時運傾！
The dusty cup shames the empty wine cask,	塵爵恥虛罍，
The cold flower blooms uncelebrated.	寒華徒自榮．
(Hightower 47)	

Hawkes presents the next couplet in "A Guest Arrives" as follows:

盤餐市遠無兼味，樽酒家貧只舊醅 [Dish-repast market far no double flavor. / Jar-wine household poor only old brewing], and translates the lines as "Because the market is far away, the dishes I serve you offer little variety; / and because this is a poor household, the only wine in my jars comes from an old brewing" (1967: 111, 112). He notes that in Du Fu's time, drinkers preferred their wine fresh. Hawkes' "old brewing" for *pei* 醅 needs comment, since *pei* indicates that the wine was unfiltered (醅，酒未漉也; Yang Lun 8.342). *Jiu* 酒 or "rice wine"—I do not accept the claim that this was "ale"—was brewed in a short period of time, at most a few days, and then drunk young. But the best wines were clear, produced by filtering. On this occasion, Du Fu was apparently only able to offer some stale, unfiltered brew to his guest.

"A Guest Arrives" concludes with a twist, in Hawkes' version: 肯與鄰翁相對飲，隔籬呼取盡餘杯 "Willing with neighbor gaffer opposite drink / Intervening fence call-take finish remaining cups," and in translation "If you are willing to sit and drink with my old neighbour, I shall call him over the fence to come and finish off the remaining cupfuls with us" (1967: 111, 112). Du Fu's seeming impropriety in inviting a third party to join Magistrate Cui and himself led Stephen Owen to claim that Du Fu viewed Cui's visit as an intrusion on his natural, hermetic life and that the poet's invitation to his humble neighbor allows Du Fu's "naturalness in human relations" to reign victorious over Magistrate Cui's "arbitrary formality." Owen concludes: "Ts'ui [Cui] cannot object; he must sit there, waiting for some old commoner to come bounding over the hedge and sit down face to face with him [and] . . . feel, as we do, that somewhere in the poem the virginal deference of his first reception has been lost" (1985: 237-242). This interpretation is possible,[17] but it goes against most traditional readings which point out that there is a bookend poem, "Bin zhi" 賓至 [An Honored Guest Arrives] in which the dominant tone is respect (*jing* 敬), whereas here the close familial, emotional ties (*qing* 情) are dominant. In the traditional understanding, the invitation is in keeping with the proposed entertainment: eating and drinking are always better in larger groups. These final lines may also call to mind Tao Qian's equally famous "Yin jiu, qi jiu" 飲酒其九 [Drinking Wine, Number 9], which opens with the lines:

I heard a knock this morning at my door	清晨聞扣門，
In haste I pulled on my gown inside out	倒裳往自開。
And went to ask the caller, "Who is there?"	問子為誰與？
It was a well-intentioned farmer, come	田父有好懷。
With a jug of wine to pay a distant call.	壺漿遠見候，
Suspecting me to be at odds with the times.	疑我與時乖.

(Hightower 137)

This guest asks Tao to reconsider his retirement, perhaps something that Magistrate Cui would ask of his relative, Du Fu. But Tao goes on to explain that "there's no turning back my carriage now" 吾駕不可回, a sentiment that Du Fu would admire at this point of his life. Therefore, although Magistrate Cui is the stated guest, it would seem that the spirit of Tao Qian may have also joined this scene.[18]

The third poem for discussion is another well-known piece, "Deng lou" 登樓 [On the Tower] (Hawkes 1967: 125-128). This is one of a number of poems Du Fu wrote in the *topos* of "ascent and contemplation of the past," as Hawkes points out.[19] Hawkes also tells us that the poem was written a little later than "A Guest Arrives" in the spring of 764 after the capital had been retaken from the invading Tibetans and Emperor Daizong had returned to the palace. However, citing Hawkes again, "in the spring of that year the Tibetans still occupied parts of Western Szechwan and the North-West. Hence the gay spring scene revealed to Tu Fu as he gazes down from his tower fills him not with elation but with gloomy apprehensions" (1967: 126). Hawkes then gives us the first couplet literally followed by his usual prose translation: 花近高樓傷客心，萬方多難此登臨。[Flowers near high tower hurt visitor's heart / Myriad-directions many troubles this climb-look-down], which becomes "Flowers near the high tower sadden the heart of the visitor. / It is a time when the Empire is everywhere beset by troubles that he has climbed up to see this view." Line one resembles Lu Chi's 陸機 (261-303) second line in his "Beizai xing" 悲哉行 [A Sorrowful Sigh], which reads "For a traveler away from home in a fragrant spring grove, / Spring's fragrances sadden the heart" 遊客芳春林，春芳傷客心 (*Wenxuan* 28.1307). Lu Chi's poem is about wanting to return to his home, however. For line 2, Hawkes notes that "the grammar ... is perhaps a little puzzling. *Deng-lin* is the main verb and *ci* an adverb of manner: 'I mount like this', i.e., 'I make this ascent.' *Wan-fang duo nan* is a subordinate clause modifying the main one: 'I make this ascent *at a time when* everywhere there are many difficulties'" (1967: 126-127). Perhaps *ci* suggests "in this situation," but that would make the line even more untranslatable.[20] Yet in recalling Du Fu's famous line *gan shi hua jian mu* 感時花濺淚 [moved by the times flowers bring tears to my eyes] from "Chun wang" 春望 [Spring Prospect], it would seem that Hawkes' idea that *ci* is temporal is correct. However, in "Chun wang" we have the more normal sequence of learning what is wrong with the world before the poet is moved to sadness by flowers. This has led some critics to suggest that a kind of reversed logic in this opening couplet adds to the artistry of the poem.[21]

The next couplet again seems to suggest inversion: 錦江春色來天地，玉壘浮雲變古今; Hawkes' word-for-word version reads "Brocade-river spring-colours bring heaven-earth / Jade-fort floating-clouds change ancient-modern," yielding a translation of "The Brocade River scene, dressed in spring's colours, / brings a whole universe before his eyes, / whilst the floating clouds above Marble Fort Mountain seem to unfold all time in their mutating shapes" (1967: 127, 128). Hawkes comments: "In this couplet the poet describes a quasi-mystical vision of all nature and all time. Tu Fu often approaches closely to a mystical experience when contemplating the grandeurs of nature; but as a rule he is rapidly twitched out of his vision by some domestic of political consideration, or by the importunity of some bodily infirmity" (127). While such a vision is a possible reading, it seems important to point out that both a diachronic and a synchronic reading are possible here. Diachronically, while spring is part of an eternal seasonal cycle, the floating clouds are ephemeral, coming and going from day to day.[22] Synchonically, the spring scene on the Brocade River suggests Du Fu's reclusion in the Thatched Hut. The Jade Fortress (Hawkes' Marble Fort Mountain) overlooks a fortified border-crossing between Tibet and the Tang lands established during the early years of the dynasty. The floating clouds that emerge from the mountains may symbolize the sycophants at court who obscure the ruler's judgment as they do in the "Jiu bian" 九辯 [Nine Arguments] in the *Chuci* 楚辭 [Songs of the South]: "How the floating clouds drift over everything, / See how they suddenly cover up the bright moon" 何氾濫之浮雲兮，焱壅蔽此明月.[23] Alternatively, they may refer-

metonymically evoked by the pass to Tibet–to the "unpredictable raids" of the Tibetans, as David McCraw argues (1992: 108).

The third couplet is 北極朝廷終不改, 西山寇盜莫相侵. Hawkes' word-for-word version is "North-pole court in-the-end not change / West-mountains raiding-brigands do-not invade," which he translates as "The court of the Northern star remains unchanged. / Let the marauders from the Western Mountains cease their raiding!" (1967: 127, 128). Hawkes' comments: "The Pole Star keeps to a fixed place in the sky whilst all the other stars revolve around it and do it homage, hence it symbolizes the Emperor or the Imperial government–which is, incidentally, in the far north in relation to Ch'eng-tu. Tu Fu says of the Imperial government that 'in the end it didn't change' because in spite of the brief interregnum when the Tibetans set up a puppet emperor of their own in Ch'ang-an, the metropolis is now once more in Chinese hands and Tai-tsung restored to his throne" (127). Though this leads to a convincingly enhanced reading, it is possible that the second line of this couplet may be stronger, something like "Let not the maurauders from the Western Mountains raid the borders."

The final couplet continues the dichotomy between the past and the present in a pair of allusions: 可憐後主還祠廟, 日暮聊為梁甫吟. The pony "Pitiable Second-Ruler still-has temple / Day's-eve want make Liang-fu song" becomes "Even the poor Second Ruler still has his shrine. / As evening falls I shall sing a song of Liang-fu" (127). Hawkes unpacks line 7, noting that it "is thought to contain a veiled criticism of Tai-tsung, whose misplaced confidence in eunuch advisers was held responsible for many of the Empire's current difficulties. Even the effete Second Ruler of Shu is still honoured, says Tu Fu, thanks to the greatness of his predecessor and the brilliance of his famous minister, Chu-ko Liang. So there is some hope for Tai-tsung yet" (127-128). Du Fu was living in Chengdu, which had been the capital of the former state of Shu, one of the three regional states that were created at the end of the Latter Han dynasty in 220 CE. The Second Ruler of Shu was Liu Chan 劉禪 (207-271), who succeeded his father, Liu Bei 劉備 (161-223), the First Ruler of Shu. Zhuge Liang 諸葛亮 (181-234), who had advised the First Ruler, attempted to help Liu Chan gain ascendancy over the other two states, but died in an attack on the northern state of Wei. After his death, Liu Chan relied on the advice of the eunuch Huang

Hao 黃皓, and as a result the Shu state was quickly conquered by Wei. Zhuge Liang is one of Du Fu's favorite figures, referred to in a number of his late poems. The warfare of the Three States Era is reflected in the turmoil surrounding the decade-long rebellion against the Tang that began in 755. Daizong, who took the throne is 765, is in a sense also a "Second Ruler," since he is the second emperor to rule after the restoration of Tang rule in the early 760s. Du Fu's modifier for the Second Ruler, *kelian* 可憐, seems to suggest "pitiful" rather than Hawkes' "poor" here, given the tone of this last couplet.

The final line produces another strong interpretation from Hawkes. He write: "The *Liang-fu-yin* was a dirge-like folksong which Zhuge Liang was fond of singing when he was still living as a young man in his home in what is present-day Shantung. Line 8 therefore has an enhanced meaning: (1) as evening falls I should like to make a poem about my musings on the top of the tower. (2) I wish that in this dark and difficult hour I could be given a position of trust like that held by Zhuge Liang, save the state, and make myself and my ruler famous for all time" (128). Indeed, yet the content of "Liangfu yin," which Hawkes does not mention, is a key to fully understanding the line. The original song depicted how Yan Zi 晏子, the chief advisor to Duke Jing of Qi 齊景公 (r. 547-490 BCE), devised a plan to trick three powerful men who threatened to overthrow the state of Qi into taking their own lives.[24] Zhuge Liang sang the song when he was out of office, wishing that he could devise a means to remove some of the courtiers of the Second Ruler; Du Fu himself must have thought that freeing Daizong from the influence of his own eunuchs, especially Cheng Yuanzhen 程元振 and Yu Chaoen 魚朝恩, was of paramount importance. Yet *liao wei* 聊為 in line 8, "I can do nothing but sing the 'Liangfu yin,'" suggests that although Du Fu had felt helpless even after thinking about the dilemma until the sun set. Huang He 黃鶴 claims this poem was written shortly after Li Guangbi's 李光弼 (708-764) death and that Zhuge Liang thus refers to him.[25]

The final poem I would like to discuss is "Su fu" 宿府 [Spending the Night at Headquarters],[26] which was written a few months after "On the Tower" in the summer of 764. Laurence K.P. Wong discusses this poem in his reading of Hawkes' *Primer*, but he finds the final line a cinematic "zoom-in" on the specific, the "single branch," a reading that in my opinion misses the point of the poem (2012: 50-51). To return to Du Fu and Hawkes, however, "Spending the Night" was written earlier in the same spring of 764 as "Deng lou"—William Hung dates it to 11 February 764 (1952: 204)— following closely on Emperor Daizong's appointment of one of his Chief Ministers, Yan Wu 嚴武 (726-765), Military Governor of Jiannan Province with his base in Chengdu. Du Fu had met Yan Wu when the poet was at court in 757 and Yan was a high official only thirty years old. Du Fu probably knew his father, Yan Tingzhi 嚴挺之, as well. Yan Wu was appointed in reaction to the aggressiveness of the Tibetans, who had sacked Chang'an in late autumn 763. Yan Wu had been a protégé of the powerful official Fang Guan房管 (696-763), whose demise in 757 led to Du Fu's dismissal from court as well. Shortly after Yan Wu arrived in Chengdu, he appointed Du Fu as a Military Advisor [*Canmou* 參謀], also procuring for him a nominal title conferred by the emperor as Consultant Auxiliary Secretary of the Ministry of Public Works.

Having summarized the background, let us turn to the poem itself, which opens in Hawkes' literal version: 永夜角聲悲自語, 清秋幕府井梧寒, "clear autumn general-headquarters well *wu-t'ung*-trees cold / Along spend-night river-city wax-candles consumed," or in the translation "In the clear autumn air, the *wu-t'ung trees* beside the well in the Governor's headquarters have a chilly look. / I am staying alone here in the River City" (1967: 130, 131). Hawkes' exegesis here only explains *mufu* 幕府 as a "military headquarters." Yet although these lines focus on the *wutong* tree and the candles in Du Fu's office, they emphasize the poet's loneliness in "spending the night alone" [*du su* 獨宿]. *Han* 寒 [feeling cold] and *can* 殘 [burning low/exhausted] can easily be applied to Du Fu himself, still awake late at night.

The second couplet follows: in Hawkes' word-for-word glosses "Long night bugle sounds sad self-talk / Mid sky moon-colour good who looks" 永夜角聲悲自語，中天月色好誰看 followed by his translation: "Through the long night distant bugles talk mournfully to themselves, / And there is no one to watch the lovely moon riding in the midst of the sky" (1967: 131-132). The exegesis directs the reader back to Hawkes' reading of lines 3-4 in poem #16, "Shu xiang" 蜀相 [The Chancellor of Shu], where Hawkes admits to difficulty in understanding the couplet (1967: 107). He unpacks the lines as follows: "the bugles talk to themselves and the moon shines unseen" (131). The syntax, like Du Fu, is tortured here. The modern scholar Huo Songlin 霍松林 argues that the lines should be parsed 4-1-2 (instead of the usual 4-3) and mean "In the long night the bugle's sound, so sad, speak only to each other; / Mid the heavens the moon's image, so beautiful, for whom to see?" But the third line may also reflect Du Fu's disappointment with the Tang government's inability to deal more forcefully with the Tibetan threat–the army is ready, but it just needs a strategy. William Hung believes Du Fu wrote many memoranda to the new Governor General Yan Wu on how to deal with the Tibetans—one of which is still extant (1952: 209). But in line 4, 中天月色好誰看, the subject shifts back to the Du Fu's isolation in the late-night headquarters. The moon high in the midnight sky suggest this was the mid-autumn festival full moon—the phase of the moon that appears in the middle of a midnight sky is always the full moon—thus also suggesting here Du Fu's desire to return home to Chang'an.

The third couplet 風塵荏苒音書絕，關塞蕭條行路難，glossed as "wind-dust interminable news-letters cut / Passes-frontier desolate travel-roads hard," is translated as "Protracted turmoils have cut us off from letters, / And travelling is difficult through the desolate frontier passages" (1967: 131, 132). The exegesis merely explains *feng chen* 風塵 here as "'troubles,' especially when warfare is involved" (131). Other than the need to substitute "winds of war prolonged" for Hawkes' "protracted turmoils," the lines seem ideally presented.

The final couplet, 已忍伶俜十年事，強移棲息一枝安, glossed as "already endured tribulations ten years affairs / Forcibly move roost-rest one branch peace," is translated as "having endured ten years of vexatious trials, / I have perforce moved here to roost awhile on this single peaceful bough" (131, 132). This couplet brings together the several themes of this poem–working late, the military situation, and Du Fu's discontent. Hawkes' exegesis notes that *shi nian* 十年 is "a round number depicting the eight and a half years since the outbreak of the An Lushan rebellion" and that "the 'single peaceful branch' on which Du Fu so reluctantly perches is . . . his post under Yan Wu" (131). However, the final line gives rise to two questions not answered by Hawkes. First, what is the significance of the tree branch? Second, what is the meaning of the final word, *an* 安, which Hawkes glosses as "peace" and translates as "peaceful" (modifying the branch)?

The "single branch" is an allusion to the second passage in the received version of the *Zhuang Zi* 莊子 ("Xiaoyao you" 逍遙遊 [Free and Easy Rambling]), which relates that when Yao 堯 wanted to cede the empire to his minister Xu You 許由, Xu refused the offer, explaining through naturalistic analogies that he had no such grand aspirations: "the wren which builds her nest in the deep wood uses no more than one branch; the mole that drinks at the river takes no more than a bellyful" 鷦鷯巢于深林, 不過一枝; 偃鼠飲河, 不過滿腹。歸休乎, 君 (Chuang Tzu 1968: 32). Du Fu has just taken on his position as military advisor to Yan Wu, but now finds himself working late at night and unable to return to his Thatched Hut outside the city walls. He was reluctant to take on this position and now is regretting the decision. In this final line he is very likely echoing the final poem of a series "Yong shi" 詠史 [On History] that Zuo Si 左思 (ca. 250-ca. 305) wrote. Zuo's poem begins: "Trying to fly up, the bird in a cage, lifts its feathers to strike (bump?) against the four corners" 習習籠中鳥, 舉翮觸四隅, and ends "[the mole that] drinks at the riverside restricts himself to a bellyful; content, he doesn't want more; the wren in the woods nests on a single branch—both can serve as the model for a man who understands things" 飲河期滿腹。貴足不願余。巢林棲一枝, 可為達士模 (*Wenxuan* 21.991-992). The poem is about wanting less and curbing one's ambition. Perhaps both *Zhuang Zi* and Zuo Si were on Du Fu's mind (or his study table) when he wrote "Spending the Night at Headquarters."

The same images seem to have still been on his mind a short time later after he had been allowed to leave his position and return to the Thatched Hut, as his "Yimen fengcheng Yan Gong, ershi yun" 遣悶奉呈嚴[武] [鄭]公, 二十韻, or "Twenty Rhymes Presented to the Duke [Zheng] Yan [Wu]":

> I am the traveler with the fishing pole on the bright waters,
> The gaffer with the crane-white hair in this clear autumn.
> Why did I come to work in your headquarters?
> The Yellow Scrolls register of service is truly like law.
> The blue robes are also from your honor.
> My old wife worries that sitting will make me rheumatic,
> My young daughter inquires about my headaches.
> Even on level ground I am liable to fall,

With my colleagues I've caused differences.
Grateful for your courtesy I try to apply my failing strength,
My intentions correspond to yours.
Earlier I won your friendship through discussions of poetry,
Now your military glory is reflected on me.
Your kind indulgences have kept me on despite my clumsiness,
Your thoughtful assistance has answered my needs . . .
In truth I'm like a tortoise who let himself be caught in a fisherman's net,
I've simply acted like a bird who peers at a cage . . .
Early morning I come to work as the vermillion gates just open,
At dusk I don't return until the bugles finish sounding.
I have not yet found a country estate,
Nor dared to give rest to my humble body.
The magpie waits anxiously at the Milky Way (which it bridges [*Huainan Zi*]),[28]
The nag is in fear of the brocade saddlecloth (which it does not deserve),
I hope you will allow me to regain my dignity,
And soon release me to lean against my own *wutong* tree.

白水魚竿客，清秋鶴髮翁。胡為來幕下，只合在舟中。
黃卷真如律，青袍也自公。老妻憂坐痺，幼女問頭風。
平地專欹倒，分曹失異同。禮甘衰力就，義忝上官通。
疇昔論詩早，光輝仗鉞雄。寬容存性拙，剪拂念途窮。
 . . . 信然龜觸網，直作鳥窺籠 . . .
曉入朱扉啟，昏歸畫角終。不成尋別業，未敢息微躬。
烏鵲愁銀漢，駑駘怕錦幪。會希全物色，時放倚梧桐。[29]

This poem is Du Fu's direct appeal to his superior Yan Wu to release him from his position as military advisor. Faced with the images of the bird and its cage as well as the *wutong* tree, the reader can perceive a poetic tapestry between the *Zhuang Zi* account of the bird which needs only a single branch, Zuo Si's poem, and "Spending the Night at Headquarters." This poem expands on Du Fu's "Spending the Night," tying the *wutong* tree in the headquarters yamen that Du Fu says is "cold" in the late night to that in Du Fu's "Thatched Hut." It also suggests that the final line of "Spending the Night," 強移棲息一枝安, should be read "Forced to move to roost and take comfort [*an* 安] on a single branch." Moreover, just as

"Spending the Night" ends with an allusion to *Zhuang Zi*, so this long poem also refers to *Zhuang Zi* in the image of the persona "leaning on a tree" [*yi shu* 倚樹]. In the chapter "De chong fu" 德充符 [Signs of Power Fulfilled], Zhuang Zi is explaining to Hui Zi 惠子 the nature of a man with "no emotions" [*wuqing* 無情]:

> Zhuang Zi said:
> The Dao gives him his personal appearance,
> Heaven gives him his bodily form;
> he does not by his likings and dislikings
> to his body do any internal harm.
> But now you, Sir, treat your spirit as something external,
> subject your vital powers to toil.
> You intone [texts or songs], leaning against a tree,
> Or propped yourself up at a study table[30] till your eyes close.
> Heaven selected for you the bodily form,
> but you chirp about what is hard and what is white (1968: 76).

> 莊子曰:「道與之貌, 天與之形, 無以好惡內傷其身。今子外乎子之神, 勞乎子之精, 倚樹而吟, 據槁梧而瞑。天選子之形, 子以堅白鳴!」

Du Fu closes his appeal to Yan Wu by hoping that he will be allowed to "lean against a *wutong* tree" in his home where he can intone his own verse, instead of being propped at his desk in the office, nodding off in exhaustion.

Thus the apparently simple poem "Spending the Night at Headquarters" offers levels of meaning that reveals a great deal of the complexity of Du Fu's mind and his habits. It is part of a coordinated line of thought, centered upon Du Fu's desire to leave his position as advisor and return to his family in the Thatched Hut, which troubled the poet in the fall of 764. It also suggests that Du Fu may have been reading or thinking about Zhuang Zi and Zuo Si at this time. Finally, the subtlety with which Du Fu addresses his hope to leave his position and retire to the Thatched Hut suggests the poem may not have been intended for other readers (much as "Juan ye" 倦夜, a lament written about this time).

Conclusion

The suggestions made in this article are for the most part speculative. Of course, it is possible to read Du Fu without delving into the poems he read and alludes to. But this is to read the poems in lower-case type, to skim meanings off the surface of deep pools. The discussions of allusions and resonances above are suggested in part by Hawkes' notes. Thus they are intended to demonstrate both the complexity of Du Fu's verse and the meticulous accuracy and literary sensitivity of David Hawkes' comments on that verse. Ultimately, the question is not whether we can nitpick this or that line in Hawkes' presentation, but whether *The Little Primer* remains as useful today as it was when it was first published in 1967. My reading of the book in a recent seminar on Du Fu that I taught at the University of Wisconsin convinces me that *The Little Primer* continues to be the starting point for any Western student studying not only Du Fu's poetry, but Tang verse in general.

Endnotes

[1] While Hawkes is probably the most outstanding translator of Chinese into English in the latter half of the 20th century on that side of the Atlantic, Burton Watson must surely be considered the doyen of American translators.

[2] After having written this paper, I discovered that Laurence K.P. Wong had earlier assessed David Hawkes' *A Little Primer of Tu Fu* in his lengthy and interesting piece entitled "Surprising the Muses" (Wong 2012: 33-113). Wong discusses most of the poems in the Primer, whereas I should only like to examine four of them. Fortunately, Wong takes a much different approach than mine.

[3] Cao Xueqin's lone novel is more commonly known as *Dream of Red Mansions* than as *Story of the Stone*.

[4] Since Tang poets were accustomed to composing poems to set rhymes (it was one of the requirements of the *jinshi* 進士 examination), the idea of coldness [*han*] may color the entire poem.

[5] Commentators such as Qiu Zhao'ao have pointed out that *kan* 看 is here read as a *pingsheng* 平聲 [level tone] (Du 1979). Satō Kōichi 佐藤浩一 notes that Qiu added 11,035 phonetic glosses in his annotation

intending to guide the reader to the proper understanding of Du Fu's verse (Satō 2006).

⁶Erwin von Zach has provided a German translation: "Mein alter Wirt sprang über de Hofmauer und flüchtete; die alte Wirtin öffnete die Pforte, um nachzusehen, was es gäbe" (von Zach 1952: 162). William Hung paraphrases the lines as follows: "In the evening I found a lodging place at Shih-hao Village. / A recruiting officer came to take men at night. / My old host scaled the wall and fled; / His old wife went to answer the gate" (Hung 1952: 141).

⁷For example, Stephen Owen gives this rendering: "While faraway I think lovingly on daughters and sons, / Who do not yet know how to remember Ch'ang-an" (1981: 200). See also von Zach: "In der Ferne sehne ich mich nach dem kleinen Sohn und dem Töchterchen, die es noch nicht verstehen, an ihren in Ch'anan zurückgebliebenen Vater zu denken" (1952: III.9, 86).

⁸Perhaps Du Fu even echoes, intentionally or inadvertently, Xie Tiao's "Yujie yuan," a poem that portrays the separation of lovers from the lonely female's point of view.

⁹In other words, back via the Yuefu tradition.

¹⁰Thus Stephen Owen renders the last couplet: "When shall we lean in the empty window, / Moonlit together, its light drying traces of tears" (1981: 200).

¹¹Tsu-lin Mei and Yu-kung Kao also point to the tactile nature of Du Fu's reference to his wife in the third couplet of this poem (1971: 74).

¹²The original note read "Delighted that Prefect Cui has come by" 喜崔明府相過.

¹³Qiu Zhao'ao has referred to this relationship in his headnote to the poem on this relationship (Du 1979).

¹⁴*Hanyu da cidian*, 9.511a; citing the *Song shu* biography of Yuan Kai 袁顗. The earliest poem that I have been able to locate using "wicker gate" was Bao Zhao's 鮑照 "Yuanzhong qiusan" 園中秋散.

¹⁵Translation modified from Hightower 1970: 27.

¹⁶On brewing rice wine during the Tang, see Benn 2002: 141-143.

¹⁷Perhaps the resonance of *ge li* 隔籬 [across the fence] to the following passage in *Baopu Zi* 抱朴子 supports Owen's reading: 抱朴子曰: 輕薄之人, 跡廁高深, 交成財贍, 名位粗會, 便背禮判教, 托云率任, 才不逸倫, 強為放達, 以傲兀無檢者為大度, 以惜護節操者為澀少。於是臘鼓垂無 賴之子, 白醉耳熱之後, 結黨合群, 游不擇類, 奇士碩儒, 或隔籬而不授/接.

Light and frivolous men make tracks for the high and the deep. They gain connections with men of wealth and become rich. Their fame and position come to be great. They go against propriety and [sagely] teachings, saying that they are following what is natural to them. Their natural talents do not exceed those of others. They deliberately let themselves go and [claim to] attain naturalness. They consider haughtiness and uncontrolled conduct to be magnanimity. To nurture carefully one's moral purity is taken to be pettiness. During the Laoba Festival, and at the end of the spring when summer is welcomed and drums are beaten, local rascals with ears red from too much wine form parties and gather in cliques. They consort with friends unwisely chose. Though [or "sometimes"] separated by but a bamboo fence from exceptional scholars and learned Confucians, [these ruffians are] unwilling to meet them (Sailey 1978: 143-144).

[18]Wong primarily provides a critique of Burton Watson's version of this poem and has almost nothing to say about Hawkes' exegesis or translation (2012: 95-97).

[19]This exact wording can be found in an excellent article on the subject (Frankel 1973: 346).

[20]McCraw translates *ci* as "here" in his rendition of the poem: "Troubles too many & multilateral: here I ascend to look out" (1992: 108).

[21]See the comment in *Xianyong shuo shi* 峴傭說詩 [The Hired Man of the Mountains on Poetry], Shi Buhua 施補華, ed. (Shanghai: Wenming shuju, 1916 [1887]), cited in He 1997: 870.

[22]On floating clouds as a symbol of the ephemeral, see the opening to Du Fu's "Li Chao bafen xiaozhuan ge" 李朝八分小篆歌 [Song on Li Chao's Eight-segment and Small-seal Style Calligraphy], Du 18.1550: "The forms of characters change [over the years] like the floating clouds" 字體變化如浮雲.

[23]*Chuci zhangju* 楚辭章句, *juan* 8.

[24]The story can be found in *Yan Zi* and the song in *Yuefu shiji*.

[25]Huang He 21.7a.

[26]Du 13.1172.

[27]See his reading of the poem in Cheng 1983: 557-558.

[28]*Tian he* 填河. It bridges the Milky Way to allow the Weaving Girl to cross to her lover.

[29]See also the translation by Hung 1952: 213-214.

[30]An alternate reading for *gao wu* 槁梧 is "a rotten *wutong* [stump]."

Works Cited

Benn, Charles. *Daily Life in Traditional China: the Tang Dynasty.* Westport, CT: Greenwood Publishing Group, 2001.
Bian Lianbao 邊連寶. "Du lü qimeng" 杜律啓蒙 [A Beginner's Guide to Du Fu's Regulated Verse]. In *Dianjiao "Du lü qimeng"* 點校杜律啓蒙. Han Chengwu 韓成武 et al., eds. Jinan: Qi Lu shushe, 2005.
Cao Xueqin 曹雪芹. *The Story of the Stone.* Vols. 1-4. David Hawkes, trans. London: Penguin, 1974, 1977, 1981, 1982.
---. *The Story of the Stone.* Vol. 5. John Minford, trans. London: Penguin, 1986.
Cheng Qianfan 程千帆 et al. *Tang shi jianshang cidian* 唐詩鑒賞辭典 [A Dictionary for Appreciating Tang Poetry]. Shanghai: Shanghai cishu, 1983.
Chou, Eva Shan. *Reconsidering Tu Fu: Literary Greatness and Cultural Context.* Cambridge: Cambridge University Press, 1995.
Chuang Tzu (Zhuang Zi) 莊子. *The Complete Works of Chuang Tzu.* Burton Watson, trans. New York: Columbia University Press, 1968.
Du Fu 杜甫. *Du shi xiangzhu* 杜詩詳註. Qiu Zhao'ao 仇兆鰲, ed. 5 vols. Beijing: Zhonghua shuju, 1979.
Frankel, Hans H. "The Contemplation of the Past in T'ang Poetry." In *Perspectives on the T'ang.* Arthur F. Wright and Denis Twitchett, eds. New Haven: Yale University Press, 1973. Pp. 345-365.
Graham, A.C. *The Book of Lieh-tzu.* London: Murray, 1960.
Han Yu 韓愈. "Tiao Zhang Ji" 調張籍 [Written Playfully to Zhang Ji]. http://www.poetrynook.com/poem/調張籍
Hawkes, David. *Ch'u Tz'u: The Songs of the South: An Ancient Chinese Anthology.* Oxford: Clarendon Press, 1959.
---. *A Little Primer of Tu Fu.* Oxford: Clarendon Press, 1967.
He Xinhui 賀新輝, ed. *Quan Tang shi jianshang cidian* 全唐詩鑒賞辭典 [A Dictionary for Appreciating the *Complete Tang Poems*]. Beijing: Zhongguo funü, 1997.
Hightower, James Robert. *The Poetry of T'ao Ch'ien.* Oxford: Oxford

University Press, 1970.

Huang He 黃鶴, ed. *Buzhu Du shi* 補注杜詩 [Supplementary Notes to the Poetry of Du Fu]. Taipei: Taiwan shangwu yinshuguan, 1983.

Huang Sheng 黃生. *Du shi shuo* 杜詩説 [On Du Fu's Poetry]. Hefei: Huangshan shushe, 1994.

Hung, William. *Tu Fu, China's Greatest Poet*. Cambridge: Harvard University Press, 1952.

Kern, Martin. "Lost in Tradition: the *Classic of Poetry* We Did Not Know." *Hsiang Lectures on Chinese Poetry, Vol. 5*. Grace S. Fong, ed. Montreal: Centre for East Asian Research, McGill University, 2010. Pp. 29-56.

McCraw, David R. *Du Fu's Laments from the South*. Honolulu: University of Hawai'i Press, 1992.

Mei, Tsu-lin and Yu-kung Kao. "Syntax, Diction, and Imagery in T'ang Poetry." *Harvard Journal of Asiatic Studies* 31 (1971): 49-136.

Owen, Stephen. *The Great Age of Chinese Poetry: The High T'ang*. New Haven: Yale University Press, 1981.

---. *Traditional Chinese Poetry and Poetics: Omen of the World*. Madison: University of Wisconsin Press, 1985.

Sailey, Jay. *The Master Who Embraces Simplicity: A Study of the Philosopher Ko Hung, A.D. 283-343*. San Francisco: Chinese Materials Center, 1978.

Satō Kōichi 佐藤浩一. "Kyū Chōgō Toshi shōchū no onchū ni tsuite" 仇兆鰲杜詩詳註の音注について. *Nihon Chūgoku gakkai hō* 日本中國學報 58 (2006): 171-187.

Shang Zhongxian. *Liu Yi and the Dragon Princess: A Thirteenth Century Zaju Play by Shang Zhongxian*. David Hawkes, trans. Hong Kong: The Chinese University Press, 2003.

Von Zach, Erwin. *Tu Fu's Gedichte*. 2 vols. James Robert Hightower, ed. Harvard-Yenching Institute Studies, VIII. Cambridge: Harvard University Press, 1952.

Wen xuan 文選. Shanghai: Shanghai Guji, 1986.

Wong, Laurence K.P. "Surprising the Muses." In *Style, Wit and Word-Play: Essays in Translation Studies in Memory of David Hawkes*. Tao Tao Liu et al., eds. Newcastle upon Tyne: Cambridge Scholars Publishing, 2012. Pp. 33-113.

Yang Bojun 楊伯鈞, ed. *Lie Zi jishi* 列子集釋 [Collected

Interpretations of the *Liezi*]. Beijing: Zhonghua, 2004.

Yang Lun 楊倫, ed. *Du shi jing quan* 杜詩鏡銓. Shanghai: Shanghai guji chubanshe, 1980.

Photo Courtesy of Andrea Augé

16

For Burton Watson

Gary Snyder

Before I had read Dr. Watson's translations, like many first-time readers of Chinese literature, I was taken by T'ang poetry and the writings of Lao Tzu and Chuang Tzu. Then I studied Watson's translations of the great Chinese lyric poets and was transformed again. But it was the tireless and downright courageous further scholarship of Burton Watson that became my real education in East Asian culture. The heavy pragmatism of players in Ssu-ma Ch'ien's historical narratives, the intellectual sophistication of the Buddhist philosophers, the great diversity of Chinese literary productions over the centuries—and the perspective on contemporary China a fuller picture provides—all this I owe to Dr. Watson's remarkable life work. Nine bows indeed.

17

The Moment Lasts Forever

Philip Rowland

anchor
i
tic

~

for all these storms and streams no north of the present

~

index of moments I'm neither here nor there

~

fleeing the
moment lasts
forever

About the Contributors

Stephen Addiss (b. 1935) is a scholar-artist whose paintings, calligraphy, haiku, and haiga have appeared widely. His books include *The World of Kameda Bôsai*, *Tall Mountains and Flowing Waters: the Arts of Uragami Gyokudô*, *Cloud Calligraphy*, *A Haiku Menagerie*, *The Art of Zen*, *Haiga: Haiku-Painting*, *The Art of Chinese Calligraphy*, *Haiku People*, *A Haiku Garden*, *Haiku Humor*, *Tao Te Ching*, *Japanese Calligraphy*, *Haiku: An Anthology*, and *The Art of Haiku*.

Duncan M. Campbell, a New Zealander, is presently Curator of the Chinese Garden at The Huntington Library in San Marino, California, having previously spent many years teaching Chinese language and literature (modern and classical) and aspects of Chinese history and culture at universities in New Zealand and Australia. He first went to China in the mid-1970s.

Jonathan Chaves is Professor of Chinese at The George Washington University. His work as translator of Chinese poetry has been nominated for the National Book Award, and in 2014 won the ALTA Stryk Award for Best Asian translation. As a scholar, he has presented the first books in English on a number of important poets, and focused on interrelationships among poetry, painting and calligraphy in China.

Timothy Clifford is a Ph.D. candidate at the University of Pennsylvania, Department of East Asian Languages and Civilizations. His forthcoming dissertation is a study of literary anthologies and "ancient-style prose" (*guwen* 古文) in Ming dynasty China.

Yoko Danno is Japanese, and has written poetry solely in English for decades. She is the author of several chapbooks and books of poetry. A new collection of her poems, *Aquamarine*, was published by Glass Lyre Press (2014), and her translation, *Songs and Stories of the Kojiki*, was published by Ahadada Books (2008) and Red Moon Press (2014). URL: http://www.ikutapress.com/danno3.html

Robert Epp was born in 1926, and received his A.M. and Ph.D. at Harvard University. He has taught at Columbia University, Stanford University, Indiana State University, and most recently UCLA, where he is Professor Emeritus of Modern Japanese. He has published translations of and studies on ten modern Japanese poets.

Jesse Glass has lived in Japan for almost twenty-four years. His painted books of poetry are part of the artist's books collection at the Tate Gallery, Britain. His books include *The Passion of Phineas Gage, Lost Poet; Four Plays* and *Black Out in My Left Eye, a Novel*.

Sam Hamill translated *Crossing the Yellow River: Three Hundred poems from the Chinese*, Lu Chi's *Art of Writing*, Basho's *Narrow Road to the Interior*, and recently published *Habitation: Collected Poems*. He lives in Anacortes, Washington.

Robert E. Hegel completed the Ph.D. in Chinese Literature at Columbia in 1973; he was a student of Burt Watson there during the turbulent 1960s. He teaches Chinese fiction and theater, along with translation studies, at Washington University, St. Louis, where he is the Liselotte Dieckmann Professor of Comparative Literature.

Lucas Klein's work has appeared in *Jacket*, *Rain Taxi*, *CLEAR*, and *PMLA*, and from Fordham, Black Widow, and New Directions. Assistant Professor at the University of Hong Kong, his translation of Xi Chuan won the 2013 Lucien Stryk Prize. He is translating Tang dynasty poet Li Shangyin and seminal contemporary poet Mang Ke.

Hua Li is Associate Professor of Chinese in the Department of Modern Languages and Literatures at Montana State University. Brill published her monograph *Contemporary Chinese Fiction by Su Tong and Yu Hua: Coming of Age in Troubled Times* in 2011; she has also authored several journal articles on the fiction of Yu Hua and Su Tong and on Chinese cinema. She is currently carrying out research on Chinese science fiction.

Victor H. Mair (University of Pennsylvania) specializes in Buddhist popular literature and the vernacular tradition of Chinese fiction and performing arts. He has led a research project on the prehistoric mummies of Eastern Central Asia and authored numerous publications (including several works from Columbia University Press). He is the editor of *Sino-Platonic Papers*, the ABC Chinese Dictionary Series, and Cambria's Sinophone World Series, and blogs frequently for Language Log.

William H. Nienhauser, Jr. is Halls Bascom Professor for Classical Chinese literature at the University of Wisconsin. Among his publications are seven volumes of what is to become the first annotated translation of Sima Qian's *Shiji* and a number of studies of traditional Chinese narratives.

Philip Rowland is a British poet and professor based in Tokyo. He is the founding editor of *NOON: journal of the short poem*, co-editor of *Haiku in English: The First Hundred Years* (W.W. Norton, 2013), and author of *Before Music* (Red Moon Press, 2012).

Hiroaki Sato and Burton Watson received the PEN American Center translation prize for the anthology on which they collaborated, *From the Country of Eight Islands: An Anthology of Japanese Poetry* (Doubleday, 1981).

Gary Snyder is a distinguished poet and translator.

Hoyt Tillman: Since receiving his Ph.D. from Harvard in 1976, he has taught Chinese thought and history at Arizona State University;

moreover, he has written and/or edited a dozen books on Chinese history. Among his honors are: an Alexander von Humboldt Foundation Research Prize (*Humboldt-Forschungspreis*); research affiliate of Peking University's Center for Studies of Ancient Chinese History; and guest chaired professor in the College of History at Renmin University of China.

Philip F. Williams has held the position of Professor of Chinese literature at a number of research universities in the U.S. and Australasia, and is currently teaching at Montana State University. He has published more than ten books, including *Village Echoes: the Fiction of Wu Zuxiang* (Westview Press, 1993), *The Great Wall of Confinement* (University of California Press, 2004), and *Asian Literary Voices* (Amsterdam University Press, 2010).

Yenna Wu is Professor of Chinese and Distinguished Teaching Professor at the University of California, Riverside. Her publications include *The Chinese Virago* (1995), *The Lioness Roars* (1995), *Ameliorative Satire* (1999), *Chinese the Easy Way* (co-authored, 1999), *The Great Wall of Confinement* (co-authored, 2004), *Remolding and Resistance* (co-edited, 2006), *Me and China* (co-authored, 2008), *Human Rights, Suffering, and Aesthetics* (co-edited, 2011), *Li Ang's Visionary Challenges to Gender, Sex, and Politics* (edited, 2014).

www.ingramcontent.com/pod-product-compliance
Lightning Source LLC
Chambersburg PA
CBHW020928090426
42736CB00010B/1071